Andy Thomas is one of the UK's leading researchers into unexplained mysteries and conspiracy theories. His many books include the acclaimed *The Truth Agenda*, which explores paranormal phenomena, global cover-ups and prophecies for these times, and *Vital Signs*, widely described as the definitive guide to the controversial crop circle phenomenon and nominated for *Kindred Spirit* magazine's Best Book Award.

Andy is founder of Changing Times, which holds events on alternative views and truth issues, and runs Vital Signs Publishing, which produced Geoff Stray's seminal book *Beyond 2012*, edited by Andy. He is also co-MC for the renowned annual UK mysteries conference, the Glastonbury Symposium.

Andy writes and lectures extensively around the world, and has made numerous radio and TV appearances. UK spots have included Channel 4's *Richard and Judy*, ITV's *GMTV*, BBC1's *The One Show* and Sky1's *Pineapple Dance Studios*; Andy has guested many times on Edge Media TV's (Sky 200) alternative chat show *On the Edge*. Andy has also featured in television programmes in many other countries.

More information on Andy, with Facebook links, can be found at: www.truthagenda.org

CONSPIRACIES

THE FACTS • THE THEORIES • THE EVIDENCE

ANDY THOMAS

WATKINS PUBLISHING

LONDON

This edition first published in the UK and USA 2013 by
Watkins Publishing Ltd, Sixth Floor,
75 Wells Street, London W1T 3QH

A member of Osprey Group

1 3 5 7 9 10 8 6 4 2

Designed and typeset by JCS Publishing Services Ltd.

Printed and bound in China

A CIP record for this book is available from the British Library

ISBN: 978-1-78028-508-5

www.watkinspublishing.co.uk

Distributed in the USA and Canada by Sterling Publishing Co., Inc.
387 Park Avenue South, New York, NY 10016-8810

For information about custom editions, special sales, premium and
corporate purchases, please contact Sterling Special Sales
Department at 800-805-5489 or specialsales@sterlingpub.com

ACKNOWLEDGEMENTS

Andy Thomas would like to thank:

Helen Sewell for manuscript proofing, endless patience and for being my dearest love and heartfelt inspiration; Piers Adams for early manuscript checking and valuable suggestions; Pavel Mikoloski for alerting me to the project; Jordan Thomas for support and much-appreciated practical help; Richard Smith for additional information; Edge Media TV (Sky 200) and Ian R Crane for support and opportunities; Marcus Allen of *Nexus Magazine* for the many formative conversations years ago, without which this book would not exist.

CONTENTS

INTRODUCTION

Pick a century, any century. Or a decade, a year, a month. In each you will find significant and seemingly indisputable events occurring, the kind that can change the course of human history. Yet, for every one of them, somebody, somewhere, will loudly dispute the 'official' account, doubting that the truth has been told. Conspiracy theories have been with us since civilization began, always whispering from the fringes, begging to be taken seriously. In certain centuries they have been, sometimes to disastrous effect, while at other times ones that perhaps should have been listened to have been perilously ignored.

In today's environment, with trust in authorities at an all-time low, and where communication has been profoundly transformed, conspiracy theories have found a new currency, with websites and social networking ensuring they receive a wider and more rapid spread than ever before. Is this a curse or a miracle? With no editorial filters or peer approval required to send them out to the world, the strangest ideas can now catch like wildfire and a steady torrent of challenges are thrown down against establishment spin – ones which reach the public almost as readily as the mainstream media.

There are signs that the authorities are fighting back. Surely threatened by those who would deconstruct their every word and accuse them of deception, cover-up and mass murder, the strategy would appear to be to use television, radio and print to persistently ridicule the self-styled 'truthseekers', who are portrayed as misguided eccentrics, prone to dangerous fanaticism. This retaliation has been successful to a degree; of all groups marginalized in recent decades, believers in conspiracies must be fairly near the top of the list, to the point where the term 'conspiracy theorist' has become an abusive label, one desperately avoided by those who would be taken seriously. This has simply driven underground something which might be more healthily expressed in the open, and has not lessened the strength of conviction over the issues themselves, as evidenced by remarkable poll statistics, which show a notable tendency towards conspiracy thinking among everyday folk.

Conspiracy theory, therefore, in its strictest definitional sense, is a brand that perhaps needs to be reclaimed for the good. For while holding *every* significant event to be a conspiracy may be to risk psychosis, some of the theorizing has – without question – helped identify several areas of genuine concern which deserve more attention. To the reviled truthseekers, it is the puppet masters of the establishment who are as likely to bring the world crashing down through their own streak of dangerous fanaticism.

How do we separate truth from imagination? Which criteria can be used to identify the propositions that should be legitimately pursued from those simply rooted in dark musings of paranoia? Was Diana, Princess of Wales, murdered, as a large number of people think, for all the official denials? Did NASA really go to the Moon, when anomalies in the photographic record suggest otherwise to a vocal minority? Were there other gunmen present at the shooting of JFK? Could 9/11 really have been set up by agencies within the USA itself? Are all our lives governed by a secret ruling elite planning a 'New World Order' of surveillance and control? It is often difficult to tell, when authorities deny but belief persists.

Evidence, therefore, not conjecture, might seem to be the best yardstick from which to find clarity on the likelihood or otherwise of all the many claims. Yet the academic sphere, which filters much of what reaches the mainstream, too often shows a curious reluctance to engage with that evidence, preferring to attack the conspiracy mindset rather than understand its reasoning. This was concisely illustrated by a remark made at a British Humanist Association conference – held specifically to discuss conspiracy theories – when a speaker declared, 'I'm not going to debate the evidence for or against particular conspiracy theories; this is not the place for that.'[1] The problem, it seems, is that for authorities, media, and the world of academia, that place is never found. The continued avoidance of seriously considering the basis of truthseekers' beliefs is what prevents the public debate moving forward in any useful direction.

Much of this book, then, establishes the fundamentals of conspiracy thinking, but also explores an often missing element: the evidence itself. Throughout my two and a half decades of research, specific theories have consistently surfaced as areas of public fascination, and these are the ones focused on, occasionally balanced with resonant cases which may not have received the coverage they deserve. The torturous controversies around religion and climate change have been left for another time, for the most part, and the chapters do not attempt to cram in all the theories ever spun, which would take away space from the more salient areas. Nor (unlike a number of conspiracy tomes masquerading as balanced studies) do they try to explain away the selected topics with easy answers and dismissive attitudes.

Conspiracy theories are frequently subscribed to by quite normal, approachable people with a genuine passion to uncover the detail of what they see as areas of legitimate anxiety. They are not, on the whole, the sad extremists falsely portrayed in the media, supposedly wearing tinfoil hats to prevent enforced mind control. Understanding what compels people to spend long and precious hours investigating corruption, cover-ups and hidden agendas with mind-blowing implications would reward civilization better than condemning them. The standard judgemental approach *is* a kind of mind control. If people believe in unusual things, there are reasons why, and sensibly comprehending those reasons, without necessarily agreeing with them, might be wise.

Ultimately, readers must decide for themselves where the truths behind the theories lie. Many most likely fall somewhere between the polarities of total belief and complete denial, but occasionally the evidence drags probability just a little further one way or the other. Nearly always, there is more to things than may at first meet the eye.

This book is an opportunity to sift through some of the intriguing, inspirational, sometimes gruesome and often shocking possibilities presented by conspiracy thinking. Inevitably it goes to some shadowy places at times, but if all that the speculation achieves is to help the reader forge a determination to create a better world founded in truth, positivity and real freedom of expression, then it will have been worth the journey.

Andy Thomas

CHAPTER 1

WHAT IS CONSPIRACY THEORY?

What, exactly, constitutes a 'conspiracy theory', and why does the mainstream hold in such low regard those who believe in them? Despite widespread dismissal, belief in global conspiracies is greatly on the rise. Are the theorists, as many academics would have us believe, psychologically damaged in some way? Or are they simply asking reasonable questions about glaring anomalies in the 'official' versions of certain events? Can a middle ground be found between the extremes of those who hold that virtually everything is manipulated or engineered for dark purposes, and those who refuse to believe that conspiracies exist at all?

I) DEFINING CONSPIRACY THEORY

Precise Definitions

When does news cease to be news? *Answer*: When it becomes conspiracy theory.

In recent years a fascinating phenomenon has developed in the mainstream media. Exposés of 'sleaze' and abuses of power amongst individuals are gleefully splashed across screens and newspapers with alarming regularity, yet any further suggestion that similar actions might be coordinated by *groups* of individuals is almost universally swept aside as being nothing more than 'conspiracy theory'. The tones employed in these moments are invariably tinged with contempt at the very idea that corruption might be institutional or serve a wider mandate than one person's misguided ego.

Is this marginalization of conspiracy theory fair? And does it follow that anyone who believes in it is inherently flawed in their thinking, as such treatment would imply? Those who routinely dismiss conspiracy theory often lack clarity about what they mean by the term, allowing an easy sidelining of what could be important areas for scrutiny. Is this merely lazy journalism or, as some would have us believe, a deliberate distraction?

To assess the true value of anything, establishing its key principles is always an important starting point. Here, then, are three different definitions of 'conspiracy theory' from mainstream sources:

> *The belief that the government or a covert organisation is responsible for an event that is unusual or unexplained, especially when any such involvement is denied.*
>
> *Collins English Dictionary*

> *A theory seeking to explain a disputed case or matter as a plot by a secret group or alliance rather than an individual or isolated act.*
>
> *American Heritage Dictionary of the English Language*

> *The idea that a group of people secretly worked together to cause a particular event.*   *Macmillan Dictionary*

Based on these definitions, it is difficult to understand why the media and authorities are so rigidly dismissive of the notion of conspiracy theory. Indeed, by applying these descriptions to many events throughout history, it is clear that not only are conspiracies of all kinds rife, but that they are an inevitable component of human civilization. Does anyone seriously dispute the existence of covert organizations, whether they be criminal cabals or corrupt cliques active within governments?

Why, then, has it become such a major taboo to discuss how these components might be working within our world today? How is it that the academic world appears to accept multiple examples of internal subterfuge within the Roman Empire (*see* chapter 2) as likely conspiracies, for instance, yet it has such trouble believing that comparable things might still occur now? Human civilization, for all its technological leaps, has not moved on so much from the social structures of its ancestors.

We can perhaps obtain an insight into to why we might have been conditioned to ignore modern-day conspiracies by hearing a rather less balanced description of conspiracy theory:

> *Conspiracy theories exist in the realm of myth, where imaginations run wild, fears trump facts, and evidence is ignored. As a superpower, the United States is often cast as a villain in these dramas.*[1]

This is the opening shot on the pages of the official US government's website dedicated to debunking conspiracy theories about itself. That these overly defensive pages exist at all is significant, indicating that the many accusations that are indeed aimed at the US authorities (widely seen as main players in the 'New World Order' project, explored throughout this book) are beginning to sting. The fact that, in 2009, Barack Obama had to (albeit off-camera) retake the presidential oaths just one day after fluffing the placement of the word 'faithfully' in his public decree, to 'avoid conspiracy theories', says much about how sensitive authorities have become to the growing list of indictments.

Is it, therefore, going too far to consider that, if Western governments are concerned about the proliferating doubts surrounding their integrity, they might instil a campaign of psychological conditioning and propaganda to attempt to discredit their accusers? The media, prone to arrogance and afraid to lose its necessary close contacts with the voices of power, could be easily manipulated (if not directly influenced by strings from above) into sneering on cue when something crucial is touched upon that risks lifting the lid on a hidden layer beneath. Thus the assertion that a deliberate taboo has been created around any serious mainstream discussion of conspiracy theory has become yet another conspiracy theory in itself.

Who Is a Conspiracy Theorist?

Through the entrenched device of treating with ridicule those who openly consider that certain events may be directed by covert factions, an understandable but perhaps misplaced defensiveness has crept into the language of those who are, by the simple dictionary definitions, conspiracy theorists. The adoption of the term is often strenuously avoided, however, lest anything they say be routinely ignored, which sometimes results in the unfortunate spectacle of researchers squirming with contrived affectations of academic status to avoid a tag that is generally placed on them in any case – usually by the very groups to which they would aspire to belong. The application of terms such as 'truthseeker' or 'truther' is perfectly acceptable as an alternative (and used in these pages), but does little to assuage the derision of the opposition. The fact is that marginalization of conspiracy theorists by the mainstream has been successful enough that no replacement term nor aspiration to a higher social standing is likely to have much effect on the critics once certain topics are breached – at least not currently.

4

It would seem that a new strategy is required for this topic to be accorded higher status. Instead of seeking a respectability that will not arrive without some major social overhaul, those who find themselves bracketed as conspiracy theorists might do better to stop worrying about what others think and plough on with grounding their chosen field of study in reality as convincingly as they can. Only through this will interest deepen and a wider public conviction grow. The less discerning conspiracy thinkers, who scream each new perceived horror as a given without proper evidence, rooted more in paranoia than factual observation, are those who have helped bring the area into disrepute in the first place. The best remedy must be to match speculation with serious research – and to use less strident tones. This way, there would, in time, be no reason to feel angst over being called a conspiracy theorist. Better, perhaps, to follow the line that George Fox's movement, the Religious Society of Friends, took after its formation in the 1600s. Branded 'quakers' as a term of abuse (because they were seen as misguided fanatics who 'quaked in the sight of God'), members simply adopted the insult as their official title, and so became the 'Quakers'. The negative intent of their critics was immediately neutralized, creating general bemusement but, ultimately, a new and lasting public respect.

Beyond the standard conspiracy strongholds, there *are* a few dedicated researchers in wider circles who have managed to gain respect for their personal convictions that specific events may be influenced by secret cabals but, even then, the reception of their work is muted. When Norman Baker, MP, published his brave book *The Strange Death of David Kelly* in 2007, which straightforwardly examined the substantial evidence that it was more probable that the controversial UN weapons inspector was murdered than took his own life (*see* chapter 5), the award-winning politician was from then on branded as a 'maverick' (enabling presenter Jeremy Paxman, in an entirely unrelated *Newsnight* debate, later to dismiss Baker with the words 'Well, you'd find conspiracy in a cup of tea').

Another example is David Ray Griffin, a US professor and Christian theologian, whose conscience would not allow him to leave the many anomalies of 9/11 uninvestigated in his meticulous writings. He has become one of the more convincing of all the many questioners of the attacks, leaving no stone of logic unturned, nor resorting to sensationalism. Griffin never considered himself a conspiracy theorist, and his previous track record showed few signs of such tendencies. Yet even he is regularly dismissed in the mainstream as a 'conspiracy guru'. So the tag seems unavoidable in such areas. Given that polls in 2011 (which, tellingly, received minimal coverage) demonstrated that a significant proportion of the world's population now doubts the official story of 9/11 in some capacity or another (*see* p. 171), Griffin needn't be too concerned. In some matters, at least, it is clear that a large number of us are, in fact, conspiracy theorists.

The reality is that to veer even a little towards certain subjects is to *be* a conspiracy theorist in the eyes of the mainstream, no matter what caveats are presented. It is clear that the world we are presented with from our newspapers and screens is rather different to the reality of what many of us truly think, as is demonstrated by the 9/11 opinions and polls on everything from David Kelly and Diana conspiracies to ghosts, UFOs and astrology, which show a sustained public belief in areas unremittingly debunked by most media pundits. Thus the truth so passionately spoken of by the theorists must be sought outside the mainstream for now, with the internet being its primary tool.

Finding the Middle Ground

What, however, is the 'truth'? Defending the study of conspiracy is not to support the view that all the theories that spring from it are correct. The purpose of this book is to explore some of the more widely held beliefs in the hope of attaining a constructive overview.

In attempting to establish a middle ground between the polarities of thought around the selected examples, some conspiracy staples stand out as being genuinely compelling, while others bring themselves into question by illogicality or lack of evidence. But this is not to make a conclusive judgement on anyone's personal views. The very problem with the establishment's treatment of conspiracy theory is that opinionated and often uninformed rushes to judgement on both sides help no one but those who, it would seem, prefer us not to scrutinize certain areas.

What does become clear when we illuminate some of the key issues is that even if some of the more extreme elements of conspiracy study are prone to going too far, the blanket dismissal of conspiracy theories that the establishment has perpetrated is equally unfair and misleading.

A Specific Kind of Conspiracy Theory

From the dictionary definitions of conspiracy theory, it is likely that there are many examples of covert groups in society scheming for their own small-minded agendas that would technically fall under the term. These areas are already well served by available sources on criminology and corporate corruption; much of this book investigates instead a broader and more specific angle that has come to embody the more typical media interpretation of 'conspiracy theory', i.e. the belief that major world events are being deliberately engineered by an undeclared but very influential ruling elite that may be using us as pawns in a long game which seeks dominion over the entire human race.

The core of this angle is that control and surveillance agendas are being indelibly installed through geopolitical power games. Manipulation through fear, war, economic subterfuge and, in the eyes of some, the application of occult knowledge and the influence of secret societies are the tools with which the ultimate goal of a 'one world government' might be achieved, a system where ultimate power is placed into the hands of a select few, operating people as puppets in a grand Orwellian nightmare. The general term applied to this perceived master plan is the 'New World Order' (NWO). Given that a desire for precisely this has been openly boasted of in surprisingly bold public addresses by major politicians, and that the ultimate shape of its aims do seem to risk – in a worst-case scenario at least – becoming exactly what the truthseekers fear, the New World Order seems a reasonable umbrella term to use for this strongly prevailing strand of conspiracy theory.

The many different ideas discussed throughout, from state-sponsored terrorism to political assassinations, from depopulation theories to hidden official belief in paranormal forces, while at first seeming perhaps to be entirely separate, may in truth make up a wider web of interconnecting threads which mask a much broader agenda that, if shown to have substance, would certainly deserve serious attention.

II) WHY DO PEOPLE BELIEVE IN CONSPIRACY THEORIES?

The Conspiracy Mindset

These pages are not the place for a detailed psychological analysis of the polarized mindsets which traditionally come head to head over conspiracy. But a brief summing up may be valuable.

The academic position on conspiracy believers can largely be summarized thus:

- They exhibit signs of mental instability, often having resentment towards authority, usually rooted in childhood experiences and family dysfunction. This leads them to blame others for all personal setbacks and to develop an eventual blanket suspicion towards authority figures on a global scale.

- They usually lack the quality of discernment and have low 'acceptance thresholds' of what they consider to be convincing evidence; i.e. they have a tendency towards gullibility (Cass Sunstein and Professor Adrian Vermeule describe this as a 'crippled epistemology', whereby beliefs are based on very limited information) and see patterns in events ('apophenia') that are not really there or, conversely, they draw sweeping conclusions from isolated anomalies taken out of context.
- Their lack of discernment makes them prone to 'social cascades' whereby the more people around them who hold to a certain view, the more likely it is that they will adopt the same belief, regardless of the weakness of the original evidence.
- Their tendency to question the official position in one area leads to a pathological inability to believe any scenario presented by the establishment, creating a general bent towards fanatical views and, in extreme cases, leading to anti-social behaviour or even involvement in terrorism in a misguided attempt to 'correct' situations.
- The perceived social isolation created by their 'unusual' views on the world is seemingly remedied if they become fervently dedicated to either actual or online communities that share the same focused views. This restricts their exposure to other ideas or evidence which might challenge their viewpoint and thus increases the tendency towards extremism.

More could be added to this list, but it distils the main points which tend to come up in most psychological treatises on the conspiracy mindset. Deep down, elements of all these may well contribute to the psychological make-up of many truthseekers. However, to hold to the notion that these questionable attributes are *all* that give rise to conspiracy theories is overly simplistic and pays no heed whatsoever to the more empirical events and situations that such minds are drawn to point out do actually occur all around us.

A similar list outlining the personality patterns of academics and psychologists might well uncover just as many qualities that bring into question their own rigid fervour in highlighting the weaknesses of others. Indeed, further contemplation makes it quickly apparent that critics of conspiracy theorists are often equally guilty of narrow-mindedness and of falling prey to 'social cascades' among their peer group. It has become a wide source of amusement, for instance, that arch-sceptic Richard Dawkins cannot see, as most outside observers can, that his fiery determination to destroy belief in religion, astrology or mysticism is as generically fanatical as that displayed by his targets.

In opposition to the academic position, the conspiracy believers themselves – whatever psychology may drive them – consider that their stance is valid, based on actual evidence that their critics seem reluctant to address.

The theorists' position on their own basic beliefs can be summarized thus:

- They have the ability to see glaring anomalies in official situations that the mainstream ignores or avoids, and only they have the courage to speak out about them.
- They are able to demonstrate that evidence for conspiracies most certainly does exist, and many examples throughout history, both ancient and modern, demonstrate clearly the role that secret cabals have played in nefariously shaping global events.
- Contemporary institutional corruption is so rife at every level of societal management, as acknowledged even in the mainstream media, that the notion that it is *not* also going on at higher levels is blinkered and unrealistic.

- The establishment's continued assault on those who believe in conspiracies is in itself an indication that a programme of official distraction and marginalization is in place, thus giving greater credence to their conviction that important areas are being covered up and withheld from the public.
- The common but incorrect characterization of all theorists as being right-wing fanatics or uneducated misfits is another suspicious demonization, when, in fact, conspiracy believers hail from all walks of life and are often highly qualified professionals.
- The accusation that truthseekers crudely take events in isolation and fashion new conspiracy theories from them is unfair. They cite instead their identification of *patterns* of related occurrences that go beyond mere chance in indicating the high probability of wider programmes of manipulation.

As with the earlier list, it is hard to dismiss every one of these points. It is, after all, clear that we live in a world where we are routinely denied the truth, and that obfuscation and corruption are very likely endemic at every level. To refute continually that this could also be taking place on a larger scale does seem obstinate beyond wisdom.

Herein lies the problem; both sides of the argument plainly have something interesting to say, but neither wants to consider the opposing view, while the general academic opposition to addressing the evidence for conspiracies has become the subject of suspicion in its own right.

A long-standing criticism levelled at conspiracy believers is that their position is too often self-protecting. In other words, the belief that their mainstream marginalization is an institutional plot risks making them impervious to any outside challenges or official denials as they employ the catch-all retort, 'Well, you would say that, wouldn't you?'. However, the academic world can be guilty of employing similar mechanisms of self-defence. A middle ground must, surely, be found if the stalemate of the current stand-off is to be broken.

Factions within Factions

One of the inherent difficulties in creating a level plane of consensus is the tendency of peers to turn against each other, even within their own social groups. This is especially true in the alternative realms, where those who hold the most extreme views on the global conspiracy are prone to accusing more moderate elements of being 'shills' or 'working for the other side'. This hostile intolerance towards any view that does not entirely concur with theirs serves to isolate the extremists further from exposure to any logical argument which might challenge their rigidly fixed beliefs. It also enables them to characterize people who might otherwise be supportive allies as simply being one more face of 'the opposition', creating a world of lazy discrimination in which the crucial art of discernment never has to be nurtured and polarization is guaranteed. By observing this self-destructive component, the psychologists admittedly score points, and it is the loud minority that give the truthseeker movement a bad name. It is a mistake, however, to tarnish all of its adherents with the same brush when a significant proportion are generally fair in their reasoning.

The fanaticism that generates factional in-fighting often afflicts the more far-right contingencies of conspiracy thinking. For instance, those who are convinced that the core of the New World Order plot lies in a fervent Zionist agenda quickly lose patience with others who maintain an open-mindedness about its ultimate motives. They can be savage in their attacks on supposedly fellow questioners, openly accusing those not fully in the anti-Zionist camp of living in fear of the Jewish Anti-Defamation League; or they go a step further and promote their targets as being Mossad agents and suchlike. This narrow refusal to countenance any belief but their own in turn gives unfortunate fuel to the likes of media pundit David Aaronovitch, whose public attacks on conspiracy theorists (especially through his book *Voodoo Histories*) frequently revolve around the misguided charge that most truthseekers are inherently anti-Semitic. (The highly contentious area of Zionist conspiracies is discussed further on pp. 32–4.)

Another major source of in-fighting concerns the paranormal-versus-geopolitical debate. Some truthers are happy to embrace extra-terrestrial incursion theories (*see* chapter 7) as part of the possible motives for global cover-ups and political strategies, while others make great capital of the mysticism within the forceful secret societies that may underpin the New World Order (*see* chapter 8). However, those seeking public credibility for more grounded exposés (which have even crept quietly into the mainstream media in recent years) on outfits such as the crucially influential but entirely undemocratic Bilderberg Group, and who wish to keep investigations firmly on a political basis, cringe with embarrassment at those screaming about occult owl ceremonies (which do in fact occur – *see* pp. 242–3) or infiltration from alien bloodlines among the ruling elite.

Meanwhile, 9/11 truth campaigners – who have presented some of the most plausible conspiracy hypotheses – can, in turn, find themselves grappling with a small but loud subsection of theorists who insist that the planes which struck the buildings were in fact holograms, or that secret energy technology must have been used to bring down the towers, etc. This generates divisive friction, especially from conventional scientists who feel they may be on the cusp of attaining a credibility which is damaged by such arguments. Some counter that in the absence of establishment truth, then all possibilities, however novel, must be considered on an equal basis, but others hoping for even a little mainstream validation soon turn on those they perceive as bringing their efforts into disrepute, thus creating public squabbles that can risk discrediting the campaigners in outsiders' eyes yet somehow seem unavoidable.

Even among the more geopolitical thinkers, hostile subdivisions can appear. This was illustrated succinctly by the opening panel at the 2011 State and Corporate Crimes Against Democracy conference in London, which turned inwards on itself within minutes, as one firmly real-world political activist poured scorn on another panellist who risked referring to the 'Illuminati', one of the key NWO-related conspiracy staples. Anyone who dared mention extra-terrestrial agendas would doubtless have been escorted from the premises.

These internal conflicts among the truth community are inevitably one of the main difficulties created by the crowding of so many disparate subjects under the sole umbrella of 'conspiracy theory', and those who find the term unbearably claustrophobic fight tooth and nail to avoid it, usually to no avail. The regrettable fact is that anything which questions the sanctity of the spoon-fed status quo *is* currently lumped together in the eyes of the outside world; it is hard to see an immediate solution, until the day that each branch of what is currently seen as 'fringe' investigation is afforded its own category of respectable recognition. But such a development seems some way off yet.

Academic Friction

If factional divisions are prone to erupt between truthseekers, they are certainly not exclusive to them; conflict can also well up among academics who risk even examining the alternative world. Investigators who cling firmly to judgemental psychoanalysis seem safe enough, but those who stray into investigating the actual *evidence* for conspiracy beliefs can soon find themselves ostracized from their peer group if any kind of empathy is expressed.

The late Harvard professor of psychiatry, John E Mack, for example, was professionally secure in his fascination with those who claimed to have been abducted by extra-terrestrials as long as his focus lay purely in the realms of personality assessment. However, when Mack began to use hypnosis to unlock claimed memories and expressed the (surprising, even to him) view that many of his subjects were simply relaying something that was entirely real to them, whether they were physical or hallucinogenic experiences, he was met with overt hostility and calls for him to step down from his post. He narrowly avoided losing his job in 1994 after the dean of Harvard Medical School set up a committee to investigate his methods and beliefs, but it was a sobering lesson for other academics who might be considering delving into alternative paradigms. Ironically, Mack was killed in 2004 when an apparently drunken driver ran him over on a London street – creating a whole slew of new 'Manchurian candidate' (i.e. mind controlled) style conspiracy theories, implying that he was assassinated by authorities afraid of a respectable figure getting too near the truth.[2]

Another professor, the US physicist Steven E Jones, also found himself in hot water when he decided to use his skills to examine the mystifying total destruction of the World Trade Center after the attacks on 9/11 (*see* chapter 6). After publishing a highly influential 2005 paper entitled 'Why Indeed Did the WTC Buildings Collapse?' and presenting a seminar which supported the view that internal combustibles and explosives must have been deployed to bring down the towers, Jones soon found himself suspended from his position at Brigham Young University. This was followed by scrutiny from both the American Association of University Professors and the Foundation for Individual Rights in Education, among other bodies, questioning the scientific skills and ethics of a man formerly considered an expert in his field. Never able to return to his post, Jones elected to take early retirement in 2007, but he refused to recant and was confident enough in his beliefs to help found the influential organization Scholars for 9/11 Truth & Justice. The curtailment of his career was another demonstration of the grave consequences for those in the academic world who decide to go public with unconventional views, no matter how much they may be supported by empirical evidence (although Jones was also attacked by a few truthers themselves, dismayed at his dismissal of the energy technology theories).

With funding and reputations hanging on the accepted, if unspoken, agreement that certain lines of 'acceptability' will never be crossed and that peer consent must always be maintained, the academic world ensures, as much as the extremist conspiracy mindset, that nothing can threaten its self-imposed boundaries. Those who choose to challenge this must embrace the hard reality that trying to change anything from within will almost certainly result in ostracization, leaving only the dreaded course of becoming a 'maverick', as Jones, Mack and others have discovered.

Those conspiracy theorists unswayed by the fanatical critics from within their own ranks and who embrace the probability that mainstream respectability will never be afforded to them at least have the comfort that, as they are considered dissidents from the very start, there is little to lose by pressing on fully with raising awareness for their heartfelt beliefs. The academic world, on the other hand, is forever hamstrung by fear for professional credibility and the dilemma of whether to go public with something that challenges peer prejudice. Yet history records that it is the mavericks who often propel human evolution the furthest.

Evidence, Not Beliefs

A common truthseeker retort heard towards those who refer to conspiracy theories is: 'It's not conspiracy *theory* – it's conspiracy FACT.' Sometimes this is technically true (9/11, for example, was factually a conspiracy, whether perpetrated by al-Qaeda or contrived as a covert 'inside job'), but more often than not such a defensive exclamation is rooted only in opinion, which may or may not be correct. This speaks greatly of the passionate and sometimes impressive faith of truthers in their own convictions, but doesn't help convince an outside world conditioned to see these people as delusional. A bridge across this divide, therefore, has to be found and, taking the oft-vaunted merits of the 'scientific method' as a model (albeit one often breached by scientists themselves, masked with fudge factors and caveats), it is surely only evidence, and not belief, that can be seriously considered when trying to justify allegations of conspiracy. This does not mean that a well-represented theory will necessarily be afforded any more mainstream respect than the more unsupported ones, to begin with at least, but it does make it more likely that its plausibility will gradually seep into the wider public consciousness (as with 9/11, David Kelly, JFK, etc.). Indeed, this slow filtration process may be the bottom line in identifying the wider consensus on specific conspiracy assertions.

It could be argued that the majority of people once appeared to believe that the Sun revolved around the Earth, but that 'consensus' on this didn't make it true. However, many minds had, in fact, long challenged the geocentric model, although its public expression was suppressed by religious and political authorities. That much of the population will happily allow itself to go along with an official decree while it is more convenient or safer to do so isn't the same as something having validity. When convincing alternative information is presented, people are quicker to change their views on things than authorities would like us to believe. It may yet be that future history records a number of the supposed 'fringe' beliefs of our times as having turned out to be valid.

As the likes of Galileo showed in the face of institutional condemnation, it is the diligent accumulation of proper evidence, guarded for posterity, that ultimately speaks for itself. The truth will, in the end, surely be championed by this, rather than by the blinkered prejudices of a passing era, creating an even greater imperative to gather sensible and convincing data if conspiracy theory is ever going to become conspiracy fact. This requires an approach that uses discernment and reasoned analysis. Neither knee-jerk condemnation nor blind support for a hypothesis of any kind is of the slightest help without the application of these qualities and the presentation of meaningful evidence.

III) HOW FAR SHOULD CONSPIRACY THEORIES GO?

Paul McCartney: A Conspiracy Case Study

With the above observation about evidence in mind, the quest to balance *apparent* evidence with discerning analysis is, conversely, where the dividing lines between potentially credible conspiracy scenarios and wilder fantasies can become blurred, throwing up the strangest synchronicities. A fascinating example (as astrologer John Green has pointed out) is the relatively lightweight but luridly obsessive theory that ex-Beatle Paul McCartney was, in reality, killed in a car crash around 1966–7 but that his death was covered up, his place thereafter being taken by a stunningly convincing and equally talented lookalike. The suggestion runs that the surviving Beatles didn't want their careers destroyed so early by this tragedy, hence the plot, but that they couldn't help themselves leaving tantalizing clues to the events in their lyrics and record sleeve artwork thereafter. The Paul-is-dead scandal began as an apparent joke rumour that took off in US college campuses and radio station phone-ins in 1969, but gathered credence as more 'clues' were found, rapidly growing into a global phenomenon.

On the surface, the McCartney hypothesis seems so ludicrous, and indeed hilarious, that it doesn't even fall onto the radar of many serious conspiracy believers. However, in one of the weirder twists of fringe investigation, when reasons to support the theory are sought, even when the most tenuous and contentious connections (and there are lots of these) are discarded, tantalizing and almost disturbing points of potential validation do somehow manage to present themselves.

McCartney did, as a matter of record, have a minor moped accident in 1965, resulting in a chipped tooth and lip scar, and in 1967 his Mini Cooper car was written off in a motorway crash. There is evidence that the details of this latter incident were indeed obfuscated, although this may simply have been to cover up the possible involvement of hallucinogenics – and the fact that McCartney had loaned the car to a friend that night and was therefore not present. Or so it is claimed.

Some of the many Paul-is-dead 'clues' are demonstrably bogus or can be taken as curious chance. For example, the second line of the number plate on the VW Beetle car behind the zebra crossing on 1969's *Abbey Road* sleeve reads '281F' and is said by some to mean that Paul would have been be 28 'if' he had lived (1F being read as IF) – but actually he was then 27. Likewise, the mumbled coda of 1968's 'I'm So Tired' is often taken as 'Paul is a dead man, miss him, miss him, miss him', but in truth the master tapes reveal the line as 'Monsieur, monsieur, how about another one'. Meanwhile, the claimed (and almost unintelligible) spoken phrase 'I buried Paul' at the end of 1967's 'Strawberry Fields Forever' is, according to John Lennon anyway, simply 'cranberry sauce'.

What, however, do we make of the fact that, even recently, compellingly convincing and professionally qualified forensic comparisons of photographs before and after the supposed time of the fabled accident have been produced that apparently demonstrate quite a different facial and head structure in the post-1966 McCartney, along with other anomalies to do with height and voice tones?[3] Also, some of the numerous and more substantial 'clues' from the Beatles pantheon are admittedly very odd. Is it merely coincidence that the repeated spoken refrain of 1968's 'Revolution 9' played backwards produces the uncannily clear phrase 'turn me on, dead man'? Or that placing a mirror in the middle of the bass drum on the front of 1967's *Sgt. Pepper's Lonely Hearts Club Band* album sleeve produces, unquestionably, the phrase 'one he die', interspersed with Roman numerals (which some say give the date of McCartney's death, November 1966)? The same picture also includes, among its many celebrity cut-outs, an image of arch black magician Aleister Crowley, who famously recommended that learning to speak backwards or in code was key to the path of spiritual mastery.

McCartney himself is often singled out on the later album sleeves: he is the only one with his back to the camera on the rear cover of *Sgt. Pepper's*; he wears a black carnation in 1967's *Magical Mystery Tour* ballroom sequence, when the other three wear red ones; most famously, only he is bare-footed on the zebra crossing cover shot of *Abbey Road* (allegedly an allegorical 'funeral procession'). There are numerous other examples, endlessly pored over by Beatles fanatics, while several strange and morbid lyrical references also intrigue. 'He blew his mind out in a car' in 1967's 'A Day in the Life' is but one example, or the almost blatantly direct spoken line 'He hit a light pole and we better go to see a surgeon' in 1968's 'Revolution 9', together with its sung alternative, 'You were in a car crash, and you lost your hair', from the same year's 'Don't Pass Me By'. Some say the car crash references are more to do with the death of wealthy socialite and Beatles friend Tara Browne, who *did* die by hitting a lamp post in 1966 – the claimed inspiration for the 'A Day in the Life' verse – but the overt and repeated car crash themes elsewhere do seem oddly highlighted. There is a multitude of websites and books available which explore much more.[4] Taken together, it seems that there is, at the very least, an intriguingly unusual stock of coincidences that are hard to dismiss entirely when trying to assess this especially peculiar conspiracy theory.

What could it all mean? Could the death of such a prominent public figure as McCartney really be covered up so successfully? Even less likely, could the substitution of someone so like him, with almost identical talents, be effected so perfectly that not only the public but even his close friends and relatives didn't notice? (The extreme end of this theory runs that the somewhat disastrous introduction of Heather Mills into McCartney's life in the early 2000s was a deliberate attempt to stop his now-doubting doppelganger from lifting the lid on his real identity, and that covert forces employed her as a romantic trap through which to subject him to mind-control techniques which guaranteed his silence – of such darkly entertaining confections are some conspiracy theories made.) Are the compelling patterns formed by all the clues and mysteries, then, merely a crazed example of 'apophenia' at work ('the spontaneous perception of connections and meaningfulness of unrelated phenomena', according to the online *Skeptic's Dictionary*), as John Green has suggested, or is there a middle-ground solution?[5]

Those who find themselves unable to sweep aside all the inter-connecting references to a mysterious accident have suggested that there might have been a certain level of reality to the dropping-in of the clues, in that the whole thing was nothing more than a publicity stunt that got out of hand. The Beatles themselves continually denied this, with ever-wearier and characteristic sarcasm, but at the same time it is well-documented that their Apple enterprise, conceived in 1967 and officially founded in 1968 as the band's record label and promotional outlet, was often staffed by eccentrics or chemically enhanced opportunists. Could others have manipulated some of the artwork decisions, at least (as their involvement wouldn't explain the lyrical references), even if *Sgt. Pepper's* pre-dated the full arrival of Apple? If nothing else, it is possible that the rumours may have been actively, if quietly, encouraged to proliferate: sales of Beatles albums notably soared when the Paul-is-dead hysteria peaked. It is not hard to imagine the likes of the ever-cynical John Lennon deciding to stir the madness further (as his mischievous and self-referencing 'Glass Onion' in 1968 proves: 'The walrus was Paul', etc.).

Would anyone really go to such lengths (including, apparently, reconstructing McCartney's entire skull) just to shift a few more LPs, however? Beyond the perhaps secondary gain of the sales boost, others have suggested a more serious mandate to the whole affair. Even now there are some who consider that the whole Beatles phenomenon was in fact a state-sponsored social experiment in seeing how far youthful minds could be engineered into obsessively following (and copying by example) the development of fresh-faced entertainers through days of innocent fun into mass hysteria, passing to drug-induced fantasies and world infamy (Lennon's Beatles-bigger-than-Christ furore) and, finally, into recrimination and disillusionment (the Beatles' break-up). By this, the dangerous and inherently authority-challenging new creative energy of an entire generation may have been successfully neutered, having been taken on a ride from hope to disempowerment. To such morose theorists, the wonderful music and exhilarating journey through the 1960s was one big, if artistically valid, dirty trick. Seen through the lens of the Beatles' odyssey being a hugely ambitious 'psy-ops' (psychological operations) experiment, it can be better understood how promoting McCartney as a kind of fallen-but-resurrected messianic figure in the religious tradition might be perceived as an important component of a darker and more all-encompassing design.

Madness? Very possibly. This discussion is not included to support any particular belief around the Paul-is-dead theory, but employed as an important demonstration that anomalous phenomena and seemingly unsolvable conundrums can sometimes arise when seeking validation for certain hypotheses. Often, corroborative evidence exists nowhere beyond the fanciful mind of an individual and perhaps some easily influenced supporters. Yet, on other occasions, surprisingly compelling pieces of data present themselves, and then the journey must begin to work out what they mean. Is it simply apophenia conjuring patterns out of unrelated but coincidentally synchronistic events, or is a genuine phenomenon making itself known? In truth, it must always be the continuous accumulation of non-subjective evidence, and a solid inner logic, that tip the balance. That above all is what must be sought when trying to identify real conspiracies and cover-ups. The McCartney case thus intrigues, but doesn't fully pass above the probability threshold, leaving it in a curious grey area of its own. Other examples, however, even in the absence of firm conclusions, can certainly be seen to weight the scales in definite directions, as shall be demonstrated in later chapters.

As for McCartney himself, after a sullen silence on the issue for some months following the initial hysteria, he was finally cornered by journalists who arrived at his farmhouse in late 1969, and the singer was eventually happy to confirm that he wasn't dead. Curiously, he never said *Paul McCartney* wasn't dead, though. Because, of course, if the 1969 version was in fact a replacement for the real man, having successfully taken on his identity, assets and talents, then he would hardly be likely to admit it. And so the conundrum remains. McCartney – if it was still McCartney – should have known, regardless of one's own experience, that if the public wants to believe you are dead, then you are, in its eyes, dead, and anything beyond that is not your business. Why would people choose to believe the world runs in such a nefarious fashion, though? Perhaps because it's simply more fun that way, but also, maybe, for deeper reasons.

The Roots of Mistrust

In Ralph L Rosnow and Gary Alan Fine's 1976 essay 'The Paul McCartney Rumor', one of the key reasons they give for so many people being drawn to the whole Paul-is-dead phenomenon was a lack of trust in authority. They also point out that the assassination of John F Kennedy (*see* chapter 5) and the clearly unsatisfactory Warren Commission report on his death (which essentially dismissed wider conspiracy speculation and settled on the lone gunman theory), together with the subsequent eliminations of further inspirational figures such as Robert Kennedy and Martin Luther King, had left an entire generation with an underlying cynicism that anyone willing to stand up and shine might be destined for similar martyrdom. The apparent demise of such an inspirational youth culture figure as McCartney thus appeared to give him more societal validation. Though genuine tears were shed by fans over his perceived passing, it also elevated the artist to an untouchable level of sainthood, a mythic figure who would forever be unsullied by an otherwise inevitable decline into old age and mediocrity. At the same time, this also meant, on a psychological level, that public figures became essentially replaceable – one might be brought down, but another would always appear to take its place.

Thus, beyond the generally acknowledged entertainment value that the seemingly preposterous McCartney case undoubtedly brought with it (finding the clues became a compulsive hobby for some, while others simply enjoyed the very idea that such an ambitiously elaborate plot might be hatched at all), this new cynicism meant that the belief that someone so famous might die and then *actually* be replaced by a lookalike – with all the necessary deceptions to support it – was not as ridiculous a notion as might have seemed a decade before. After all, if the grassy knoll witnesses could be ignored and sidelined, and blind eyes turned from all the many anomalies surrounding Lee Harvey Oswald and his own mysterious killer, Jack Ruby, then, in the minds of many (the McCartney rumour was believed by millions across the USA in particular), anything was now possible, however bleakly underhand. This seam of mistrust, felt especially by youthful minds, had been further fed by the shockingly violent put-down of the 1968 student peace protests at Columbia University, and would intensify further with the acceleration of the Vietnam conflict, followed by the proven conspiracy behind the Richard Nixon/Watergate affair (*see* chapter 4). This in particular would quickly infect all generations with doubt about political leaders and stir a new awareness of the lies they might be being fed in other areas.

Herein lies the underlying stimulus that fuels most conspiracy theories: the seemingly unending combination of demonstrable falsehoods and unsolved mysteries that have been given ever more public exposure since the 1960s have resulted in a loss of faith that has gradually stripped away the quaintly innocent presumption that authority figures have our best interests at heart. The media façade that attempts to convince us that those cases which blast apart with grand revelations are the extreme exceptions to establishment honesty (in the UK, the 2009 MPs expenses scandal, for instance, or, in the USA, Watergate) results in a society that may idly appear to go along with it, but, deep inside, the general mistrust is palpable and entrenched. This most probably explains why polls show that a remarkable number of people now doubt the evidence about even something as historically significant as the Moon landings (*see* chapter 4) – and why around half the world's population is now prepared to believe that the US government lied about an event as huge as 9/11. Consequently, the development of widespread beliefs that a covert ruling elite may wish to curtail the freedom of its citizens, and even want to wipe them all out (*see* chapter 8), becomes more understandable.

It might therefore be tempting to psychoanalyse all conspiracy theories away, as the academic world has attempted to do, but the crunch comes with the more honest recognition that actual evidence *does* exist to support some of the areas in question. Pushing this aside, in the light of the increasingly prominent role conspiracy theory is establishing in the average person's thought processes (although they may not recognize it as such), is unwise and unhelpful. If authority is unhappy with being so mistrusted, then it only has itself to blame. Only by exposing and properly examining all the evidence around contentious events in a spirit of reconciliation will this unhealthy social time-bomb be defused, revealing the real truth, however uncomfortable it may be.

As a last word on the McCartney phenomenon, it should be observed that his case is a novel exception to the rule. McCartney himself (or whoever he now is) might wryly take umbrage at the fact that conspiracy theories around famous figures usually have it that they *didn't* really die, for example, Elvis Presley, Doors singer Jim Morrison, even Adolf Hitler. The emotional denial that often sets in when cherished or, conversely, hated figures pass on (especially if there is the slightest doubt surrounding the circumstances of their deaths) frequently results in rumours of their survival with stories that they have been seen setting off for secret lives free from the public's gaze. When attachments are made to figures that become part of society's framework, the thought that they are no longer there can unsettle the geography of some people's lives, even when that figure may have been abusive. The conspiracy theories offer a safety net, a hope for a kind of afterlife that leaves them feeling more secure. But poor McCartney instead has to endure the infuriating knowledge that some people feel happier believing that he *did* actually die; that way, he remains an ethereal figure of lost genius, instead of the miscreant who went on to perpetrate 'The Frog Chorus'.

John Lennon's own generally undenied martyrdom at the hands of a psychotic gunman in 1980 has given rise to a number of conspiracy theories of another kind, however, with many believing that killer Mark Chapman was under the influence of another Manchurian candidate-style mind-control programme sponsored by authorities keen to see a curtailment of the singer's comeback onto the world stage, with all his somewhat inconvenient politics of peace. This illustrates, once again, that virtually every conspiracy notion one can imagine is subscribed to by someone, somewhere. The question is, where does it stop? And *should* the process be stopped if there is evidence of any kind to consider?

Avoiding Hard Reality?

One of the secondary gains from subscribing to certain conspiracy theories is that they enable believers to put themselves at a more comfortable remove from harder everyday concerns. Some are drawn to belief in oppressive deception, either because (as previously noted) this situation is familiar to them from their own childhood, or because it fires them with a motivation to kick against something and thus develop their personality in new directions when this stimulus is otherwise lacking in their daily lives. However, the attraction to a good-against-evil psychological battle, while not without usefulness, can also result in an avoidance of attending to practical matters closer at hand.

In the run-up to the much-discussed mystical date of 21 December 2012, for example, with end-of-the-Maya-calendar doom-mongering rife in the alternative world, all number of imminent disasters were prophesied and speculated on. For all the attempted debunking, a 5,125-year cycle is, without doubt, embedded into several calendrical systems around the world and may speak of some wider cosmological or solar cycle, while the sense of a shift into a new era is certainly felt by many, even if the events may take decades to unfold. But by early 2012 some of the gloomier apocalyptic predictions which had been flagged up to occur *before* the December pivot had remained unfulfilled. Perhaps unsurprisingly, most of these were based on rapidly distributed internet rumours from generally unspecified sources – never an encouraging sign.

One of the more sensationalist scares involved the return of the mythic planet Nibiru, based on a Sumerian legend concerning the lost planet of the gods that, according to the late (and controversial) alternative historian Zecharia Sitchin, re-enters our solar system every few thousand years from a vast elliptical orbit, creating gravitational havoc and general upheaval as it does so. A specific take on this erupted in 2010–11, when an otherwise unremarkable comet named Elenin was widely endorsed as being, in reality, Nibiru, on its way to Earth at last. Websites swelled with alarming information on the potential effects of Elenin, and millions of hits were made on YouTube clips allegedly showing Elenin/Nibiru in the sky – plainly defocused shots of Jupiter, Venus and even the Moon. The unlikelihood that such a blatant phenomenon could somehow be covered up by a gigantic conspiracy of both professional and amateur astronomers (and the strange silence of the general population, none of whom apparently ever looks at the sky) seemed not to dissuade the faithful. Claims from NASA – not always reliable, admittedly – that nothing remotely spectacular could result from such a minor comet did little to still the interest. But, sure enough, Elenin eventually disintegrated into a smudge of dust, and nothing of note resulted. The voices behind the hysteria, of course, without pause for breath or apology, acted as if nothing had ever been said about Elenin and simply turned their attentions to other Nibiru candidates, be they errant 'brown dwarf' stars invisible to cameras, or other wandering celestial bodies. Others claimed that Elenin had been secretly nuked by world authorities.

The strange thing about such fear-mongering in the conspiracy world is that it seems to award primary status to tenuously speculative threats to humanity, based on the word of highly questionable or unknown informants, while far more ominous – and verifiable – events lie much closer at hand, yet go largely unremarked upon. While all the Nibiru/Elenin hysteria was going viral, for instance, official NASA reports on the very strong possibility that the Sun might soon throw out a huge electromagnetic solar flare, with potentially devastating consequences for global electricity grids and the entire technological infrastructure of the planet, were barely mentioned in alternative realms. The widely publicized 2010 gathering of the world's leading defence ministers and government scientists in the USA to discuss NASA's concerns about the worst effects of such an event, and the fact that the Sun had indeed broken records for sunspot and flare activity in the previous ten years, seemed not to count for anything among those more distracted with mystery comets and dubious internet images.[6] The forementioned deep-rooted mistrust in authority now automatically results in any declaration issued through it being treated with suspicion or subdued interest in some quarters. Yet the Sun's erratic behaviour can be observably confirmed as one of the biggest potential threats to our civilization today.

What is the root of this tendency to promote more fantastical ideas above threats that are closer to home? Perhaps as long as the mind can hold onto something in a realm of fairytale-like potential rather than face colder realities, a strange safety zone sets in, occupying the imagination and enlivening otherwise mundane lives. A similarly inherent inertia seems to be present in some of those expecting, or claiming to want, apocalyptic occurrences (something apparent in both evangelical Christian 'end-timers' awaiting the 'Rapture' and New Age thinkers seeking 'Ascension' into the Fifth Dimension). By courting hopes for earth-shattering events outside their control, they are simultaneously saved from having to make changes to their own lives, or the world's, here and now. Why do anything to improve existence when something might soon come along to turn it upside down and press the reset button anyway? This abdication of self-responsibility can be seen in the thinking behind a number of conspiracy theories. All the while imminent devastation can be speculated on, the acknowledgement of uncomfortable personal truths is held off for yet another day. And when one potential fails to deliver, another is quickly latched onto.

When some of those very earth-shattering events might show some *real* signs of arriving, it is curious to observe how a number of people unexpectedly retreat from their own position. When the kind of social upheavals long speculated on in the 2012 prophecy mindset, for example, seemingly began to erupt around the world in Arab uprisings, economic crises, riots and demonstrations, increasingly wild weather and other clusters of abnormal events, some who had been excitedly postulating on these very kinds of developments for years suddenly found different things to talk about. Others shrank away from the stark reality of what was surely always, in their own philosophy, going to be challenging to live through, and found diversions instead in the love-and-light realms or simply everyday hobbies.

The propensity to retreat in the face of unexpected confirmation is something conspiracy theorists should be wary of. If, for instance, whistleblowers suddenly proved beyond any doubt that 9/11 was indeed a New World Order-sponsored inside job, not only would there be an enormous psycho-social blow to the percentage of the population who had not previously believed this, but the political fallout would be equally devastating. One might even envisage open war erupting between various NWO factions and the rebellious masses, tearing the world apart in the process. If truthers are going to push ahead with seeking validation for their beliefs, they need to be ready to stand up for themselves in the battle that might possibly follow a wholly successful exposure – with likely retribution waiting in the wings.

The safe psychological remove that can result from speculation on the extremes of all manner of theories must, then, be brought into a fuller light of awareness if the theorists themselves are to serve their sometimes valid concerns better. The risk of retreating too far into a siege mentality that has more to do with escape than seeking empirical verification needs to be avoided. Worse, a total refusal to countenance *any* information presented by the establishment can risk taking people to places that marginalize them so far from normal society as to be harmful to their own prospects of living a reasonable life.

The question is, are all beliefs relative and therefore acceptable, or are there limits which should be imposed, or self-imposed, on how far people should take their quest for truth, and how much of it they express in public?

Drawing a Line?

To some degree, where one draws the line with alternative views on world events is a matter of sensitivity. Some are happy to explore the more likely geopolitical intrigues without too much concern, comfortable that enough evidence speaks for itself to make a serious case for conspiracy that even the public instinctively senses in its gut (JFK, David Kelly, etc.). Other ideas – however unfairly – are comfortably categorized in the popular mind as essentially harmless eccentricity (Paul-is-dead, crop circles, etc.) and are therefore tolerable as light entertainment. But the challenging of certain specific events or core dogmas can meet a sudden wall of harsh resistance and be collectively branded as unquestionably distasteful. This is where conspiracy theory enters dangerously inflammatory territory.

'Inflammatory' can, of course, constitute different things to different people. One subject that rocks between this and the novel eccentricity box, for instance – the claimed Moon landings conspiracy – crosses the threshold one way or the other, depending on an individual's emotional attachment to it. Those who viewed NASA's achievement of setting men on the Moon as the ultimate pinnacle of humankind's evolution, offsetting the unfortunate misdemeanours of the times (Vietnam, Watergate, etc.), can become passionately outraged at those who dispute the claim and believe that some or all of the supporting evidence might have been fabricated (*see* chapter 4). On the other hand, people who never really cared one way or the other about the Moon missions can be almost amused to consider that it might all have been an elaborate hoax, delighted to hear that even modern history is not beyond doubt, giving rise to an odd feeling of nihilistic liberation. As with the McCartney case, the tracking of clues and new information can become an absorbing hobby for easier-minded researchers, but the more world-weary feel the weight of such a potentially huge deception in quite a different way, aghast to learn that humanity might have allowed itself to be so manipulated, and wanting in turn to expose the situation for the long-term betterment of civilization.

Of the areas of concern that fall very firmly into the danger category, however, causing severe conflict and risking the reputations and careers of those wandering even slightly close to them, there is one primary exhibit. In recent decades, an extremist minority theory has arisen that the historical records for the Nazi persecutions of the Jewish people in the 1930s and 1940s have been exaggerated, even fabricated, to support a Zionist plot for world domination. There is a long history, of course, of animosity towards Judaism, resulting in many appalling atrocities around the world. Already scapegoated in a number of countries as being responsible for society's woes, the Jews were greatly damaged by the 1903 appearance of a Russian document entitled 'The Protocols of the Elders of Zion'. Generally held to be an outright forgery, it purported to be a record of the minutes of a meeting of Jewish elders in which they outlined their nefarious plans for global hegemony. Despite endless condemnation of the document and its questionable origins, it would nevertheless fuel the hate campaigns of Adolf Hitler's Nazis and numerous racist tracts.

Although the Protocols are largely agreed to be fake, some conspiracy theorists have claimed they embody many truths about the plans of the New World Order instead. But for the vocal minority that still believes the document to be genuine, particularly among the racist element, the notion that some or many of the claimed events of the Holocaust might have been embroidered, however astonishing this may seem in the face of the evidence, is not such a big leap for them to make.

The outrage expressed over this area, however, creates problems for those who would never subscribe to such a view, yet at the same time maintain that virtually nothing in history has ever been accurately reported without some ideological or political colouration. By loose implication (promoted by the likes of Aaron-ovitch's *Voodoo Histories*), this belief has quietly allowed the propogation of a false mainstream association which implies that the majority of conspiracy theorists are anti-Semitic at heart, by default. This in turn has been used unfairly to discredit perfectly reasonable areas of investigation, and created an atmosphere where even justified criticisms of the state of Israel and its politics (and occasionally, by association, US policies) can be slammed as racist.

This overly zealous kick back at those who question anything even remotely connected with Judaism has, by the inevitable law of polarities, actually helped stimulate a small but fanatical sect of equally hypersensitive anti-Zionists. The resulting conflict mentality, in turn, produces the problem that no speculation becomes off-limits; because neither side respects any lines in the sand, there is little left to lose by going to extremes and seeking out any minutiae that might unsettle the opponent. Hence the unhealthy development of the Holocaust denier (or questioner) on the one hand (the ultimate expression of attempting to disempower an event that was an acknowledged major factor in the rise of the Jewish state from 1948), and the view that any challenges to Israel are inherently anti-Semitic on the other.

The anti-Zionists – some of whom at least attempt to make a clear distinction between their abhorrence of extremist Zionism but toleration of normal Judaism – hold that they are simply speaking their personal beliefs and demand to know why they should not be allowed to do so. This area creates some discomfort in the Western freedom-of-expression debate, for if citizens are truly as free as their leaders like to boast, should they not be permitted to speak their thoughts, no matter how reprehensible others may consider them to be? This debate has surfaced a number of times when prominent questioners of the Holocaust (such as author David Irving, at one point incarcerated in Austria) have been imprisoned for airing their beliefs. Even people personally disgusted by these opinions have raised concern about the implications of such prosecutions, including the renowned linguistics professor and US rights campaigner Noam Chomsky[7] – Jewish himself – feeling that such legislation steers too close to the stifling principle of 'thought crime', as first imagined in *Nineteen Eighty-Four*, George Orwell's nightmare vision of absolute totalitarianism.

Conversely, some people feel so strongly about these issues that they see such laws as being justified, considering that even if the documented accumulation of factual evidence for something as significant as the Holocaust is unconvincing for a small minority, the looks in the eyes and tones in the voices of those who lived through the events tell more than enough to make picking through the fine detail a needlessly painful exercise. The problem lies in the issue of boundaries. Where should punitive censorship stop? A number of US neoconservatives, for example, have proposed similar laws to stop people questioning 9/11, laws which would bring with them accompanying small print on internet restriction, as anti-piracy copyright legislation has in recent times, creating a dangerously loose thread that could be pulled on all freedom of speech. It is perhaps not too extreme to imagine a fascistic regime coming to power that might eventually restrict opinions on almost anything it didn't like, adapting and extending existing legislation that began with the restriction of views in just one area.

These concerns illustrate the difficulties that can arise in the world of conspiracy theory, demonstrating how real extremism occurs, but also highlighting how simple *accusations* of extremism can be used unfairly to taint every – sometimes legitimate – line of inquiry. There are many sensitive issues around what constitutes genuine freedom of speech. These undercurrents are what have allowed the right-wing US politicians, in particular, to try to crush alternative political thinking. Many of them have directly accused conspiracy theorists of being not only innately anti-Semitic, but also of actively or intellectually supporting 'terrorism'. This has been especially aimed at those who believe 9/11 was coordinated by internal US sources: for if Middle Eastern terrorists are *not* solely seen to be responsible for the atrocities, the much-promoted *raison d'être* of the last decade or so of US global policy is implicitly undermined.

Polls and surveys demonstrate, perhaps inevitably, that a majority of people in the Islamic countries support the alternative version of 9/11, and it is a truth that fanatics of all persuasions do have a tendency to subscribe to conspiratorial views. However, given the underlying neoconservative implication that a large number of Muslims could, at heart, be potential terrorists, these statistics are then foolishly misused to demonstrate that interest in conspiracy theory amounts to implicit support for the likes of al-Qaeda, and that all such believers are likely to exhibit dangerous behaviour that needs to be curbed. There has already been a growing spate of Americans being sectioned under misused mental health laws for expressing fervent belief in conspiracy theories. The mindset behind this worrying caricature of truthseekers as terrorist sympathizers and therefore probable perpetrators of future atrocities was perhaps best summed up by President George W Bush's notorious and misconceived 2001 statement that 'either you are with us, or you are with the terrorists.' It was also, of course, the same president who famously exclaimed, 'Let us never tolerate outrageous conspiracy theories.'[8]

Evidence and Discernment

Why, however, should we not tolerate conspiracy theories? Because the likes of Mr Bush tell us not to? Because the media refuse to deal sensibly with them? Because academics claim they constitute a form of mental illness? Because people are frightened to hear about them? None of these stands up to much application of common sense. The motivation behind people's belief in conspiracies can be complex and subtle, and may vary from theory to theory. Sound-bite psychology that purports to explain away the conspiracy phenomenon under one umbrella does a disservice to too many human beings with intuitions, feelings and thought processes that deserve a little more respect, even if they may not always be right.

If there is perceived evidence of any kind to support a controversial belief, then it is probably wiser to allow that evidence to be examined pragmatically so that the ultimate truth of the situation can organically emerge, as it inevitably does in the absence of coercive censorship. The refusal of the mainstream to 'tolerate' any serious investigations of many of the areas covered in this book has led only to resentment and to an ever-growing proportion of the population that does not feel its views are represented or understood by an establishment that seems more concerned with navel-gazing protectionism than with presenting an accurate picture of the world. It is, in the final assessment, evidence, openness and discernment that will settle matters – not denial and avoidance.

This, then, is the purpose of the following chapters: to present a selection of widely discussed conspiracy scenarios, arranged in thematically linked categories, and to consider the evidence for them, attempting to reach beyond traditionally entrenched polarities. It would be impossible to cover every theory ever suggested, thus only those with a fair starting threshold of evidence, or which have been raised to prominence over the years, are included here. The investigation seeks to find the essence of the beliefs around them and applies logical analysis to see where the balance of probability lies, without condemning deeply felt opinions.

One of the reasons that people believe conspiracies must be rife in our world today is because history is strewn with former examples of covert plots and scandals, and it is valuable to look back into the past before turning an eye to more recent times.

IN SUMMARY . . .

Conspiracy Theory: Arguments Against

Conspiracy theorists are held in general contempt by the mainstream media and authorities – The academic world holds that belief in conspiracy is shaped by social background and psychological make-up, and not necessarily supported by evidence – There are unquestionable tendencies towards certain personality profiles within the conspiracy community – Truthseekers can lack discernment in their biased analysis of chosen areas – Claimed evidence could merely be the result of 'apophenia', of seeing meaningful patterns where there are none – The tendency to question everything can lead to extremism and socially marginalizing views.

Conspiracy Theory: Arguments For

The media's sidelining of conspiracy theories is unfair and based on an uninformed view of what the term means – The many public exposures of corrupt officials and criminality within systems perfectly fit the dictionary definition of 'conspiracy theory', making it very likely that all manner of other, more powerful, secret cabals must also exist – The academic viewpoint rarely addresses the actual evidence for conspiratorial beliefs, which can be strong in some areas – The psychological tendencies of certain people may be the very attributes that enable them to see the hidden truths behind a situation – For every false pattern that may present itself, other strange synchronicities can emerge which are harder to dismiss – The more extremist ideologies are held only by a minority – It is evidence that must be used to discern the reality of something, not beliefs.

CONCLUSION

By its technical definition, conspiracy theory would appear to be a perfectly acceptable sphere to explore. Its dismissal by the mainstream has created an atmosphere of denial that cannot be continued indefinitely. Sooner or later, the evidence to support some, if not all, of the theories will have to be properly faced if civilization is to move forward in a spirit of inclusiveness. There are some flaws in the thought processes behind conspiracy thinking, generating polarities where a self-protected extremism can grow, and academic observations do have something interesting to say about the psychological tendencies of the truthseeking community. But the reason why many people believe in conspiracy theories as often as not lies in the verifiable reality that evidence for them exists. If the intuitions that some develop through their personal background enable them to identify crucial factors in certain situations, it might be better to treat their faculties as a gift, rather than a pathology. Discernment and a conscious application of logic plainly need to be nurtured, but the characterization of all conspiracy theorists as psychologically damaged fanatics is a dangerously dismissive policy that does nothing but restrain legitimate lines of questioning in potentially important areas.

CHAPTER 2

HISTORICAL CONSPIRACIES

Those who believe that conspiracies are rife today point to the many precedents from history which categorically demonstrate that certain events have been engineered or manipulated, either to undermine regimes or to boost otherwise unachievable mandates for political or religious forces. Sometimes the mere spreading of a theory has been the conspiracy itself. Both the Roman period and the 16th and 17th centuries make for good examples that show human nature appears to have changed little over the centuries.

I) ANCIENT CONSPIRACIES

Plots of Older Civilizations

In the conspiracy pantheon there are countless theories *about* ancient times, especially concerning extra-terrestrial bloodlines being seeded aeons ago by the arrival of the 'Anunnaki' or all manner of godlike beings. It is believed by some that these visitors gave rise to alien/human hybrid races whose occult knowledge may have been handed down through generations to inform the structures of global power today; these areas are explored in chapter 7. What needs to be established in this section is that conspiracy thinking is nothing new in our world.

Conspiracies, or theories about them, have probably been present in every culture since one tribe of early hominids was accused of interfering with the running of another by stealing food and water, or by an elder doing it himself and blaming it on outsiders, justifying the massacre of local enemies. Tales of scapegoating and sleights of hands from powerful individuals to trigger desired actions that might otherwise be distasteful to the general population seem to run through most great empires, from the Assyrians to the Egyptians. Greek mythology is famously a rich source of conspiracy theories, with the wooden horse of Troy being perhaps the most famous example of a trick being used to launch an act of aggression. Even the gods were said to indulge regularly in plots and schemes with or against mankind (or among themselves) to sway opinion and mould the fortunes of war, as classic works such as the *Iliad* or *Odyssey* reveal. The Old Testament provides more tales of subterfuge and deception on a grand scale, albeit with divine retribution never far behind.

However, of all the innumerable examples, it is the Roman Empire that gives perhaps the most resonant comparison to the claimed conspiracies of today. As popular culture is fond of likening our times to the fall of the Roman Empire, with its 'bread and circuses' policies, distractive military campaigns in foreign lands and society falling into debauchery and drunkenness, it seems apt to use the Romans as the prime exhibit of conspiracies in antiquity.

Dangerous Times in Rome

Although Roman history was more often than not recorded by talented propagandists, keen to elevate or denigrate the objects of their bias, one thing is clear from the ancient texts: holding a powerful position was a dangerous game. From the start, Roman history was marred with the violent dispatch of its co-founder, Romulus, in 717 BCE by a conspiracy of senators, his sudden absence covered up with a conveniently spun legend of an overnight ascension to heaven, with the great leader apparently taken up in a whirlwind. From thereon it seemed that, for all its claims of civilized democracy (of a kind), first the Republic and eventually the Empire of Rome fell prey to an almost endless succession of plots, coups, family wrangles, machinations, poisonings and assassinations. Details of the conspiracies would often not be revealed until the deeds were done (or, if they were, it was vengeful slaves or badly treated lovers who blew the whistle), but everyone suspected the likely origins of certain events.

When Julius Caesar was stabbed to death in public by, almost ludicrously, a gang of around 60 plotters in 44 BCE, even the cover stories of divine intervention had been abandoned. The prevalence of background unrest (given that Caesar himself had unseated his predecessor, Pompey, by rebellion) must have become so ingrained in those times that conspiracy was not merely theory, but an integral, if unfortunate, component of Roman politics. Food and wine tasters and personal bodyguards were a must for anyone in a position of influence.

By the time the Roman Empire had run its course, around 35 of its emperors had been assassinated or murdered by internal cabals or rebellious factions. Despite this, the appeal of becoming emperor never seemed to fade, but the perils of the job were high. However, although such conspiracies were rife and widely recognized, these were largely assaults against society's *leaders* by other would-be tyrants. Given that much of modern conspiracy theory is centred around the concept of the state assaulting or deceiving the people themselves, what precedents for this can be found from Roman times?

In 64 CE, a notable portion of Rome was destroyed in the 'Great Fire'. Although modern scholars tend to absolve him, at the time it was widely believed that the incumbent emperor, Nero, had himself given the order to torch the area in question, hence the many, probably apocryphal, legends of his calmly playing a lyre (not a fiddle) while his own city burned. Some recorded that he sent out men feigning drunkenness to start the fire, while others claimed that soldiers or hired thugs openly went on the attack. The central allegation ran that Nero wanted to reclaim land near the Palatine Hill so that he could create his Domus Aurea palace, which was subsequently built there, and needed to rid himself of the aristocratic villas in the way, along with their obstructive occupants. Nero, in turn, blamed the early Christian community for the atrocity and, in a classic example of scapegoating, had confessions tortured out of its followers before ordering a spate of horrific executions. (Today, the plight of potentially innocent Muslim 'suspects' held captive for years without evidence in the wake of 9/11 seems not so very different to this situation.)

This was not the only fire to trouble Roman times. Later, in 303 CE, part of Emperor Diocletian's Imperial Palace was razed to the ground, generating yet another round of persecutions against the now burgeoning Christian population, which was inevitably held to be responsible. Once again, even at the time many saw Diocletian as being more likely to have ordered the fire, in his quest to find grounds on which to wipe out this alarmingly persistent band of religious fanatics. (Almost unimaginably, within their own lifetimes, the Christian survivors of these persecutions would see their beliefs embraced as the new official religion of Rome under Emperor Constantine, who decided to stop resisting the tide and instead use it to his own advantage.)

The readiness of Roman citizens to believe so widely that their own emperors might be capable of such acts against them suggests that lack of faith in our leaders was not so very different back then. Given the many other outrages, political murders and massacres (sometimes involving thousands of deaths) that usually followed each change of emperor, as alleged 'sympathizers' towards the previous regime were systematically eliminated, it is unsurprising that trust in authority was shaky. What *has* changed since then, modern conspiracy theorists would contend, is that such actions against the population are still carried out, but by more subtle means. 'False-flag' terror attacks (so named after the historical tactic of ships attacking their own fleets under the colours of the enemy to incite further hatred), social conditioning, sidelining of 'fringe' opinions and chemical suppression take the place of overt physical assaults on the population for the most part, while it is claimed that assassination continues to be used as a tool in specific cases, albeit covertly. 'Accidental' deaths such as Diana's, or numerous less well-known examples among people with potentially embarrassing details to reveal about prominent politicians, continue to raise enormous suspicions, and mysterious 'suicides' are rife among whistleblowers or witnesses (*see* p. 167). Dr David Kelly's contentious demise is perhaps the most famous recent example of the latter, as explored in chapter 5.

So the ancient world provides a clear picture that conspiracies, while less shamelessly explicit today, are nothing new, nor are the many theories surrounding them. But, lest the impression be given that a leap of 2,000 years or so might be allowed to mitigate the notion that such behaviour is still alive and (un)well in our society today, there are plenty of other historical precedents from more recent centuries. There are many that could be chosen, from numerous eras, but one period in particular provides a rich seam of illustration, albeit one that still involves Rome.

II) RELIGIOUS-POLITICAL CONSPIRACIES OF THE 16TH AND 17TH CENTURIES

Religious Unrest in Tudor Times

When dissatisfaction with his wife Catherine of Aragon's failure to produce a male heir coincided with his lust for the much younger Anne Boleyn in 1525, Henry VIII's attempts to be free from both the domestic and political restrictions of the Roman Catholic Church set in motion a chain of events that ensured a steady flow of wars, intrigues and conspiracies, some real, some merely alleged, that would last for centuries. Henry's jostling against papal authority over later controversial relationships, intensified by a desire for greater political influence, led to a wider struggle in which he effectively set himself up as God's new envoy on earth through the development of what would become the Church of England, with himself at its head. Catholic monasteries were 'dissolved', often destroyed, their occupants scattered or executed and subsequent popes were for generations characterized as tyrannical oppressors, scheming to destroy English sovereignty (as indeed soon enough they were, enlisting the likes of staunchly Catholic Spain to mount a number of famously failed invasions and attempted subterfuges).

The fuller story behind this crucial moment in history, which saw one of the most influential countries break with a force that had effectively governed the Western world for nearly a millennium, can be easily explored elsewhere. What is of concern here is the resulting chessboard, set for all manner of conspiratorial tangles that would follow.

Those who fiercely held Rome to be the unquestioned seat of God's power were aghast at Henry's challenge but, at the same time, by the early 16th century there was a growing discomfort at the political sway held over the country by a distant pontiff. This allowed resistance to the Church of England to fall away just enough for it quickly to become the official religion of the nation, while around the same time a general Protestant movement, begun by Martin Luther in Germany, was beginning to take hold in a number of European countries.

Given the strong conviction that had been forged in many hearts towards the new faith, coupled with an effective outlawing of the open practice of Catholicism, it was perhaps particularly unfortunate that Henry's eldest daughter Mary I decided that the nation should revert to Roman rule after she acceded to the throne in 1553. This might have been avoided had Henry's firmly Protestant son Edward VI not died aged only 15 (having been crowned at just 9). But, after a disastrously failed attempt to put Edward's favoured cousin Lady Jane Grey on the throne, resulting in her teenage execution, aggrieved Catholic influences returned with a vengeance to support Mary, and it was decreed that any heretics refusing to recant their Protestantism would be dealt with by public burning.

This unexpected reversal created a deep dilemma for those who genuinely felt that divine forces had spoken through Henry's actions. Rather than face potential damnation, between 1555 and 1557 a recorded 284 men and women went to the flame, while many others were tortured or died in prison. The deep resentment felt across the nation towards 'Bloody Mary' in turn resulted in a centuries-long persecution against Catholics when Mary died suddenly in 1558 and the country was converted back to the English Church by her half-sister Elizabeth I. In truth, Elizabeth probably had more Catholics executed during her reign than Mary did Protestants, but – fairly or unfairly – it is the 'Marian persecutions' that carved the most heartfelt memories of religious strife into the English collective memory, igniting a string of underhand conflicts that would ensure conspiracy theories became an indelible part of English life over the next two centuries.

Elizabethan Scheming

With much of Europe standing against Elizabeth's England, which was now firmly set on Protestantism, several covert schemes were mounted to undermine it. Many of these centred around attempts to place Elizabeth's Catholic cousin, Mary Stuart ('Queen of Scots'), on the throne instead. Consequently, numerous conspiratorial plots and counter-plots erupted around Mary, both with and without her knowledge, although she herself spent much of her life under English house arrest or imprisonment.

In 1570, Roberto di Ridolfi, an international banker (of the kind widely held to be behind much of the alleged global conspiracy today) who had already been involved in the 'Northern Rebellion' – an earlier failed attempt to foment a Catholic uprising amongst earls in the north of England – mounted an assassination/invasion plot against Elizabeth. Despite strong Dutch and Spanish backing, loyalists made party to the conspiracy managed to expose it before it could come to full fruition. In 1584, a similar attempted coup by Sir Francis Throckmorton, this time with French support, was also foiled.

Things came to a major head with the 'Babington Plot' of 1586. Double agents had already managed to set up an ongoing entrapment scheme with the confined Mary Stuart, by which incitements to Catholic insurrection were directly encouraged. Coded messages from Mary were 'smuggled' out to her supporters – neither party realizing that every supposedly secret communication was in fact being read by Elizabeth's secretary of state, Sir Francis Walsingham, who bided his time, waiting for enough undeniable evidence to implicate the plotters and ensure a full justification for the execution of this dangerous would-be queen of England. The ploy of setting up one's enemies, pushing them to enact the very things feared of them by active stimulation, with a view to then exposing the plots for political gain or to encourage hatred against them, is a recurring feature in the conspiracy world.

Theorists believe this technique is still used today, particularly concerning activities supposedly planned by the likes of al-Qaeda, but which, on closer inspection, reveal suspicious links to Western intelligences.

When a leading member of the Catholic gentry, Anthony Babington, became heavily involved in the plot to overthrow Elizabeth, it was his damning correspondence with Mary, detailing planned events and overseas invasions (this time from Spain, France and Italy), backed up by Mary's written consent, that finally gave Walsingham his chance. With a few more incriminating references falsely added into copies of the letters for good measure (presumably to ensure the absence of any mitigating loopholes), there was no longer any question of the plotters' guilt, and typically horrific executions, torture and prosecutions followed, culminating in the final demise of Mary, convicted of treason and beheaded in 1587. With no obvious replacement to take on a rallying role for Catholicism, the rumble of threatened rebellion quietened for a while.

A conspiracy of a less overarching kind occurred in 1601, when Robert Devereux, second earl of Essex, who had fallen out of favour with the now aged Elizabeth, led an insurrection that did actually lead to military action on the streets of London. It was aimed more at restoring his own prestige at court, rather than being an attempt at all-out regime change; enough support was rallied to lead 300 armed men into the city, but the general population failed to respond to the cause, and its few followers were easily quelled, leading to Devereux's inevitable execution. Although his intentions were largely self-centred, some supporters had seen an opportunity to use the rebellion as a spark for a wider Catholic uprising – including one Robert Catesby, who, having been wounded in the skirmishes, managed to escape with a brief imprisonment and hefty fine. Four years later, as we shall see, Catesby would be at the core of one of the most famous conspiracies of all time.

The Shakespeare Conspiracy

One of the more curious tactics used by the Essex rebels was the mounting of a production of William Shakespeare's play *Richard II* at London's Globe Theatre the night before the failed coup (not *Richard III*, as Hollywood's 2011 take on proceedings had it, courtesy of Roland Emmerich's controversial Shakespeare conspiracy film *Anonymous*). The play's theme of a preening monarch, prey to dubious advisers and falling into paranoia before being deposed by rebellion and ultimately murder, was apparently intended to help stir the mob to civil unrest, in the hope that the Essex revolt would gain the people's support next day. Although its intentions failed on this occasion, it is a strong early example of propaganda and public conditioning being spread through the guise of popular entertainment.

Shakespeare himself has, in recent years, come under the gaze of several conspiracy claims, with many considering a common playwright incapable of expressing so many rich insights into human affairs and displaying such broad knowledge of courtly etiquette without at least some kind of outside input. It has been widely speculated that more venerable figures such as Sir Francis Bacon, Christopher Marlowe or Edward de Vere, the seventeenth earl of Oxford, may well have contributed to the plays, or authored them entirely, aliased to protect their names from what was then seen as a somewhat disreputable profession. Speculation has been bolstered by the absence of any substantial recorded information about Shakespeare himself. Inevitably, most academics round heavily against this view, but there has been a steady increase in the number of leading classical actors and scholars prepared to consider openly that the figure we know as William Shakespeare may have been a composite front for either another author or a committee of contributors, which may or may not have included the bard himself.

The often volatile reaction against this theory produces in itself another telling example of how ingrained establishment resistance is to anything that threatens the status quo. This was keenly illustrated with the release of the aforementioned *Anonymous* movie in 2011, which opts for the de Vere hypothesis, mixing in the Essex rebellion for dramatic purposes. What was plainly intended as entertaining distraction rather than historical depiction (which, as we have seen, is hardly to be relied upon) was nonetheless met with some of the most vitriolic attacks seen towards mainstream cinema for some time, rooted largely in sheer outrage that anyone might so publicly challenge the authority of such a great British institution. However, the movie's shrewd inclusion of famous Shakespearian actors (including Derek Jacobi and Mark Rylance), obviously happy to put their names to something fronting the controversial idea, led to one of the most overt media discussions of a conspiracy theory, albeit a light one, yet seen. This at least stimulated a little more awareness that there *are* other views to the narrow selection usually voiced in the mainstream, even if they were met by a barrage of condemnation.

The Gunpowder Plot

When Elizabeth I died in 1603, her failure to marry and produce children or to name an heir resulted in Mary Stuart's eldest son being imported from Scotland and crowned the new English monarch as James I. Although one might have expected James to bear some resentment for the execution of his mother, he dutifully maintained the Church of England. A few acknowledged Catholic sympathizers had somehow managed to retain a quiet presence at court throughout Elizabeth's reign, tolerated as long as there was no open practice of their faith, which remained a punishable offence. Some had hoped the arrival of James might free them of this shackle, but he showed little sign of initiating a full emancipation.

One Catholic unable to contain his disappointment was one Robert Catesby, the resentful survivor of the 1601 Essex rebellion. Together with the aid of several other conspirators – most famously Guido (Guy) Fawkes – Catesby formulated a plan to assassinate James, together with his court and government, by igniting barrels of gunpowder stored in a convenient undercroft that ran beneath the old House of Lords. Had it succeeded, the blast would have constituted the largest peace-time explosion then witnessed, probably wiping out anyone within an eighth of a mile (as a television experiment in 2005 demonstrated).[1] It was planned for detonation during the state opening of Parliament on 5 November 1605; the hope was that a national Catholic uprising would follow, led by forces in the English Midlands, after which James's nine-year-old daughter, another Elizabeth, would be installed as a puppet queen, loyal once again to Rome.

These machinations have been recorded by history as the 'Gunpowder Plot', perhaps one of the most famous conspiracies of all time, still commemorated in Britain in its famous 'Bonfire Night' celebrations. Although awareness of its source inspiration seems to fade with each generation, some towns still uphold its fuller traditions, such as Ottery St Mary in Devon and, most spectacularly, Lewes in East Sussex (this author's birth town). Even today, the Lewesian streets see effigies of Pope Paul V and Guy Fawkes (along with more contemporary political ogres of the moment) blown up to annual controversy, as the events of 1605, together with the Marian persecutions, are remembered with large-scale pageantry, illustrating the profound effect religious strife of old has had on the country.

The full details of the Gunpowder Plot are less important here, but it is highlighted to demonstrate an example of a conspiracy (one descended from several previous intrigues) that has become a marked fixture in the nation's calendar. England's history, in particular, is therefore indelibly defined by the recognition that conspiracies do most certainly occur. If then, why not still now?

The misplaced assertion that only in days of yore did such things happen, and that too many lessons have been learned to ever allow it today, is a weak one, given the evidence.

Harder-nosed truthseekers might point out that the Gunpowder Plot was merely yet another assassination attempt, a failed terrorist rabble-rousing on behalf of a persecuted minority, rather than a full contrivance to defraud the people, as 'conspiracy' is often defined today. However, a twist to the events of 1605 may throw another light on it.

Catesby, together with his band of co-conspirators, was ultimately undone when an anonymous informant sent a letter to William Parker, fourth baron Monteagle, warning him not to attend the opening of Parliament if he valued his life. Inevitably, Monteagle raised the alarm and Fawkes was consequently apprehended as he guarded the powder barrels in the early hours before the opening of Parliament. As ever, interrogations, torture, retreats, shoot-outs and appalling executions followed, and the day of the Gunpowder Plot was done. But perhaps not quite dusted.

Who sent the crucial letter to the baron? This question has never been satisfactorily answered. It was widely assumed that the anonymous hand was most likely that of Francis Tresham, one of the plotters. As brother-in-law to Monteagle, he might reasonably have been concerned about his welfare. But Tresham, even when dying of a mysterious illness while imprisoned in the Tower of London, continued to deny sending the letter, and his involvement was never proven. This is where claims of a 'false-flag' operation have arisen.

Even at the time, voices were raised that, just as Mary Stuart's communications with co-conspirators had been openly set up and monitored to implicate her, so also might the Gunpowder Plot have been actively encouraged or even arranged by James's advisers, with or without his direct knowledge. There were many who desired to stir firmer legislation against Catholics, and, sure enough, the revelation of the potentially devastating scheme provided justification for the stiffest sanctions against the Roman Church in many years. Although the subsequent public reaction perhaps fell short of the all-out pogroms that hardliners might have hoped for, nonetheless much of the population enthusiastically embraced the bell-ringing and firing of cannons (eventually to become the more familiar bonfire and firework frenzies) that were officially decreed must take place each 5 November as an annual reminder of the baleful dangers of Catholicism.

If the Gunpowder Plot *was* a set-up, its result was a success and the upshot was the same (just as the West made useful capital of 9/11 by gratefully making it the launch pad for a new crusade into the Middle East), even without the false-flag connotations. But continuing suspicion has fallen on Robert Cecil, first earl of Salisbury, secretary of state and 'spymaster' for the King, and a protégé of the Mary Stuart-baiting Sir Francis Walsingham. In addition to seeking greater legislation against Catholics, he was also eager to stoke new pretexts for war against Spain and Portugal, through which England could rise to new power and influence (which, several conflicts and a century later, it did, as the British Empire rose). It is said by some that Thomas Percy, one of Catesby's conspirators, was a double agent, actively working for Cecil, and that Tresham was in fact poisoned in the Tower to remove his awkward protestations of innocence – for if *he* hadn't written the damning letter to Monteagle, other hands would inconveniently have to be investigated.

John Gerard, a Jesuit priest who had been implicated as being involved in the plot despite his denials (although he was certainly connected to Catesby's circle), plainly believed it was a case of officially sponsored terrorism. In the 1606 tract *A Narrative of the Gunpowder Plot*, published after his flight into exile, Gerard wrote:

For purposes of State, the government of the day either found means to instigate the conspirators to undertake their enterprise, or, at least, being, from an early stage of the

*undertaking, fully aware of what was going on, sedulously
nursed the insane scheme till the time came to make capital
out of it. That the conspirators, or the greater number of them,
really meant to strike a great blow is not to be denied, though
it may be less easy to assure ourselves of its precise character;
and their guilt will not be palliated should it appear that, in
projecting an atrocious crime, they were unwittingly playing
the game of plotters more astute than themselves.*

Jesuits are themselves held in heavy suspicion by some conspiracy
theorists today, but a number of odd things do arise around the
official story of the 1605 plot. How, after all, were 36 huge barrels
of gunpowder transported so easily by known Catholics into the
vicinity of the House of Lords without raising suspicion? It may
be that – almost certainly unwittingly – most of the plotters were
indeed patsies, believing they were working under their own
volition, while their movements were in truth being monitored
and unrestricted until the final moment of apprehension. (Things
do not always work like this: in a similar situation Emad Salem,
an FBI double agent, claims that in 1993 he was hired to provide
dummy explosives to a group of Muslim extremists so that they
could be implicated in a plot to bomb the World Trade Center
using a truck. However, in that case, Salem asserts that the group
was inexplicably given real explosives, as a bomb *did* go off, killing
six people and injuring over a thousand others; *see* p. 177.)

It has also been noted that John Streete, the soldier who shot
and killed Catesby and Thomas Percy (reputedly with the same
musket ball) in the final siege at Holbeche House following
Fawkes's apprehension, was, unusually, granted a special pension
for his services, even though taking them alive for interrogation
had supposedly been the desired course of action. Was this a
reward for removing the two men who might have had some
potentially embarrassing revelations to make under trial? (Not
one of the captured plotters, with nothing to lose by then, spoke

of any official sponsorship at their trials, however. If a double agent, was the more-knowing Percy betrayed by Cecil to prevent any inadvertent confessions, or was his death just an unfortunate accident?)

There are undoubtedly some unresolved issues around the false-flag claims. If he was secretly working for the authorities, why did Percy not just desert the scene once the plot was uncovered, instead of risking himself by staying on to fight the siege (unless he had already sensed Cecil's betrayal, and was now genuinely on the run himself)? And would it have been such a strange thing in those times for a real plot to have arisen anyway? The false-flag theories for the events of 1605, although increasingly popularized by modern theorists, remain unproven, and academics, unsurprisingly, generally discount them, although the accusations made at the time are grudgingly acknowledged.

As with the Great Fire of Rome, it is less the ultimate truth of the events that matters here, but rather the willingness of so many people to believe in the most convenient or self-reassuring versions. Inevitably, the Catholic sympathizers of the day were quick to support Gerard's view of state responsibility, while the Protestant majority took the plot at face value and used it to full effect, setting in stone legislation that would ensure Catholics remained pariahs in some parts of the country until well into the early 20th century.

In a curious distortion of all this, it is interesting to note that in recent years (thanks largely to the 2005 movie version of Alan Moore and David Lloyd's graphic novel *V for Vendetta*) Guy Fawkes has evolved into a figurehead for positive rebellion; a symbol of freedom rather than the dark traitorous figure hated in previous centuries. The movie's plastic Fawkes masks are now, for good or ill, the *de rigueur* uniform of social dissenters, from anti-capitalists to human rights activists. The mask-wearers argue that, just as Fawkes and his allies represented a persecuted minority seeking justice and the freedom to believe in what was right for them, so too do they. However, it is also the case that Fawkes unquestionably represented a terrorist mindset prepared to indiscriminately murder for its convictions, which makes for a less savoury modern icon, while the character of 'V' kills as much for vengeance as for ideology. This is an uncomfortable paradox that has not been satisfactorily resolved in the ascent of the revised Fawkes symbolism.

It is certainly the case that, had the Gunpowder Plot succeeded (if it was ever intended to), it is unlikely that the conspirators would have gained much real sympathy amidst the wide revulsion that would certainly have been felt against such an underhand and morally questionable mass killing. Without the full backing of a poised invasion force from another country (absent, this time around), it might well have been the Catholics of England who would have ended up massacred, rather than the Protestants, with the plot having the reverse effect to that apparently intended.

Whichever way it is looked at, the undeniable aspect of this case in point is that it was very definitely a conspiracy, one which would resonate for a great length of time and give rise to numerous other conspiracies – or at least theories about them.

'Straw Man' Theories

One of the acknowledged problems with conspiracy thinking is an occasional tendency towards hysteria that goes beyond the available evidence. Clear patterns that give reasonable grounds for suspicion in one area can be seen to give the green light for belief in another for which proof may be in much shorter supply.

For example, a credible UFO sighting from a reliable witness will often give rise to a number of 'back-up' claims in the days after by excitable but less discriminating individuals keen to support the veracity of the original sighting. Some researchers then happily add the later, more questionable, accounts into the general picture to bolster the overall effect. However, if these are then exposed as cash-in hoaxes or mistaken reports of otherwise mundane phenomena, public doubt is suddenly cast on the original sighting too, bringing the whole story into disrepute. Ultimately, blending good information with bad for the sake of sensationalism is a self-defeating strategy.

With this in mind, there is a good likelihood that certain wilder conspiracy theories may be contrived 'straw man' theories (i.e. easily blown away), deliberately spread by both media and authorities to encourage wider-eyed speculators into the more bizarre cul-de-sacs of truthseeking before very publicly demolishing the arguments for them, bringing down the reputation of all conspiracy thinking by simple association. There is reason to suggest, for instance, that this strategy was employed when certain UK tabloid newspapers insisted on running endless conspiracy-flavoured 'leaks' about the official inquest into the death of Diana, Princess of Wales (*see* p. 154) in the run-up to the verdict in 2008. It was implied that all sorts of dark deeds were about to be revealed when, in truth, the final report drily rejected any such notions and plumped firmly for the mundane. Suddenly the promised scandalous discoveries were made to seem ridiculous, sending out a clear message to the population of the perils of such deranged thinking. Had it all just been a ploy to sell more papers (which it certainly did), or was something more fundamental at work?

Many other areas of conspiracy speculation, from 9/11 theories to Moon landing doubts, have almost certainly fallen victim to related tactics, with the more outlandish elements seemingly encouraged into wide prominence, allowing awareness of the more convincing areas to be eclipsed. Hence conspiracy theories can arise over the *contrivance* of conspiracy theories themselves, and once again there are clear historical precedents for this occurring.

The Titus Oates 'Plot'

Telling genuine concern from deliberately stirred hysteria is not always easy. The English Civil War of the 1640s saw long-brewing struggles between Parliament and the monarchy conflate into disastrous open conflict, culminating in the execution of Charles I and leaving a jittery and confused nation in its wake. Although the fallout from the Gunpowder Plot had apparently ensured that long-term resistance to open Catholicism would endure, some had marked reservations about the replacement king, Charles II, whose line was restored to the throne in 1660 after the short-lived Puritan republic crumbled following the death of Lord Protector Oliver Cromwell. Although Charles himself maintained the Protestant religion, his brother James Stuart – heir to the throne, in the absence of any legitimate children from Charles – had openly re-embraced Catholicism, and fear of renewed sympathies towards the old religion were seeping once again into a traumatized population. This was strongly demonstrated when the Great Fire of London swept through in 1666, devastating large swathes of the city. Scapegoats are always sought in times of crisis, with cholera or plague outbreaks throughout history habitually blamed on despised local religious or ethnic minorities having poisoned the water supply and suchlike. Thus the London blaze immediately raised charges that Catholic (specifically Jesuit) insurrectionists were responsible.

Into this smog of paranoia stepped two dubious characters: Israel Tonge and Titus Oates. Tonge had been rector of a church lost in the Great Fire. Harbouring deep loathing towards Catholicism, he subscribed to the view that Jesuits were responsible for the calamity and set about writing a series of inflammatory pamphlets denouncing Rome and accusing it of numerous conspiratorial designs. It was the tract co-authored with Oates, however, that was to create the 'Popish Plot' – one of the most insidious and harmful episodes in English history.

Titus Oates was always of questionable background. Reportedly an unintelligent bigot from an early age, what he lacked in personal finesse or achievement he made up for by attacking the reputations of others. He had already been jailed for perjury after falsely accusing his schoolmaster of sodomy, yet still managed to forge a career as an Anglican minister (although this didn't prevent Oates from later being accused of sodomy himself). At some point Oates somehow found himself being drawn to Catholicism, and actually studied at a Jesuit institution at St Omer in France. Although Oates later claimed this was merely a ploy to infiltrate Jesuit secrets, it seems likely that his subsequent expulsion from St Omer in 1678 sparked a revengeful streak in him against his former masters.

The publication of Tonge and Oates's entirely self-descriptive pamphlet, *The True and Exact Narrative of the Horrid Plot and Conspiracy of the Popish Party Against the Life of His Sacred Majesty, the Government and the Protestant Religion, etc.*, in the same year of 1678 can thus be seen in two ways: either as a foolish act of vengeance filled with personal religious hatred, or as yet another covert scheme from authorities, using the helpful lies of vicious ignorance to stir up a new wave of fear to stem a reawakened tide of Catholic influence. The torturous tract made claims that assassination plots were being planned against the King from within his own ranks, accompanied by the usual tales of massed invasion forces poised to leap upon England from foreign shores loyal to the Pope, the instigator of the scheme.

This time, however, unlike previously uncovered 'plots', there was no evidence of any kind to support the claims, which seem to have sprung almost entirely from the minds of Tonge and Oates (primarily the latter) or were rooted in nothing more than the standard fear-mongering rumours of the day, which regularly rippled through England's anxious cities. Even Charles II, confronted with news of the alleged plot, seemed dubious about its reliability and was reluctant to act without further evidence.

A lack of substance, though, did not stop the effectiveness of Oates's scheme. Word of the Popish Plot soon spread to a public ready to blame all ills on the old foe, and the renewed abhorrence of Catholics began to result in the usual depressing rounds of death, torture and persecution. With the government unable to ignore the rapidly disruptive gossip any longer, Oates was called before the magistrate Sir Edmund Berry Godfrey in September 1678 and, later, the Privy Council, where he managed to persuade it that action was needed. Rather than treat Oates's increasingly wild claims and indiscriminate naming of 81 alleged conspirators with the contempt they should have received (anticipating the similarly paranoid curve which would finally undo US senator Joseph McCarthy during his Communist 'witch-hunts' of the 1950s), instead Oates was given his own squad of soldiers, with which he tracked down and arrested suspects. All this was given further momentum when magistrate Godfrey was mysteriously murdered. No one was ever convicted of the killing. At the time it was broadly assumed to be the result of a Catholic assassination, but it is not unreasonable to consider that Oates or his supporters might have been behind it, such was the gift Godfrey's death brought to their cause. Anti-Catholic hysteria went into overdrive and Parliament declared its full acceptance of the Popish Plot, resulting in the eventual trial and execution of 15 Catholic lords, noblemen or archbishops, and further oppression of the remaining Catholic population.

Yet, underlying all of this, there remained a lingering uncertainty in some quarters, with a faint discomfort at the dogmatic zeal and obviously fevered imagination of the man at the centre of all the disruption. As executions went ahead in the face of very flimsy evidence (generally based on overly suspicious misunderstandings, or invented allegations fronted by obviously paid 'witnesses'), wiser heads began to ask questions, especially when Oates – who by 1680 had been given his own apartments in Whitehall – pushed too far with his fantasies. Outlandish claims such as those which stated that assassins were planning to shoot the King using silver bullets to inflict unhealable wounds were indicative of the hubris Oates had fallen into (although such ideas are no less strange than some of the conspiracy theories adhered to today). Doubts grew and the justice system turned against believers in the Popish Plot as, one by one, supposed conspirators began to be acquitted.

Titus Oates finally made the mistake of turning against the King himself (who had never been convinced by the plot) and was consequently convicted of perjury and sedition under the new and, as feared, Catholic-leaning King James II in 1681. Oates was imprisoned for three years and publicly whipped and pilloried on an annual basis, before eventually being pardoned under the 'Glorious Revolution' of 1688 (a virtually bloodless Dutch invasion instigated on the invitation of Parliament itself), which saw off James and restored England once and for all to its Protestant course through the accession of William of Orange and Queen Mary. Oates's reputation never recovered, but the whole episode had neatly demonstrated the unnerving willingness of the population to go down a dark avenue of imagination on the word of a tiny and prejudiced minority.

A Lasting Damage?

The Titus Oates catastrophe seems to have marked a turning point for blanket public belief in conspiracy theories, in England at least, and damaged the credibility of those who continued to support them without good evidence. Conspiracy theorizing would never go away, and has grown to prominence once more in our times, but never again would the nation allow itself to be quite so susceptible. Indeed, talk of conspiracies would instead be gradually driven underground into the unhealthy twilight existence it appears to inhabit today, whereby many people believe in them, but public expression of that belief is frowned upon and ridiculed by the mainstream. Surely there is a healthier balance to be struck. Unfortunately, Nazi-ruled Germany in the 1930s would fall victim to the same corrupting furrow of conspiracy paranoia ploughed by the likes of Oates, allowing blatant lies and ethnic hatred to give consent to oppression and scapegoating, bringing down even further the reputation of the conspiracy theorist in modern society.

As for prejudice against Catholicism, although lessons were learned from the fallout of the Popish Plot, this didn't see an end to some of the more fanciful accusations. Shortly before being ousted by the Glorious Revolution, the by-then Catholic sympathizer James II had thus far produced two adult daughters. They were seen as less threatening heirs to the throne because both had been brought up Protestant, and many were accepting of James seeing out his uncomfortably Rome-friendly reign in the hope that normal service would be resumed with the next generation. However, when James's wife, Mary of Modena, suddenly gave birth to a *male* heir in 1688 – who by law jumped the accession ladder – panic ensued, as this time it was likely that the boy would be raised a Catholic, threatening a further divided nation and yet another reversal of the official faith. Unable to accept the uncomfortable reality, a new conspiracy theory swept the nation which insisted that the boy had, in truth, been still-born and that a substitute male child had been secretly smuggled into Mary's chamber inside a bed-warming pan, to masquerade forever more as the new heir to the throne. In the event, James fled the country on the arrival of William and Mary, and this seemingly bizarre theory, which might otherwise have become a potential flashpoint further down the line, was never pursued further. (This has curious resonance with the claims that President Barack Obama was not really born a US citizen, and was thus an illegitimate ruler; *see* p. 235. Public concern about such things has a long historical thread.)

There are many more religious conspiracies, theories or claims that could be included here as precedents for the kind of situations still arising today, but enough has been presented to show that conspiracies of one kind or another have always been, and probably always will be, an ingrained part of the social and political landscape. Others might argue that the passing of the centuries has changed things, and that no one would dare enact such tactics in our more enlightened civilization. Unfortunately, even recent history demonstrates that this is very much not the case.

IN SUMMARY . . .

Historical Conspiracies: Arguments Against

History may not have been recorded accurately, therefore basing conspiracy theories around what we are today told occurred might not be reliable – People 'were simpler' in former centuries, and therefore might have had to resort to conspiratorial behaviour in a way no longer required in our more enlightened times – Some claimed conspiracies, as with the Titus Oates plot, turned out not to be true – Given the enormity of history, by the law of averages certain events can be plucked out as conspiracy examples, but does focusing on them create a disproportionate impression?

Historical Conspiracies: Arguments For

If history is considered reliable enough that children can be taught it as fact, then the clear signs of conspiracy embedded within it must be equally valid – There is no substantial difference in the basic social structures of today compared to those which appeared to be present in earlier centuries; therefore it is likely that the same kind of undercurrents which generate conspiracy are still present

– *The recurring patterns of deception and false-flag tactics, from ancient times to more recent centuries, all exhibit the same basic components.*

CONCLUSION

Conspiracy theories of one kind or another have long been with us, and there is clear evidence, even at this historical distance, to give substance to a significant number of them. Some examples are not even so far back in time as to allow that they might have taken place in an environment of notably lesser conscience.

Whilst not automatically supporting the reality of every conspiracy speculation, these episodes, along with the hundreds of others that could have been included, provide plentiful evidence that today's mainstream implication that such things couldn't possibly happen today is almost certainly mistaken.

CHAPTER 3

FALSE-FLAG CONSPIRACIES

If history is littered with numerous examples of likely or proven conspiracy, a more recent century alone provides a notable upsurge. The 20th century was rich in probable cases of false-flag attacks or manipulated incidents for military gain, events which might have paved the way for the widespread allegations that the 9/11 attacks at the beginning of the 21st followed the same pattern.

I) THE SINKING OF RMS *LUSITANIA*

One of the recurring themes of modern conspiracy thinking is that of wars being started, or misdirected, by false-flag attacks and engineered atrocities. Perhaps the most discussed potential case of this kind is now 9/11, but the 1941 attack on Pearl Harbor may have been an earlier model (below). However, others look back still further – to the 1915 sinking of RMS *Lusitania*. Indeed, questionable events of this kind often seem to involve maritime activities, as we shall see.

On 7 May 1915, in the early stages of the First World War, and with nearly 2,000 passengers aboard, the British ocean liner RMS

Lusitania was passing along the south coast of Ireland on its return to Liverpool from the USA. At 2.10pm, the ship was torpedoed by a German U-boat. Amidst panic and a chaotic evacuation, only 764 survivors were left when the vessel disappeared beneath the waves just 18 minutes later. Women, children and a large number of dignitaries never stood a chance of escape, trapped in black corridors and cabins by the almost instant electrical failure after the impact.

International outrage followed the sinking, and the horror became emblematic of the evils of the German Empire, which now had to be defeated across the network of trenches being dug in western Europe. An impressionistic image of a mother and baby trapped underwater soon appeared on posters bearing the simple word 'ENLIST'. It was a powerful tool in galvanizing support for the struggle, and was especially influential in bringing a previously reluctant USA into an active combat role. This seems fair enough, given the enormity of the atrocity against civilians, particularly at a time when killing non-military personnel, without warning at least, was greatly frowned upon. Why, then, has *Lusitania* become the focus of so many conspiracy theories over the years, casting doubt on its apparently indiscriminate targeting?

Given the importance of the *Lusitania* incident as a propaganda coup, it is easy to see why some believe it was no mere coincidence that such a sensitive event took place so early in the conflict, asserting that it was specifically contrived to help escalate the first of two globe-encompassing conflicts which numerous theorists hold were in themselves huge moves on the New World Order chessboard (*see* chapter 8).

The official position is that *Lusitania* was a purely civilian liner, but other claims suggest its hold was in fact loaded with shells and high-explosives bound for Europe, making it a prime target for German U-boats and dooming its mostly unwitting passengers to an almost guaranteed watery grave. Arguments over the ordnance onboard *Lusitania* remain unresolved to this day, although large amounts of rifle rounds and other small munitions were clearly being carried. As for the presence of larger explosives, it is apparent from German records that its vessel *U-20* fired just one torpedo, yet many surviving witnesses described *two* vast explosions – one following almost immediately after the other. If not another torpedo (as was thought at the time), then what caused the large secondary blast, which tore *Lusitania*'s hull wide open? It is widely thought that this may have been evidence of something more deadly than non-explosive rifle ammunition going up in the cargo hold, although the more orthodox view sees a breaching of the high-pressure steam generating plant as being a more likely cause.

Either way, and most importantly, the German government clearly *believed* that the ship was being used for secret military cargo and had decreed that it saw *Lusitania* as a legitimate target even before it left the USA. Aware that several German-Americans would be onboard, the German embassy had advised citizens about the dangers with this warning:

> *Notice! Travelers intending to embark on the Atlantic voyage are reminded that a state of war exists between Germany and her allies and Great Britain and her allies . . . travelers sailing in the war zone on ships of Great Britain . . . do so at their own risk.*

The notice was submitted as an advertisement to at least 50 US newspapers well before *Lusitania* sailed. However, perhaps tellingly – due, according to some, to interference from the US State Department – all but one of the papers failed to run the notice, and most passengers set off in blissful ignorance, never thinking a civilian liner would be vulnerable, even in a time of combat. Not, at least, until the torpedo struck, when it was realized that the rules of war had suddenly changed.

The conspiracy view contends that the German government had been deliberately tipped off that *Lusitania* was carrying large amounts of explosives that would ultimately be deployed against it, ensuring that *U-20* would turn its sights on the ship. Further suspicions have been raised by the observation that, as far as can be ascertained, *Lusitania* was never informed by radio that an alarming 23 British ships had been attacked (and three sunk) by U-boats since its setting off from New York – in the same southern Irish waters that it was heading into. It had not gone out of its way, therefore, to manoeuvre in a fashion that might evade enemy action as it entered the danger zone, and did not proceed at the top speed, which the captain would surely have ordered had he known of the peril nearby. The fact that records of the transmissions between the Admiralty and *Lusitania* during its final voyage remain classified today can only deepen conspiratorial musings.

All this might be dismissed as mere 'incompetence' or a foul-up, the usual lame yet often effective defence given to explain major intelligence failures (deployed especially around the events of 9/11, and the Iraqi 'weapons of mass destruction' debacle). However, taken with the fact that *Lusitania*'s military escort vessel *Juno* was mysteriously withdrawn, for reasons unknown, just as the liner entered the treacherous sector – allegedly on the orders of First Lord of the Admiralty, Sir Winston Churchill – one has to wonder at the curious nexus of threads. On its maiden voyage just two months earlier, *Lusitania* had enjoyed the consistent protection of *three* warships as it neared British waters, and lack of available fleet could not explain *Juno*'s strange disappearance on the day of the sinking, as at least four potential escorts were moored at Milford Haven without official duty.

Churchill himself, far from being seen as the great national hero of history, is held by many truthseekers to have been a key player in fomenting dubious New World Order policies. Whether Churchill specifically sealed the fate of *Lusitania* is unknown, but there is an unequivocal record which shows that Churchill was more than happy for non-military ships to be sunk if such tragedies were to change the course of the war in a desired direction. Just months before, on 12 February 1915, in a letter to Walter Runciman, president of the Board of Trade, Churchill wrote:

> *It is most important to attract neutral shipping to our shores in the hope especially of embroiling the United States with Germany . . . For our part we want the traffic – the more the better; and if some of it gets into trouble, better still.*[1]

Thus, for Churchill, the sinking or attacking of ships was without doubt seen as useful bait to bring the USA into the war. Would this extend to openly compromising the safety of one of his own country's liners, though? Critics of the conspiracy view contend that the letter directly refers to 'neutral' shipping, rather than British, and challenge the thought that even this famous political gambler would be quite as gung-ho as to put into print a wish to see some of his own vessels torpedoed. Yet it must have been in his mind. History records that when stakes are high, 'necessary sacrifices' can all too often become legitimized in the minds of those we riskily entrust with our lives.

Viewed overall, it is difficult to dismiss entirely the notion that *Lusitania*'s safety was deliberately compromised, whoever might have been responsible, and it is clear that both British and US leaders knew long in advance that such an event might be the catalyst for the acceleration of one of the most terrible conflicts in history. The official narrative, just as with the Second World War, has it that America was keen to stay out of the self-styled Great War, until the moment its own citizens were attacked. However, seasoned truthseekers believe that the 'script' was written long in advance (just as the Project for the New American Century appeared to anticipate 9/11 – *see* p. 192), to create an early step towards 'one world government', and that hints of foreknowledge were dropped enough times to be more than chance asides. A conversation in the run-up to the Lusitania incident, recorded between Colonel Edward Mandell House, one of President Woodrow Wilson's top political advisers, and Sir Edward Grey, British foreign secretary, had Grey asking:

What will America do if the Germans sink an ocean liner with American passengers on board?

House reportedly answered with:

I believe that a flame of indignation would sweep the United States and that by itself would be sufficient to carry us into the war.

It could be argued that such a course of events might be bound to follow in a time of conflict, and that likely outcomes were merely being discussed, but something about the solidity of the answer suggests a more knowing tone.

Some have suggested that the plans for *Lusitania* went one stage further, and that the ship might have been torpedoed by British forces themselves. Given other shameful moments in conspiracy history, events of such a hubristic magnitude cannot be entirely ruled out, but in this case it seems unlikely. No whistleblowers nor convincing evidence have ever come forward to support such a version of events, and records from *U-20* make it clear that the German navy was responsible for the attack.

The events that led *Lusitania* to be where it was, however, in a vulnerable position without escort, are far more questionable, and it stands as a likely exhibit of a sacrifice being made for a wider cause. What constitutes a 'cause', of course, is somewhat subjective, and the people or objects being sacrificed are more often than not simply unfortunate pawns in a wider game that cares little for human welfare – or the truth.

II) PEARL HARBOR

During the next round of global conflict, the defining moment of the apparently surprise Japanese attack on the American naval base at Pearl Harbor in Hawaii on 7 December 1941 is also perceived by many doubters as having been a contrivance. In resonance with the *Lusitania* situation, the event shows signs of having been manipulated into occurring, and it again gave the green light to bring an outwardly reticent USA into active combat.

There is little doubt that American politicians knew well that an attack would come sooner or later, if only through their own open provocation of Japan, responding to that country's severe hostilities in the Far East. This included the banning of Japanese oil exports earlier in the year, and other measures guaranteed to generate a reaction in a world at war.

Although the official view is that enemy action was first expected in the Philippines, hence US astonishment over the supposedly unexpected targeting of Pearl Harbor, the growing accumulation of evidence over the years, including undisclosed intelligence reports and obfuscated code-breaking of Japanese transmissions, suggests that there was more than sufficient advance warning for greater protective status to have been accorded to Hawaii. Public awareness of this has seeped through enough that the theory of the pivotal attack being deliberately allowed is now widely subscribed to, even beyond the conspiracy fringe – to the fury of American patriots.

It is well-known that President Franklin D Roosevelt – seen as another major player in the NWO agenda by conspiracy theorists – was keen to enter the struggle against Japan's Nazi allies in Europe, but faced resistance from internal political and corporate influences. Many Americans had strong business interests in Germany and remained far from convinced that it would lose the war. But the loss of nearly 2,500 US servicemen at Pearl Harbor, with many more injured, together with the destruction of 18 warships and over 200 aircraft, soon encouraged their consent.

Some observers felt this was a manufactured situation, even at the time. Of the days in the run-up to the attack, Vice Admiral Frank E Beatty wrote:

Prior to December 7, it was evident even to me . . . that we were pushing Japan into a corner. I believed that it was the desire of President Roosevelt, and Prime Minister Churchill, that we get into the war, as they felt the Allies could not win without us and all our efforts to cause the Germans to declare war on us failed; the conditions we imposed upon Japan – to get out of China, for example – were so severe that we knew that nation could not accept them. We were forcing her so severely that we could have known that she would react toward the United States. All her preparations in a military way – and we knew their overall import – pointed that way.[2]

So the political environment in which the attack occurred was clear. The question is whether the precise location of Pearl Harbor was anticipated as the main flashpoint. On this, arguments continue, although it seems hard to believe, given the clear hints available at the time, that US intelligence could have really been *that* unsuspecting that Pearl Harbor might be the place. It has also been argued that the best vessels in the US fleet were absent from the Hawaii base that day, as if being preserved from harm, although this is hotly contended by military sceptics. Whatever the details, plainly, as with Churchill's letter on the benefits of 'neutral' shipping meeting trouble during the First World War, Roosevelt, having lit fuses in a number of directions, was just waiting for the inevitable retaliation, although his aides professed that perhaps it came harder than expected. Of the President's reaction, his administrative assistant, Jonathan Daniels, wrote:

The blow was heavier than he had hoped it would necessarily be . . . But the risks paid off; even the loss was worth the price.

This statement in itself unequivocally illustrates that provocation was expected to bring action, although this was never openly declared. From the comments of numerous other officials, it is also likely that a number of insiders knew well where and when the 'blow' would take effect, with Vice Admiral Libby writing:

> I will go to my grave convinced that FDR ordered Pearl Harbor to let happen. He must have known.

In times of conflict, naturally, there is always confusion, and a need to conceal information from the enemy. But it is transparent from a myriad of examples such as the Pearl Harbor events that the 'fog of war' let-out is used over and again to obscure knowledge of events that appear to have been engineered for strategic purposes, sacrificing human life once more for a prioritized cause. Some would argue that such sacrifices may be essential in times of crisis. Yet where does one draw the line? Does falling back on such a caveat not risk the outwardly righteous party crossing the line into behaviour equally befitting the fascistic foe? For, just as outrage over Pearl Harbor-type incidents may have been used to galvanize otherwise reluctant support (removing resistance to more totalitarian policies along the way, in the name of public safety), something similar may well have aided the ascension of the very enemy Europe was facing in the 1940s.

III) THE REICHSTAG FIRE

We have already seen (*see* chapter 2) how public fury over questionable fires in Roman times was, on more than one occasion, used to crush resistance and enflame persecutions, with one side blaming the other for the blazes, while London's catastrophe in 1666 generated similar responses. Even in the 1930s, the same game was being played.

Great damage was inflicted on Germany's economy when the Allies imposed reparations following the armistice which ended the First World War. Thousands of German citizens were left disillusioned and in severe poverty. The conditions were therefore ripe for the rise of fascism, with all its apparently easy answers and tough talking. Sure enough, by 1933, disillusioned war veteran, convicted insurrectionist, anti-Semite and self-styled saviour of the nation Adolf Hitler had led his National Socialist German Workers' Party – the Nazis – into a crucial role in the ruling coalition. Yet ultimate power still eluded him. Ruthless intimidation, masked by militaristic pageantry and social discipline, had taken the Nazis almost, but not quite, to the top, with Hitler sworn in as chancellor in January of that year. The 'Enabling Act' the Nazis wanted, which would effectively grant the chancellor absolute power over the Reichstag parliament (meaning 'imperial diet', or assembly), was being held back by justifiably concerned voices, especially among the Communist opposition. Without a catalysing event to justify the desired Act – lawful only in times of extreme emergency – forcing through such a measure while holding only 32 per cent of the Reichstag seats was going to be difficult. Serendipity, however, suddenly made that task easier.

In the early hours of 27 February 1933, a fire broke out in Berlin's Reichstag building. The flames soon gutted the central structure and caused substantial damage. Inside the building, police apprehended the Dutch Communist and political agitator Marinus van der Lubbe. Four leading members of the Communist Party were soon rounded up and arrested for good measure. To Nazi propagandists the situation was categorical: the fire clearly marked the first phase of a major Communist uprising which threatened to destabilize the country and undermine parliament. Emergency legislation took effect almost immediately, with mass detainments across the country, while already-diminishing civil liberties vanished overnight. The removal of the Communist

Party from both the chamber and the political landscape gave the Nazis the majority they had sought, and Adolf Hitler was, without obstruction, granted the absolute power he craved.

The circumstances of the Reichstag fire have long raised the question of whether it was, in truth, a Nazi false-flag operation, rather than a Communist plot. Why, after all, would the Communists want to compromise their own position in parliament, when savage persecution would be sure to follow? Indeed, it has now become a conspiracy staple to use the phrase 'the burning of the Reichstag' in the same breath as describing an event which smells even slightly of underhand manipulation to benefit the reputation of a 'wronged' party.

For all this, despite the Nazis' infamous reputation, unlikely to inspire trust of any kind in their direction, their responsibility for the fire has never been entirely proven. Van der Lubbe was a known arsonist, certainly, and prone to unpredictable behaviour. Most agree that he, at least, probably had a hand in starting the blaze. Other defendants were acquitted during the subsequent trial, but van der Lubbe was found guilty and executed. According to a British journalist present when Hitler arrived to inspect the burned-out Reichstag, the Führer appeared genuinely uncertain about what had occurred, and what it meant for Germany, while his propaganda minister, Joseph Goebbels, reportedly did not at first believe the fire story when telephoned with the news. Given these characters' propensity towards sly deception, none of this absolves their potential culpability, but questions have nonetheless been raised about who, precisely, instigated the event.

Was van der Lubbe a patsy, set up by Nazi backers, or simply a lone maverick? Or was he genuinely fronting an ill-advised Communist plot, as the official Nazi story goes? It has been asserted that a whole group of arsonists must have been present for the fire to have taken so quickly and effectively (using self-lighting incendiaries). Some researchers claim that clues derived from Gestapo archives now held in Moscow make it very clear that the Nazis were directly responsible, albeit through circumstantial records, but others dispute this. If it *was* a false-flag event, of course, it does not necessarily follow that Hitler and his closest cronies were personally aware of what was going on. If engineering by New World Order operatives was occurring, as some have alleged, they may have been the unwitting beneficiaries of a manufactured scheme to elevate the Nazis in the hope of guaranteeing a major European conflict further down the line. Either way, the fire was an undisputed gift to Hitler, who described the event as a 'sign from heaven', and it tipped Germany into irreversible despotism for over a decade.

It is interesting to note that probable Nazi responsibility for the Reichstag fire has, on the whole, gained mainstream acceptance, despite many unanswered questions, yet similar false-flag claims regarding politically useful atrocities such as 9/11, for which there is more substantial evidence, are dismissed by the media as deranged fantasies, despite many fundamental restrictions on freedom also having resulted from them. Society is greatly influenced by popular archetypes of 'goodies' and 'baddies', and our responses appear to be very easily conditioned.

Sometimes, however, potential plots to manipulate conflicts and conflagrate world events may not always go to plan.

IV) THE USS *LIBERTY*

Between 5 and 10 June 1967, long-brewing tensions between Israel on one side, and Egypt, Jordan and Syria on the other, boiled over into open conflict through what became known as the 'Six-Day War'. Israel's decision to launch pre-emptive air strikes against its Arab neighbours rather than wait for incoming action gave the Jewish nation an upper hand which back-footed its enemies and granted it a decisive victory. Yet, in between the many complex controversies of the war, which still cause division today, a particular incident stands out in the pantheon of conspiracy theories and is held by most truthseekers to be one of the most likely modern attempts, albeit a failed one, at a false-flag manoeuvre.

On 8 June 1967, with the war raging inland, the US navy 'technical research ship' USS *Liberty* was cruising north of the Sinai Peninsula in international waters. Officially, the USA maintained a neutral status during the Six-Day War, but was monitoring military communications nonetheless. That morning, several Israeli planes overflew *Liberty*, and the crew assumed that its identity as an American vessel was clear. Yet, around 2.00pm, the ship was suddenly assailed by apparently Israeli forces, from both air and sea. Mirage jets strafed the deck with a variety of deadly ordnance, including napalm, followed by offensives from a flotilla of three torpedo boats which arrived shortly after. Unsure at first about who was attacking, the largely unarmed *Liberty* briefly returned fire with machine-gun rounds. But five torpedoes were launched by the Israelis, one of which struck the vessel, holing the research department and causing heavy casualties. *Liberty* was relatively lucky – it stayed afloat. The ship would almost certainly have been sunk had the four other errant torpedoes hit home. Further cannon and ammunition fire were received before the assault was halted.

By the end of this unexpected drama, 34 US crewmen had been killed, and 171 injured, while the ship itself was heavily damaged. But why? With its culpability now undeniable, apologies were quickly transmitted to the US authorities by Israel, claiming that it had all been a terrible mistake. Confused intelligence reports had led them to believe *Liberty* was, in fact, an Egyptian warship. In the heightened state of tension, they couldn't take chances and so acted decisively. Compensation was soon offered, and rounds of diplomatic smoothing began. Despite the misgivings of a number of high-level US military staff and politicians, President Lyndon B Johnson quickly accepted the official apology, and appeared to wish to sweep the whole matter under the carpet as quickly as possible.

It is interesting to note that, in Johnson's later autobiography, the *Liberty* incident warrants no more than a passing mention, with even the casualty figures substantially and mysteriously lowered from their true numbers, seemingly to dilute their significance.

Others, however, did not go along with the proffered explanation, not least the majority of *Liberty*'s surviving crewmen, who remain convinced that the Israeli forces must have known full well that the ship was of US origin. Conspiracy theorists have long been convinced that the attack was a botched attempt to escalate a local war (if a serious one) into a full-blown international crisis. However, given that Americans are generally supportive of Israeli versions of events, especially among the military classes, it is notable that the USS *Liberty* Veteran's Association also firmly maintains the false-flag stance, and continues to campaign for justice and a fuller investigation.

With 'friendly-fire' tragedies and disastrous intelligence errors apparently a recurring and inevitable part of any large military conflict, what, then, are the main objections to seeing the *Liberty* event as just another example of such confusion?

The crew's conviction that the Israelis must have positively identified the US origin of *Liberty* lies in the fact that several low fly-bys were made by Israeli planes in the hours before the assault (as film and photos attest) – low enough that the noise from one of the slower propeller craft actually rattled the infrastructure of the ship. Some claim that the pilots even waved to deck crew as the plane passed. All this time, with just one brief interlude during a change-over, records show that, alongside other clear English-language markings (significantly different to Arabic characters), very visible US flags were flying – something denied by Israeli reports. The torpedo boats, at least, in close proximity to *Liberty*, should have realized immediately that it was not an Egyptian adversary.

It is known for certain that at least one Israeli pilot reported the vessel's identity as American just before the attack, confirmed by a radio communication intercepted by the US embassy in Beirut

– yet the planes were still ordered to fire. It has been implied by Israel that even if the pilots and naval captains in question *were* aware that the vessel was American, their intelligence reports may not have been passed through the chain of command correctly, in true incompetence-as-caveat tradition, thus failing to stop the onslaught in time. But this is challenged by a number of important observations.

One of the routine combat techniques used by Israeli forces was to employ signal-jamming devices to block emergency transmissions from their targets, and *Liberty*'s records show that this occurred during the offensive. But such jamming can only take place when an enemy's precise frequency has been identified, which requires extensive pre-attack monitoring of signals. As each ship in the US navy – as a defence against blanket jamming – always uses an individual transmission frequency, the *Liberty*'s own must have been listened to, analysed and clearly identified in advance, or the jamming could not have taken place. This vital point in itself is seen by many researchers as evidence enough that the 'accidental' hypothesis cannot be correct and that Israeli commanders should have known full well what they were firing at. Significantly, they have never responded to the issue of the signal jamming.

Other areas raise doubts over the official version of events. *Liberty* was not cruising at a speed which would have identified it as a warship, and Israeli intelligence allegedly compared reconnaissance images of the ship taken during the morning fly-bys with internationally available data on military vessels (*Jane's Fighting Ships*). Israel claims that the US naval attaché in Tel Aviv was contacted to verify the identity of *Liberty*, which informed them that no US ships were in the region; thus it attacked on the basis that the ship must therefore be an Egyptian intruder. But the USA denies that any such enquiry was made. One side or the other would appear not to be telling the truth. This raises the double spectre that either covert forces within the USA were secretly manipulating *Liberty* into a vulnerable position (*à la Lusitania*) in the hope that it would be attacked for sinister reasons of their own, or that the Israelis lied to cover connivance or incompetence.

Why would Israel want to launch an assault against its staunchest ally, however? Several ideas have been put forward. One hypothesis states that *Liberty* had been scanning communications that might too soon have revealed Israel's plans to cross into Syria via the Golan Heights if they had inadvertently been leaked from the USA to the Syrians, thus losing the crucial element of surprise. Evidence suggests that the Golan attack (a key element in the ultimate victory of the Israelis that would have benefited from happening sooner rather than later, although it was a move opposed by the USA) may have been postponed until after *Liberty* was disabled, thus allowing the action to go ahead unmonitored.

Another version of events runs that the Israelis were keen to conceal a shocking massacre of Egyptian prisoners of war that may have been carried out illegally by the Israel Defence Forces (IDF) that day in the North Sinai town of El-Arish. Such an atrocity – entirely denied by the IDF – would have outraged the international community at a time when Israel needed moral support, and might have been revealed by *Liberty*'s radio monitoring, necessitating the ship's neutralization. Although a massacre has never been proved, nor perpetrators identified, a mass grave containing the bodies of 30 Egyptian soldiers, most likely from 1967, was uncovered in the relevant area in 2008.

The most adhered-to theory behind the *Liberty* incident, however, remains the one which identifies it as a likely attempt to escalate the conflict into an international war against Egypt, drawing in the USA first by sinking one of its ships with action hoped to be seen as Egyptian. In the event, Israel would not need outside help to secure its victory, but this outcome was far from certain at that point in the six-day conflict, and anything that weakened the reputation of its enemies would in any case be helpful to Israel's long-term security.

All this, of course, assumes that US intelligence was entirely a victim to the events, whichever version one subscribes to. However, with New World Order theories never far behind, some hold that the incident was a component of 'Operation Cyanide', a clandestine attempt to increase Israel's power and give a stronger US foothold in the Middle East against the encroaching influence of the Soviet Union. In this view, *Liberty* was the necessary sacrifice proffered by the USA. It has even been suggested that the original intention may have been to implicate the Soviets directly, rather than the Egyptians, perhaps to initiate a third world war.

If global escalation was the true motive, then it would seem that the critical assault at its core was seriously mismanaged – a noteworthy point usually raised against the theory. Taking out *Liberty*'s effectiveness to monitor communications with relatively moderate action that could be easily written off as accidental would be less risky, but implementing a full false-flag scenario to engineer world opinion would surely require the ship's total destruction and, preferably, an absence of any survivors to cast doubt on the identity of the attackers. Why, then, did *Liberty* remain afloat, with the majority of its crew left alive to teli the tale? Perhaps, suspecting the real purpose of their mission, or at least doubting the morality of their orders, the Israeli pilots and captains simply couldn't find it in themselves to turn the full required fury on allies, and virtually unarmed ones at that. Why, after all, did four out of the five torpedoes aimed at a wounded vessel fail to reach their target? Was there a half-heartedness at work which unwittingly compromised the intentions of those giving the orders? If the attack *was* planned to sink the ship and thus trigger wider repercussions, it would appear to have been critically undermined either by sheer military incompetence or unexpected reluctance among those at the front line.

If, on the other hand, the action took place merely to compromise *Liberty*'s ability to monitor signals, more sense is made of the restrained tactics used against it. It might be argued that, rather than resort to such drastic measures, Israel could instead have just explained its plans to its closest ally, but maybe it was leaving nothing to chance, especially if Washington was not fully supportive of the strategies used.

Whatever the primary aim of the attack, it seems that there *was* some kind of intention, if an ambiguous one, to obfuscate awareness of who was carrying it out. The planes that struck *Liberty* were, according to the crew, unmarked. There does also seem to have been a loose attempt to wipe out some of the survivors, with claims that the torpedo boats strafed the life rafts as they were launching. But, given that these vessels *were* clearly identifiable as Israeli, again there is the suggestion that not everyone involved in attacking *Liberty* may have been made party to the same agenda – otherwise, why not disguise the torpedo boats too and make a better job of wiping out everyone, ensuring that the ship and its occupants vanished more conveniently beneath the waves?

The failure to destroy *Liberty*, for whichever reason, must have necessitated some fast backtracking and policy reversals. Some say a US-backed invasion of Egypt was abandoned at this point, requiring a drastic redrawing of NWO plans, which would find new focus in the events surrounding 9/11.

There are, without doubt, several grey areas at the centre of the *Liberty* mystery. But a conspiracy of one kind or another was very likely at work, unless one believes the Israeli claim that it was indeed an unfortunate mistake. To accept that, however, means placing blind faith above many unresolved anomalies.

Despite President Johnson's acquiescence, Dean Rusk, the US secretary of state at the time of the incident, certainly didn't believe the official verdict, writing:

> *I was never satisfied with the Israeli explanation. Their sustained attack to disable and sink Liberty precluded an assault by accident or some trigger-happy local commander. Through diplomatic channels we refused to accept their*

explanations. I didn't believe them then, and I don't believe them to this day. The attack was outrageous.

Many other officials had similar misgivings. The subsequent US Naval Court of Inquiry, hastily convened in the days following the attack, weakly concluded that it was all most likely a simple case of 'mistaken identity', but there is a wide belief that the hearing was a whitewash, if not an overt cover-up. In the way of most official inquiries, it failed to address some of the key evidence, heard no statements from surely crucial Israeli sources, and had no remit by which to apportion culpability anyway, thus rendering it meaningless.

As for President Johnson, his priority seemed to be one of drawing a veil over the whole thing, even as the events were occurring. Some testimony suggests that, on hearing that *Liberty* was being assaulted – and on supposedly making the assumption that the attackers were Egyptian – Johnson had planes launched from a Mediterranean-based aircraft carrier to mount a retaliatory assault on Cairo. When it became plain that the ship was still afloat and that the Israelis were undeniably responsible, the fighters were recalled at the last minute. If true, these actions can be seen in three ways: either the events occurred as the official story would have it; or Israel felt it had achieved enough by crippling *Liberty*'s monitoring capabilities and so made clear its 'accidental' role, perhaps afraid of what intensified US action against Egypt might bring to the region. Or, in the full false-flag/NWO view, Johnson was just about to step up the conflict as part of its intended widening, when the unexpected failure to completely erase *Liberty* and its crew necessitated a rapid change of plan.

Either way, it would seem that Johnson had little regard for the welfare of his own men and was more concerned with not humiliating Israel than saving lives. When it became clear that *Liberty* had been attacked, very probably by Israeli 'friendly fire', it is said that Johnson blocked rescue orders and ordered a recall of the support aircraft that were automatically dispatched to aid the vessel, as if happier to see it sink without trace. When a new independent inquiry into the incident was finally held in 2003,[3] Rear Admiral Lawrence ('Larry') Geis quoted Johnson as saying:

I want that goddamn ship going to the bottom. No help – recall the wings

Another telling statement attributed to Johnson had him telling the 6th Fleet Commander that he didn't 'give a damn' if the ship sank: 'We're not going to embarrass an ally.'

Allowing for the potential unreliability of paraphrased recollections, the flavour of the remarks nonetheless make it plain that few tears were shed in Washington for the crew of *Liberty*, and that the survivors, with all their awkward questions and memories, must have been most diplomatically tiresome. What conspiracy theories do always unambiguously reveal among the myriad uncertainties is the disheartening reality that the one thing which always results from the deceptive power games of those we allow to govern us is human misery.

It has been said that, with the Cold War at its height, perhaps Johnson was merely making tough choices, worried maybe that the incident could risk enflaming an already tense stand-off with the Soviet Union (especially if the USA at first thought it might have been responsible for the attack). Moscow was an open supporter of Israel's enemies, supplying arms and intelligence, and some have even suggested that the Soviets may have deliberately helped accelerate the situation into the Six-Day War to give them grounds to bomb Israel's nuclear facility at Dimona, thwarted only by Israel's unexpectedly swift victory. But this is largely conjecture, adding one more layer to the enduring enigma of the *Liberty* incident.

Appropriately like Russian dolls, we have yet another situation here of false-flag accusations within false-flag accusations, vying for space with middle-ground scenarios and countered by denials and probable cover-ups at the other end of the spectrum. There are many other instances of maritime dubiousness, such as the sinking of USS *Maine* in 1898, which mysteriously exploded while moored at Havana during a Cuban revolt against Spanish rule, killing over 270 of its crew and precipitating a US–Spanish war. Some say it was a simple accident, others that it was sunk by Spain, and, of course, there is the popular view that the USA sank it itself as a pretext for war. Yet again, confusing evidence supports more than one of the possibilities, which remain unsettled to this day, but a 'meta-analysis' of all such incidents does begin to reveal a repeating pattern that is hard to brush aside as mere coincidence.

V) THE GULF OF TONKIN INCIDENT

The *Liberty* incident was at least an attack that *did* take place, despite the disputed details. Yet some major conflagrations begin merely with *claims* of an attack. Just three years before the Arab–Israeli clash, a worse conflict erupted in the form of the Vietnam War, when a tense stand-off erupted into full-blown combat following a supposed attack by North Vietnamese Communist forces on American destroyers in the Gulf of Tonkin. A moderate and not unprecedented skirmish had taken place between USS *Maddox* and three torpedo boats, and been easily repelled, on 2 August 1964. But the second, supposedly more serious, attack on 4 August was the one that tipped President Johnson into openly bombing targets in North Vietnam the next morning, despite having officially informed the Soviets the same day that he had no intention of escalating a dangerous situation in Vietnam. Thus began a war that would see many thousands of lives lost on both sides, dividing Western opinion and the American nation itself on a scale previously unseen.

Yet it is now accepted that the second Gulf of Tonkin event, the primary fuse which set off this appalling chain of events, never actually occurred.

How could this be? As an internal US National Security Agency document, declassified in 2005, clearly states:

> *It is not simply that there is a different story as to what happened; it is that no attack happened that night . . . In truth, Hanoi's navy was engaged in nothing that night but the salvage of two of the boats damaged on August 2.*

Alleged sonar errors and unusual weather conditions apparently had USS *Maddox* and USS *Turner Joy* firing on targets that simply weren't there. It might be said that, in an anxious situation, as with the *Liberty* attack, nations might be forgiven for acting rashly in their own defence, and that sometimes vital information comes too late. But in this instance it was known almost immediately after the false pursuit of the 'Tonkin ghosts' that a mistake had been made. Intelligence confirming this was cabled to Washington within a few hours. Time enough, perhaps, to halt a war. But when a pretext is required, nothing, it would seem, will stop the wheels of conflict, certainly not the truth. Ignoring the qualifying messages, yet almost certainly aware of the real situation, Johnson, ever the pacifist, issued this statement:

> *The determination of all Americans to carry out our full commitment to the people and to the government of South Vietnam will be redoubled by this outrage.*

Less than two hours after these words, the bombing had begun. A reason to go to war had evidently been required, and so one was found, distorted enough that the years it would take for the details to emerge would dull any subsequent concerns into a collective fog-of-war shrug. In the immediate aftermath, what had begun as a fiction soon became distorted into a full-blown media fantasy, the 'Gulf of Tonkin Incident' luridly recounted as evidence of evil Communists launching pre-emptive attacks on the high seas.

Given the very clear indications available even at the time, it is hard to see the Gulf of Tonkin event as anything other than a deception, if simply one of opportunism taken over a serendipitous military error. The conspiracy theories around it find their root as much in the decades of obvious cover-up since as in the claimed events themselves, and provide one more important instance in which public consent was programmed by information filtering – and blatant lies.

Yet, interestingly, for all the deception foisted upon it by authorities and a complicit media, popular opinion is not always as easily swayed as might at first be thought. For there are other events in recent history that, despite endless official denials, appear to make conspiracy theorists out of much of the general population, as we shall explore next.

IN SUMMARY . . .

False-Flag Conspiracies: Arguments Against

The public struggles to believe that governments would place their own people in peril for political advantage – Would such cherished patriotic figures as Sir Winston Churchill or Franklin Roosevelt really wish to sacrifice their own shipping or military bases to enemy action? – Surely only tyrants such as Hitler would consider false-flag strategies – The USS Liberty *incident was just a regrettable mistake with coincidental anomalies – The misrepresentation of the Gulf of Tonkin events may have been a necessary strategy in the face of the threat from Communist forces.*

False-Flag Conspiracies: Arguments For

History shows that governments, or at least covert forces within them, do have an unfortunate record of seeing lives as expendable when political advantage is required – Many theorists consider that the actions of high-profile politicians may often be determined by wider New World Order agendas, allowing them to put aside their personal scruples in the face of a perceived higher cause – The Liberty *attack displays so many suspicious elements that it is almost impossible to believe that it was purely accidental – The plain misuse of the Gulf of Tonkin false alarm displays a callous disregard for both the truth and life itself.*

CONCLUSION

The grey areas that surround even some relatively recent historical events, often due to intentional concealment, give reasonable grounds for believing that underhand scheming continues to colour the geopolitical landscape and that false-flag tactics are considered fair game when strategies demand them. Absolute proof for particular events may be elusive, but enough clues stand out to justify the contemplation of conspiracy theories around them.

The Gulf of Tonkin deception by itself illustrates something of the essence of our elected leaders and what they are prepared to do when power is at stake. The population is perhaps too trusting to think that people would never be sacrificed if circumstances demanded it.

CHAPTER 4

POLITICAL CONSPIRACIES

Some conspiracy theories become so mainstream that the media ceases to label them as such. Yet the 1970s Watergate scandal, for instance, which saw Richard Nixon resigning the US presidency, was by definition a conspiracy. Although a relatively minor one, the subsequent public disillusionment it generated helped pave the way to widespread doubt about the trustworthiness of authorities, leading to even huge achievements such as the Moon landings falling under doubt. Other events, including the Iraqi weapons of mass destruction debacle, the WikiLeaks exposures, revelations over Parliamentary expenses and the wider implications of the News International phone-hacking cover-ups, have further eroded faith in the political world, creating a climate in which conspiracy theories are guaranteed to proliferate.

I) WATERGATE

From Fringe to News

The authorities would have the public believe that everything they tell it is of impeccable reliability. Yet in their hearts most people know that the questionable personalities who have often clawed their way to the top through brinkmanship and lobbying, if not underhand dealings, rarely present them with the full truth of anything. With livings to earn and families to raise, apathy or a sheer lack of time among everyday folk are the main factors that allow political and financial obfuscation to roll forward unchallenged. Some argue that this situation is openly cultivated to further enable the New World Order agenda.

However, every now and then an indisputable event takes place which cracks open the establishment façade, and the truth of what may well be its inherent nature leaks out to rounds of journalistic shock horror. These are the moments when conspiracy leaps the divide, crossing briefly into the realms of mainstream acceptability, although it is interesting to note how quickly the word 'conspiracy' vanishes from the lexicon in the process. The offending event is generally reclassified as an exceptional outrage, one which could surely never happen twice, and is then relabelled as a mere 'scandal' – usually with '-gate' appended to its title to create a catchy media tag, in memory of one of the best-known, if at first comparatively slight, conspiracies of recent history.

Watergate Revealed

On 17 June 1972, five intruders were discovered and arrested inside the Democratic National Committee headquarters at the Watergate office complex, Washington, DC. The exact purpose for the break-in has never been satisfactorily established (although one idea is discussed below), but it is clear that some kind of political espionage was intended as the burglars were attempting to install wiretapping facilities when they were apprehended. The subsequent investigation and trials of the men responsible quickly revealed that they had been working on behalf of key opposition Republicans with close ties to the incumbent president, Richard Nixon.

To general disbelief, Nixon denied to his death that he had any knowledge of the original crime, but was undone as much by the cover-up instigated by him and his immediate staff as by the original action. Despite several public addresses protesting his innocence ('I'm not a crook'), the revelation in 1973 that Nixon had ordered several important White House cabinet rooms and private offices to be fitted with secret tape-recording equipment dealt the final blow. When the investigating Senate Committee finally subpoenaed the tapes (after much legal blocking by the Nixon camp), the recordings included a number of blatant conversations which implicated many named individuals, but moreover proved Nixon's role in attempting to withhold the details of the original break-in. The matter of whether his cabinet set up the burglary remained unresolved, but enough damage had been done.

Day by day, the tortuous legal and media investigation into the plot revealed evidence of ever-wider corruption among not only political players but also lawyers, who had been persuaded to perjure themselves to protect the President. This had a profound effect on both the collective psyche of US citizens and, to a degree, the entire Western world's as, for the first time on such a scale, the extent to which elected leaders could run amok when left unchecked was exposed. Even more injurious, perhaps, the profane language and callousness displayed by the President and his colleagues in the widely published transcripts of the Washington tapes dismayed decent folk, as the everyday attitudes of power-mongers were laid bare. Any lingering illusions about a cosily caring and upright patriarchal authority, which were already wobbling due to the extensive public doubts over the morals of the ruinous war in Vietnam (which in itself began with a huge deception, as we saw in the previous chapter), were soon dissipated.

Wider Implications

Beyond the depressing but essentially mundane aspects of corruption revealed through the Watergate conspiracy, layers of darker scheming were also hinted at. Nixon's use of the term 'Bay of Pigs' in several of the taped conversations, for instance, may have referred to the infamously botched attempt by John F Kennedy to deploy a CIA-trained force of Cuban exiles against Cuba itself (with a view to unseating the rule of Fidel Castro) in 1961, but it also seemed to be applied as a mysterious catch-all reference to either other assassination plots against Castro, or to the assassination of Kennedy himself, which some conspiracy theorists have long linked to Nixon (*see* p. 136).

The most vocal of the convicted Watergate burglars was one Frank Sturgis, a man with a long history of espionage and gun-running. Initially a supporter of Castro's revolutionaries, he turned against them before becoming, according to some, a CIA double agent. Sturgis has often been implicated as one of the alleged additional gunmen who killed JFK. This was something he officially denied before his own death in 1993, but he did claim inside knowledge of the assassination, stating that Castro ordered it, later adding that the KGB were also involved. Sturgis was adamant that what were really being sought by him and his fellow Watergate intruders were potentially incriminating photos taken around Dealey Plaza in Dallas on the day of JFK's 1963 shooting. In 1977, Sturgis told the *San Francisco Chronicle*:

> *The reason we burglarised the Watergate was because Nixon was interested in stopping news leaking related to the photos of our role in the assassination of President John Kennedy.*

This plainly implicates Nixon as being one of the hands behind the murder of JFK and, if true, might make more sense of Nixon's obvious desperation to cover up his knowledge of the Watergate break-in, while Sturgis's testimony has become important to some views of the Kennedy plot (*see* chapter 5). Others have inevitably attacked his version of events.

It seems, then, that there may have been more to Watergate than the simple attempt at political point-scoring which mainstream accounts have plumped for. Other apparent code names heard on the White House tapes, such as 'the Texans', used by Nixon to refer to a conglomerate of Texas-based Republican fundraisers, which included George Bush Senior (president from 1989, and father of George W Bush), have been used by some to pull yet more threads together on the wider New World Order plot. It is possible that more damning evidence might have come from the recordings, but, rather conveniently, 18.5 minutes of one of the crucial tapes had apparently been 'accidentally' erased by Nixon's personal secretary. Later analysis suggested that a somewhat more systematic method of deletion had been employed.

Many other revelations might have come from deeper investigation into Watergate and Nixon's role in it, but the paths of inquiry were stopped in their tracks when Gerald Ford (who, as vice-president, stepped into the top position when Nixon resigned in 1974) officially pardoned his predecessor – thus 'immunizing' Nixon from any criminal proceedings against him, which might have turned up vital details in a number of dangerous areas. Ford was heavily criticized for the pardon (some say it may have cost him the next election), showing that the population at large was far from convinced that there was no more to be known, but the act had seemingly served its function of putting a lid on any further meaningful scrutiny.

So was born the classic '-gate' suffix, which has come to mean anything that appears to be corrupt or covered up – often helpfully replacing the need to apply the term 'conspiracy'. For all the obvious attempts to limit the damage, Watergate nonetheless provided a blow to the collective feeling of trust in authority – one that has never satisfactorily healed. With so many complexities and connivances having been dramatically exposed in just one small area when placed under the microscope, suddenly nothing felt reliable or secure any more.

This growing unease would be exacerbated further by the disclosure of the Iran–Contra affair – 'Irangate' – in 1986, which saw US weapons being illegally sold to Iran by Colonel Oliver North and other Reagan administration staff secretly to fund an unsound group of Nicaraguan rebels. But the new era of doubt had already been set by the mid-1970s, which would in turn lead enquiring minds to re-evaluate many other fixtures of the times, and give rise to some of the best-known conspiracy theories of all, where even the supposedly greatest achievements of humankind have been called into question.

II) THE MOON LANDINGS

Man on the Moon?

One of the most iconic moments of modern times took place on 21 July 1969, when President Nixon made what officially remains the most long-distance phone call in history. With humanity's envoys Neil Armstrong and Edwin 'Buzz' Aldrin, NASA astronauts from Apollo 11, standing on the surface of another planetary body for the very first time, Nixon's voice addressed them from across the gulf of space:

> *Hello, Neil and Buzz. I'm talking to you by telephone from the Oval Room at the White House. And this certainly has to be the most historic telephone call ever made. I just can't tell you how proud we all are of what you've done. For every American, this has to be the proudest day of our lives. And for people all over the world, I am sure they too join with Americans in recognizing what an immense feat this is.*

Because of what you have done, the heavens have become a part of Man's world. And as you talk to us from the Sea of Tranquillity, it inspires us to redouble our efforts to bring peace and tranquillity to Earth. For one priceless moment in the whole history of Man, all the people on this Earth are truly one: one in their pride in what you have done, and one in our prayers that you will return safely to Earth.[1]

At this, the world breathed in with pride. Much of it, anyway. With Vietnam raging at that moment, with death and mutilation at hand, the line about bringing 'peace and tranquillity to Earth' ran hollow to some. Just a few years later, as Nixon fell into disgrace and the USA faced the hard reality that power does indeed corrupt, the context of the entire speech began to be seen through rather different filters, as even civilization's noblest feat became fair game for reassessment.

A tiny minority, unable to accept the magnitude of the Moon landings, had already sought reasons to doubt NASA's claims, citing apparent glimpses of Coke bottles rolling across the supposedly lunar landscape, and flags waving in wind that shouldn't exist in a vacuum. But the holders of such extreme views had been written off, literally, as lunatics. With the huge psychological blow that Watergate inflicted, however, many new conspiracy theories were born (as rumours of Paul McCartney's death had similarly gone viral when the Vietnam conflict spiralled), and the Moon landings were one of the first targets.

Given the dramatic monetary costs of the ongoing Vietnamese situation, aside from the toll in lives, the new sense of global consciousness that had been forged in the heady days of 'flower power' ensured that the financial drains alone of the preposterously expensive Apollo missions were suddenly cause for concern in a world of famine and poverty. How had such a frivolous and risky venture been afforded primary status when people were still dying for want of basic needs? Other, more cynical, misgivings also began to creep in: had the 'Moon Shot' programme, far from being 'one giant leap for mankind', actually been more about scoring points over the Soviet Union, as yet another strategy in the ongoing Cold War, the already absurd but perilous stand-off which by now had the whole planet in perpetual fear of nuclear destruction?

Yet the lunar missions had effectively been sparked by John F Kennedy's famous speech of 1961, in which he declared America's intent of 'landing a man on the Moon and returning him safely to the Earth' by the end of the decade.[2] With the outpouring of grief over the iconic president's tragic death, what true patriot would not want to see those intentions fulfilled, and avoid a nation's humiliation over the 'space race'? (It is clear, though, that scientists working for both the Soviets and the USA – many of them cribbed from the same pool of quietly pardoned Nazi rocket pioneers – covertly shared more space science with each other than was ever admitted at the time.)

Thus, for some, the six Moon missions between 1969 and 1972 were a brief beacon of hope for the human race, an example of the positive things that could be attained with a united and peaceful planet. For others, they began to be seen as just another US flag-waving exercise and a convenient distraction from the horrors of the time. Had it, in fact, all been too good to be true? This thought soon began to solidify into what has become one of the best known, most ridiculed, and most persistent conspiracy theories of all time: the question of whether the Apollo missions really happened at all.

Is it really possible that the lunar expeditions, as some contend and a surprisingly large percentage of people believe, could have been an elaborate face-saving hoax, faked in a studio to cover for scientific inadequacies that simply could not guarantee success at the time? Worse, could it have been one huge staged psy-ops stunt in the first place, intended simply to hypnotize the masses with false images of US grandeur, enabling public excitement to fill coffers that were in truth siphoned off for black budget military space programmes that would never otherwise have been sanctioned? Or did NASA somehow make it to the Moon, but fail to bring back enough convincing evidence, with photographs blurred by x-rays and temperature extremes, a problem never solved in any of the six missions, requiring extensive augmentation or restaging to convince the world that it *had* been there?

These questions, bitterly attacked by astronomers and scientists, needless to say, would at first seem to exhibit the most insane form of denial, a mistrust in authority taken to the maximum. However, the staying power of this theory may be explained by the unsettling reality that at least some of the evidence presented by the lunar conspiracy believers is hard to dismiss entirely.

Opinions on the Lunar Hoax Hypothesis

As the 1970s progressed, a series of booklets on the Moon landings began to appear in American fringe circles, generally self-published and with political disillusionment well to the fore. They promoted the extraordinary hypothesis that the Apollo missions were elaborate hoaxes; they picked apart the details and challenged NASA to provide more evidence that astronauts really did stand on the Moon. As time went by, these doubts found increased public attention, and more-professional publications appeared, taking the allegations further. The eventual explosion of the internet in the 1990s provided a much wider voice for 'minority views', freed from the shackles of having to seek publishers or meet print costs, and the lunar questioners gained one of the biggest conspiracy platforms. By 1999, a Gallup poll showed that a not insubstantial 6 per cent of US citizens (almost double the percentage of American vegetarians, for instance) believed that the Moon landings had been faked, with a further 5 per cent saying they were 'undecided'. Ten years on, for the 40th anniversary of the Apollo 11 mission, a 2009 poll conducted by the magazine *Engineering and Technology* demonstrated that by then an astonishing *25 per cent* of British people no longer had any faith in the official story.[3]

Mainstream responses to such polls are fairly predictable. The academic world reacts, as we saw in chapter 1, by pontificating on profound psychological reasons for such a widespread state of denial, while popular astronomers tend to abandon any decorum and rant about the general ignorance of the population, claiming that better 'education' is needed. But is this a fair position? 'Educating' usually translates as debunking the fringe, but this strategy invariably falls into the trap of attacking the straw man theories, which are indeed easily dealt with (stars would *not* be visible in the lunar photos because of camera exposure levels, flags 'flew' straight because they were wired, etc.), while failing to address the more serious issues, some of which are explored below.

So is every person who challenges the NASA record – some of whom are themselves academics, qualified engineers and photography experts – simply in need of re-education or psychological therapy? Or could it more straightforwardly be that there are a number of fundamental anomalies in the official evidence that genuinely require some better explanations than those routinely (if resentfully) offered?

The Physical Evidence

The evidence that calls aspects of the Apollo missions into question is often technical and complex, and is extensively available elsewhere, but the basics can be summarized.

Of the three levels of available proof to show that NASA went to the Moon, only one really has any verifiable currency. The first, the testimony of the astronauts, is written off by conspiracy theorists as unreliable because of the long history of military personnel fronting false stories (Gulf of Tonkin, etc.) under orders, oath or threat. Military is what the astronauts were, for all NASA's pretence of being a civilian outfit. Curious inconsistencies in these pioneers' claims appear to be mutually exclusive. Some say the stars were bright and brilliant when seen from space, while others say they were disappointing and barely visible. Some affect tones of wonder at having stood on another sphere, while others seem subdued and oddly reticent about their experiences (the late Neil Armstrong, especially). Simple differences in personality? Or something more suspicious? Either way, words do not constitute proof – several early mountaineers, for example, were later found to have lied about their claimed conquests.

The second level of proof cited is the rock supposedly gathered by astronauts. But, if a rock is claimed to be from the Moon, how many people, in truth, would know the difference? Some of the samples donated for lab analysis or exhibition have turned out to be rather more terrestrial, in any case. Astrobiologist Andrew Steele, of the University of Portsmouth, having finally obtained permission to examine what was claimed to be lunar soil, was disconcerted to find that it in fact exhibited very earthly contaminants (Teflon, remains of microorganisms, etc.) which should not have infiltrated closely guarded samples kept in sterile conditions. Meanwhile, the Dutch Rijksmuseum in Amsterdam was irritated to find that a piece of 'Moon rock' donated by a visiting US dignitary in 1969 was, on closer analysis 40 years later, merely petrified wood. Were these rare procedural slip-ups, or something more conniving? Aside from these controversies, real lunar material might have been obtained using unmanned probes (as Russia did), and it is said to have fallen to Earth as meteorites in quite substantial quantities over the aeons, so the possession of Moon rock does not prove definitively that astronauts retrieved it and cannot be used as a reliable criterion.

With the weaknesses of these areas in mind, what we are really left with as the most overt evidence that NASA visited the Moon is the photographic record, which at first glance seems to be glorious and substantial, with colourful and pin-sharp portraits of conditions on another world. Yet the photographs have been the most assailed aspect of all.

The Photographic Evidence

Recent satellite images, purporting to put to rest the lunar hoax theory, claim to show the remains of the lunar landers and 'rover' tracks, etc., as interesting dots and smudges. But in an age where even the most basic pictures are routinely manipulated with easily available software, a photograph – especially one taken by NASA itself – is no longer enough to constitute proof of anything. Even if the aerial shots are genuine, and objects are indeed up there on the Moon, which they may well be, this does not unequivocally demonstrate that direct human activity placed them there several decades ago, particularly given the modern skills available with remote-controlled craft. Nor does it mean that the pictures we are told were achieved by men at a ground level were actually taken on the Moon, even if they did walk there themselves. As a glance at Jack White's substantial deconstruction of the Apollo image bank at www.aulis.com will reveal, numerous astronauts' photos are highly debatable or raise more questions than they answer.

Many of the difficulties inevitably revolve around lighting. As NASA claims that no artificial illumination was used, it follows that all the photographs must have been taken in harsh unfiltered sun, without clouds or atmospheric conditions to alter a uniform light. Yet in a number of shots it is far from uniform, displaying instead inexplicable pools of light, usually centred on the main subject. One of the most famous photos of all time – Apollo 11's Buzz Aldrin standing on the Moon, as taken by Armstrong – is a case in point. Especially when the contrast of the shot is increased, it reveals a much brighter area to the rear right of Aldrin, with a strange and sharp fall-off of light backwards towards the horizon, but also just a few feet forward, towards the camera. The strong impression with such lunar images is that spotlights have been used to enhance the main subject.

Equally anomalously, this pool of light appears to throw a jet black shadow forward left of Aldrin, so dark that it is devoid of any detail in the Moon dust – yet Aldrin's body, technically in silhouette with the light behind him, is well illuminated, the features on his suit captured perfectly. If this is, as NASA implies, due to reflected light bounced from the ground before him, then why isn't there also enough ambience to show at least a little texture in the ground shadow? It could be argued that taking up the exposure of the camera might have helped reveal the suit front, but if that had been done the whole landscape around Aldrin should be glowing bright (not relatively subdued, as it appears), and detail in the shadow would, without question, be visible. These anomalies are repeated throughout the NASA image bank, leading many theorists to surmise that either artificial lighting was used or that the pictures were taken not on the Moon, but in more earthly studio conditions.

The same image of Aldrin presents a further issue – also visible in a number of other shots – whereby the height of the horizon line appears, very pleasingly from a compositional viewpoint, to cross directly behind his helmet, with the *reflected* horizon line on the visor continuing at the same level. However, that same reflection plainly shows Armstrong standing on flat ground, taking the photo with a camera strapped to his chest, as were the vast majority of the lunar images. Simple experiments (see especially Mary Bennett and David Percy's 1999 book *Dark Moon*) demonstrate the impossibility of this horizon line being at helmet level if taken by a chest-held camera. When calculated, the horizon should be much lower, passing behind Aldrin's own chest. So this photo, and the others like it, appear in truth to have been taken from just above head height, looking downwards, as can be demonstrated by the fact that the *top* of Aldrin's backpack is also visible, which would be impossible at chest height. Therefore Armstrong could not have taken this picture. If that is the case, who did, and how, with only two people ever on the Moon at any one time? As neither a person nor a suspended camera is visible above or behind Armstrong, were these air-brushed out of the published photo? No convincing official explanations have ever been offered to account for these issues, which are usually ignored while the straw man 'errors' are loudly derided.

Lighting anomalies become even starker when examining back-lit shots of the Lunar Excursion Module (LEM, or lunar module). A number of photos display large areas of deep black shadow cast into the foreground by sunlight indisputably coming from behind the LEM – yet the detail in the shadow side of the module itself is often brightly lit, almost ridiculously so in some shots, exhibiting intense luminosity that couldn't possibly be bounced from the surface. Indeed, little bright reflections, seen on the heels of emerging astronauts' boots, or gleaming off the shiny foil surfaces of the LEM, demonstrate clearly that light is being shone in directly from the side, and not from ground level – again suggesting the presence of artificial lighting.

The cameras themselves (Hasselblad 500 ELs) raise another issue. Although they were of high calibre, they were also relatively basic, with no viewfinders, having been designed for chest use. Astronauts operated them wearing thick pressurized gloves and in helmets from which they could barely look down. Each photo was taken with no guarantee that everything was in view, even allowing for wide angles. This would not generally be considered the best way to obtain good pictures. Yet the Apollo record displays a large number of perfect compositions, expertly lit.

A number of professional photographers have expressed puzzlement over the mostly faultless exposures alone. This is particularly pertinent to the first landing, Apollo 11, when the lighting conditions that would be found on another planet were effectively unknown until the moment the first shots were taken.

Yet the record shows that no 'bracketing' (the taking of several photos using different light settings to ensure that at least some come out correctly) was carried out at any point, despite the importance of doing so with only manual metering available. The contact sheets from all the missions demonstrate that the astronauts simply exited the LEM and started snapping, with no consideration of the exposures. By happy chance, they got them right virtually every time. Defenders claim that the astronauts were simply well trained, but this doesn't explain the complete absence of procedures that any photographer would have customarily used at the time.

Additional Visual Issues

Other challenges that have been made to the Apollo images concern the backgrounds of slopes and distant mountains, as much as the objects in front of them. The strange, hard lines that sometimes seem to mark a division between the foreground as it recedes towards the horizon and a rise in the land behind it suggest to some doubters either the use of scenery flats or denote gaps where large screens might rise up to be used for 'front projection'. Front projection is a technique whereby high-definition images are beamed from an oblique angle up onto huge screens (successfully used by Stanley Kubrick in the 'Dawn of Man' sequences of his classic 1968 film *2001: A Space Odyssey*), which players can perform in front of without casting shadows, avoiding the need for later superimposition or 'matting' shots.

NASA says that the hard lines merely denote natural folds in the ground, but there is evidence in a number of shots of the *same* backgrounds appearing in what should be mutually exclusive locations or angles, suggesting either that a piece of scenery has simply been reused, or that an identical background slide has been projected. Perhaps the Moon is simply more uniform in its terrain than here on Earth, as has been argued, but that does not explain photos where the backgrounds to close-ups of objects such as the LEM still look exactly the same in pictures supposedly taken several hundred yards further back in wider sweeps, with no angle, height or perspective change, which seems peculiar. Critics have also pointed out that even allowing for the smaller diameter of the Moon to the Earth, mountains on the horizon often seem closer than they should be, or are hazy and out of focus, when, without any atmosphere to fog the view, they should be crystal clear.

Scale problems again present themselves when different images of the same landing locations are shown from varied distances, with certain objects suddenly seeming to be bafflingly larger or smaller in relation to the ones next to them, compared with other photos. It might be said that these are optical illusions caused by the lack of surrounding reference points, but theorists claim they could be equally, if not better, explained if they were in fact achieved using sophisticated model shots where the relative scales of the different models were not quite consistent (a phenomenon commonly noted in science fiction movies by keen-eyed viewers). Even pictures of the astronauts themselves suggest that *they* might be models in certain scenes, a possibility heightened by the notable inconsistencies of the suit details in some photo sequences. Apparently unremovable features sometimes seem to oddly disappear or rearrange without explanation from shot to shot, when they are supposedly the same astronauts on the same lunar walks.

The Videos

It has been asserted by halfway-defenders that if the photographs may be questionable, then the famous video sequences of apparently low-gravity bounces across the lunar landscape, and 'rover' drives across seas of dust prove that men did walk on the Moon. Yet even these are not universally considered reliable. Bright flashes which occasionally appear above the heads of astronauts strongly suggest the presence of wires to some, and sometimes men appear to 'dangle' in a seemingly impossible way, even allowing for reduced gravity. (This is especially visible in an Apollo 16 sequence showing an astronaut attempting to get up from the ground.)[4]

In 2009, celebrating the 40th anniversary of the Moon landings, BBC1's generally conspiracy-baiting prime-time television programme *The One Show* decided to see how successfully 'low-gravity' sequences could be achieved in a studio using wires and slow-motion techniques. Contrived to debunk nonsensical hoax theories, instead it did quite the opposite, as even the amused presenters had to admit, producing footage that mirrored the NASA videos almost perfectly. Indeed, when lunar footage is simply sped up a little, the results appear to exhibit quite normal movements, so it is not impossible that sequences might have been filmed in terrestrial conditions before being slowed down to give an other-worldly impression.

The gravity issue seems particularly pertinent in videos of the lunar rovers. Given the tales of Moon dust being so dry and fine that it could fly around the heads of the astronauts for several minutes before settling again, there is no evidence to demonstrate this in any of the video footage. In the biggest disturbances of dust that we see, as the rover churns its way across the surface, the lunar soil appears to fall quickly back to the ground in sandy swathes, a phenomenon that is even more obvious when the footage is accelerated to 'normal' speed.[5] Other rover anomalies have also presented themselves, particularly in still shots showing the supposedly used cars sitting on terrain with no visible wheel tracks in the dust leading to them, suggesting they have merely been 'placed' there as set dressing.

Moments where videos *and* photos were supposedly taken at the same time, which might provide supporting evidence of the official version of events, can also fail to inspire confidence. The famous 'jump salute', where Apollo 16 astronaut John Young leaps up to be momentarily suspended a foot or so above the ground while saluting the American flag, was allegedly photographed from the front at the same time as being videoed from behind. Yet a simple comparison of the high-resolution still shot with the video demonstrates that they must have been staged separately, as different flag angles, a distinctive flap on Young's backpack (sticking up in the still, flat in the video) and dust anomalies (clearly visible beneath his feet in the video, absent in the still) make plain. A minor issue perhaps – clearly the jump was mounted more than once to get two good images – but when NASA says it is one thing, and the truth is clearly another, it can hardly complain when conspiracy theories arise.

Proven NASA Fakes

If it could be shown that NASA had never in its existence manipulated an image, all might be well here, and the hoax claims could be swept aside as the madness that the mainstream insists it is. However, disconcertingly, this is not the case. A much-reproduced photograph supposedly showing astronaut Michael Collins spacewalking from Gemini 10 in 1966 was in recent years exposed as a proven fake when the original image (albeit horizontally flipped) was unexpectedly unearthed in the NASA image bank – revealing its original background of a zero gravity-simulating test aeroplane. The photo of Collins had merely been cut out and pasted onto a black background to give the impression of being in space. Curiously, the photo largely vanished from circulation after this discovery.

Similarly, a famous image of Apollo 14 astronauts playing golf on the lunar surface was found to be another demonstrable 'cut and paste', collaged from a number of different photographs. The shot was in any case impossible, showing the two astronauts at play from a high angle, with the LEM in shot behind them (with no automatic still cameras, who took the photo, and from what platform?). The identification of the source material used for the montage also saw this picture fall out of public circulation.

Even that most famous of images, the aforementioned portrait of Buzz Aldrin, was manipulated for public consumption from the start, as the briefest of comparisons with the original shot and the one issued by NASA Media Services shows. The 'classic' version is cropped at the sides and a large slab of black sky has been added at the top.

Thus NASA has never been above playing with its own photographic record for publicity purposes. The problem is: if it can happen two or three times, why not four or five – or several hundred?

Further Options and Questions

The very fact that the lunar hoax hypothesis has to be attacked so frequently in the mainstream speaks not only of its dogged public appeal, but also of its power to shock and annoy. Did the Moon landings really never happen at all, or is such thinking just deranged gibberish? Is there a middle ground to be found?

It is worth considering what the real motivation might have been behind a hypothetical lunar deception of any scale, large or small. Was it that there was never any real possibility that the missions could work, or were there genuine intentions to head Moonwards that were thwarted by unresolved technical issues with the craft? After all, not one LEM ever worked successfully during terrestrial training, with one errant module nearly killing Neil Armstrong. After the Apollo 1 fire (in itself contentious; *see* page 109), further dead astronauts would be an unacceptable publicity disaster in the political climate of the time, a serious consideration which might have led to a Plan B of pure theatre.

Conversely, did NASA somehow successfully achieve its objectives as claimed, but fail to obtain enough convincing evidence due to unexpected photographic issues with x-rays and cosmic radiation, requiring the hasty setting up of studio-staged 'back-up' material? Experiments with the extremes of heat and cold found in sunlight or shadow on the Moon, matched with the effects of unfiltered radiation, suggest strongly that the film stock might not have survived. Even the low-orbiting International Space Station keeps its IMAX films in thick lead-shielded cases today, but no such protection was available on the Apollo craft, and they were far beyond the Earth's protective belts.

As for the total-hoax scenario, no one argues that rockets didn't take off – that is undeniable, given the public spectacle of their launches – but whether anyone was aboard, and where they really went if they were, has been the subject of much debate. Did the occupants spend days in Earth orbit, or just secretly splash down immediately after launch, to reappear for the press receptions after? Those who doubt the whole story point out that, aside from effects on film stock, the astronauts themselves would probably have been detrimentally affected by all the unusual radiation they were exposed to if they had really gone to the Moon, yet there seems to be no more tendency towards cancer among the lunar visitors than in any other demographic.

Some have even challenged the ability of the otherwise impressive Saturn V rockets to have carried the weight claimed, questioning everything from the colour of the launch exhaust to their technical specifications. Attention has similarly been drawn to some intriguing anomalies with the properties of thruster exhaust in space. In no Apollo footage – such as when the top of the LEM is seen to ascend from the lunar surface, supposedly with its rocket at full thrust – is there a visible effect of any kind, when all NASA space ventures since (shuttle manoeuvres, for instance), using exactly the same fuel, have displayed an unmistakable glow.

Lunar Whistleblowers?

For all these admittedly fascinating discussion points, however, could something as *big* as the NASA missions really ever be faked? With thousands of qualified minds involved in setting them up, clearly with the best of intentions and believing it all to be possible, could that many people be so easily manipulated? And if so, why go to such lengths to keep going with a deception covering six missions that would surely have risked exposure at every turn? Some truthseekers would argue that it *is* gradually being exposed, of course – hence the high profile of this particular conspiracy theory. It has even been suggested that those uncomfortable at being forced to participate in such a deception *did* try, subtly, to leave clues that would in time reveal the fraud; clues which are now being unearthed by all the analysis. Perhaps those behind a hoax might simply not have considered that something so significant would ever be questioned, and consequently allowed a sloppiness to set in, but there are certainly some curious statements made by the astronauts at times, which could be interpreted as half-heartedly bitter attempts to drop in deliberate hints at their exasperation. Apollo 12's Pete Conrad, for instance, makes some very exaggerated statements about the Sun being 'like somebody is shining a bright spotlight on your hands!'

In answer to why no open whistleblowers have come forward to expose what must have been such a widely staffed deception, it has been countered that in fact only a few committed conspirators may have been needed to have faked a studio set-up and keep it secret (as Peter Hyams's resonant 1977 fake-mission-to-Mars film *Capricorn One* postulates). Convincing mock-lunar landscapes were constructed for training purposes before the missions, and might easily have been augmented for later photographic sessions. With payments made, oaths sworn or threats made, just a small camera crew and one or two directing authorities might have made it possible to keep such sessions under wraps to all but the chosen few. If the whole venture was mounted as a full and real-time hoax, on the other hand, broadcasts could have been made as live from the anonymous studio, with mission control and other global operatives making the reasonable assumption that the signals were coming from the Moon, especially if they were routed cleverly enough. As it happens, the lunar transmissions were indeed sent through a highly convoluted series of relays around the world.

The dearth of whistleblowers may also be explained by the possibility that there could have been an implicit understanding among NASA staff that raising awkward questions about their own project might not be wise, not least because two men who vocally questioned the technical ability of Apollo in the run-up to the first mission had met with unpleasant ends. Virgil 'Gus' Grissom, an experienced astronaut originally intended to have been first on the Moon, had been a loud critic of the unreliable technology being developed to take them there, and publicly expressed doubts about the programme's feasibility to journalists. He knew this made him vulnerable, and even warned his wife that there might be an attempt on his life. Strange it was, then, that Grissom was one of the three astronauts who died in the launch-pad fire that raged through the oxygen-rich cockpit of Apollo 1 during training in 1967. Stranger still, years later, when his son Scott Grissom, by then a qualified engineer, managed to examine the remains of the capsule, he found evidence to suggest that an electrical fault had been deliberately rigged to cause a fire, openly declaring to the media that his father was murdered.

Investigations in the immediate aftermath of the Apollo 1 fire might have turned up this same evidence already, were it not for the fact that NASA inspector Thomas Ronald Baron, who suspected foul play and had identified unacceptable incompetence throughout the whole Apollo programme – which threatened its success, in his eyes – also met a premature end when he and his entire family died as their car was mysteriously driven directly into a train. His full and damning 500-page report was never published. These dubious factors may well have dissuaded others from calling attention to further deficiencies in the Apollo programme.

Unanswered Questions

There are many other arguments that have erupted around almost every aspect of the Moon landings, too numerous to dwell on here. Unanswered questions remain on both sides of the debate. If it was a hoax, for instance, why indeed continue on with six missions (seven, including the aborted Apollo 13 attempt, in itself seen as a contrived PR scam by some theorists), when keeping even one deception secret was surely a risk? Did they plough on in the hope that at least one mission would eventually really work? Or were the continued ventures just a PR necessity to keep the black budget funds pouring in to military projects being masked by the lunar programme, which were finally up and running by the last 'visit'? There is no question that much of the thrust of near-space exploration has been military in purpose, as the swarms of unhealthily proliferating spy satellites and experimental weaponry orbiting over our heads today would confirm, for which publicity is virtually zero.

However, in a reversal of the usual conspiracy theory, another fringe contends that a secret and successful space programme had in fact already been up and running for years before Apollo, its true achievements kept quiet for nefarious purposes (something explored in the British spoof-or-was-it ITV documentary *Alternative Three* in 1977). In this view, we had to be fed a little to keep us all happy, but what we were shown was far less impressive than the astonishing reality. Another belief considers that the evidence of what was really found on the Moon was simply unshowable, because it would have revealed the undeniable presence of extra-terrestrials visiting our planet, observing us from bases on our satellite (*see* chapter 7). Why, after all, did NASA suddenly stop going to the Moon, despite all the gifts for humanity it was claimed our presence there could bring?

For all the regularly announced lunar returns we have heard of in more recent years, some from a number of different countries (and even commercial ventures), why has not one of them yet amounted to anything other than vague and unfulfilled plans? Covert programmes notwithstanding, are we really now capable of doing something our 1960s forebears weren't, or does the full technology needed to leap human beings safely across the gulf of space still remain elusive, hence the hesitation? There are endless possibilities to all this, beyond the remit of these pages – the internet will keep the curious busy for many weeks.

Settling the Matter

What is the truth of this classic conspiracy theory, so attacked, and yet so tenacious? Concluding one way or the other as to whether humans did walk on the lunar surface would seem to be impossible without heading up there ourselves, as one day perhaps an unbiased individual will. Only an entirely independent verification that the NASA objects are there in their exact places, and with the very same lighting conditions visible in the iconic images, will settle the matter now. Aerial shots alone will not suffice.

Supportive testimony for at least some kind of misrepresentation having occurred around the Moon landings is, as can be seen here, perhaps stronger than might be imagined. Certainly, the claim that there is no evidence to support any part of this conspiracy theory is unfair.

It is perhaps in trying to grasp the sheer enormity of such a disillusioning trick being played, with all it would imply for many other areas, that some people prevent themselves from seriously considering any aspect of this theory: if something as historic as the Moon landings didn't take place as we have been told, then what did? However, as polls show, the numbers of doubters are slowly growing, and previous chapters have made clear that there are many precedents for huge deceptions which might have been kept quiet at the time, but which are coming under scrutiny now. Increasing awareness of the more questionable aspects of history can only encourage a new alertness to the potential diversions of truth which would appear to be continuing all around us today.

III) WEAPONS OF MASS DESTRUCTION, WIKILEAKS, MPS' EXPENSES, PHONE HACKING AND OTHER MAINSTREAM DISILLUSIONMENTS

Authorities Diminished

If Vietnam and Watergate blasted away significant amounts of trust in authority, leading people to question events as momentous as the Moon landings, what might the cumulative effect have been from other unfortunate revelations in the decades since? Particularly since 9/11, in the Western world at least, a steady stream of events has further eroded public faith in politicians, perhaps explaining why, by that event's tenth anniversary, a significant proportion of the world's population no longer believed the official story (*see* p. 171).

The 'War on Terror' launched by the USA in the wake of 9/11 enabled fear and patriotism to eclipse common sense in many areas, fundamentally weakening long-established civil rights and spawning a domino effect of Middle Eastern wars. It also generated developments that extensively damaged any lingering respect for governments.

Iraq and the Weapons of Mass Destruction

Given that Osama bin Laden had been officially identified as the perpetrator of 9/11 – although proof for this was never produced – the war in Afghanistan necessary to hunt him down and weaken the now-demonstrable threat from his al-Qaeda terrorist network could be justified to a degree. But when the remit began to widen out to countries with more tenuous connections, questions were raised. Once Iraq, as led by the undoubtedly cruel dictator Saddam Hussein, fell into the gunsight as the next great threat to civilization around 2002, public discomfort set in. Alleged Iraqi links to al-Qaeda barely held water, and the collective gut sensed that oil and Western imperialism, rather than terrorism concerns, were the primary drivers this time around, while conspiracy theorists smelled New World Order agendas.

As objectors against a planned allied invasion of Iraq took to the world's streets to protest in huge numbers unseen for years, something more was apparently needed to bring everybody 'on-message'. When anxiety over Hussein's contravention of his people's human rights wasn't enough, and pious talk of helping to create a new and better world failed to move the polls (with plenty of other oil-free countries under worse oppression), the old tool of public fear was reached for, championed largely by US President George W Bush and British Prime Minister Tony Blair, who loudly beat the war drum. At least avoiding a false-flag event this time around, instead a (now-infamous) 'dossier' was produced, purporting to demonstrate firm intelligence that Hussein was preparing 'weapons of mass destruction' that could be deployed within '45 minutes' against the West, maybe chemical, maybe even nuclear. The evidence for this was too sensitive to be shared with the populace, naturally, and cynicism remained. But the resulting uncertainty shifted public opinion just enough, in the USA and UK anyway, to permit military action against Iraq, which went ahead in March 2003 with devastating consequences.

The campaign itself, which saw thousands (mostly Iraqis) dead or injured, was almost eclipsed by the dismal aftermath, which, with barely a plan drawn up for its rehabilitation, left Iraq a faction-torn wasteland, with thousands more dying of disease, hunger and sectarian in-fighting in the years following. Many NWO theorists believe this masked a conscious intent: to create a weakened Iraq which would be open to greater manipulation in the grand plans for the region.

Whether through incompetence or design, the greatest public shock, as the 'liberated' Iraq was picked through, was the gradual realization that the weapons of mass destruction (WMDs), the linch-pin that had waved the action through, weren't there – just as most people had felt so strongly in their bones. Worse, it soon became evident that parts of the vital dossier had been works of fiction, almost absurdly derived in part from a student thesis found on the internet and augmented for dramatic purposes. Tony Blair and his chief spin doctor Alastair Campbell appeared to be responsible for much of it. Shuffling excuses were made about 'intelligence errors', but few felt much sympathy towards this in the light of the costly (in every way) destruction that had been wreaked, seemingly for no reason.

Even as the path to war was building, high-profile diplomats and intelligence officers had tried to signal the unlikelihood of the WMD programme, with one of the main United Nations weapons inspectors, Dr David Kelly, even having gone to the BBC to express his concern. In turn, Kelly was blasted by the Blair government as a discredited irrelevance, one so weak and remorseful he committed suicide soon after in the wake of his public shame. Or did he? Most people believe it more likely that Kelly was assassinated, to remove a dangerously vocal informant (*see* chapter 5).

Overall, it seemed patent that a war had been desired, and so a war was what we got, regardless of evidence, the opinion of experts or the views of voters. Although little sympathy is felt today towards the fate of Saddam Hussein (eventually tracked down and executed under Iraqi law in 2006), even less is reserved for Blair and Bush, both of whom are widely seen in Britain as liars and war criminals. The actual term is not necessarily heard in regard to the Iraq war, but it is by definition another conspiracy theory fully supported by the population at large, no matter how many official inquiries absolve the perpetrators.

Previous Fraud Concerning Iraq

The realization that action against Iraq was most likely encouraged by fraudulent means should not really have shocked anyone; it may already have happened once before. Back in 1990, shortly after Iraq's notorious invasion of Kuwait, tales began to circulate of atrocities carried out by the advancing soldiers. One report, which was fundamental in kindling allied action to expel Iraqi forces, concerned a harrowing tale given as a first-person account by a teenage girl called Nayirah. Testifying to the US Congressional Human Rights Caucus in October 1990, she tearfully and convincingly described Iraqi soldiers entering a Kuwaiti hospital and pulling premature babies out of their incubators, leaving them on the ground to die. Nayirah's account generated widespread horror and demands for action throughout the Western media. Several senators, together with President George Bush Senior, loudly cited it in their calls for a military response, and it was an acknowledged major factor in garnering public support. However, if the reaction was genuine, it is very possible that the story was not.

When convincing corroboration failed to materialize, and investigations following the eventual liberation of Kuwait in 1991 found only evidence of fleeing Kuwaiti doctors abandoning babies, and not Iraqi assaults against them, the 'incubator' story began to sound less like an authentic narrative and more like the classic 'atrocity' propaganda that always circulates in the face of undoubtedly unscrupulous behaviour from invaders. But by then its job had been done.

The doubts over the incubator tale were confirmed when Nayirah, the only real witness, was in fact revealed to be the daughter of the Kuwaiti ambassador to the USA, Saud Nasir Al-Sabah, and not a chance observer, as had been claimed. At this, accusations flew that she had been hired all along to front an inflammatory fiction. Although the family denied that Nayirah was lying, it soon became clear that much of the story had at the very least been heavily filtered through a PR company, Hill+Knowlton, supposedly working on behalf of Citizens for a Free Kuwait, an organization that, if it was ever real (some assert it was set up on the orders of US intelligence purely to front the atrocity claim), was hardly likely to be unbiased in its reporting.

The ultimate shape of this probable deception can be summed up by the findings of the corporate investigation firm Kroll Associates, hired by the Kuwaiti government to get to the bottom of the story. Kroll carried out around 250 interviews, including a detailed cross-examination of Nayirah, where her original account fell apart and it became clear that, even if she had been present at the hospital in question, she had perhaps witnessed seeing a single baby out of its incubator for 'no more than a moment', in very uncertain circumstances that probably had nothing to do with soldiers. Contrary to her original statement, it also emerged that she was not a hospital volunteer, but had merely 'stopped by for a few minutes' for reasons unknown. No reliable evidence to support the incubator story was ever produced, yet a spokesman for the PR company still managed to describe the essentially dismissive Kroll verdict as a 'vindication of Hill+Knowlton'.

Libya Propaganda

The revelations behind the Kuwaiti incubator story (much covered in the *New York Times*) took some years to come to light, and by then seemed historical enough to generate some public disapproval, but nowhere near enough outrage – an apathy that authorities appear to rely on to pursue similar strategies. The later weapons of mass destruction ruse thus fits into this earlier pattern of blatant propaganda with regard to Iraq, which is almost certainly maintained today when Western action is required, or merely desired, in a growing list of other 'rogue states'.

Significant disillusion was felt towards the US and UK governments in the wake of the WMD admissions yet, despite this, the arrogance of power has kept the same games rolling along since, while the public in turn, either bored or simply despairing, allows them to continue unchallenged in any meaningful sense. We perhaps have only ourselves to blame when the world fails to change in a positive direction. But the media, seen by most truthseekers as wittingly or unwittingly complicit in perpetrating or concealing conspiracies, also plays a crucial part.

On 24 August 2011, as the Western-aided 'civil war' in Libya came to a head and rebel fighters began to corner the remains of Colonel Gaddafi's army, BBC1's *Breakfast Show* broadcast 'live' images purporting to show crowds in Tripoli's Green Square, celebrating the imminent fall of their former leader; except that slightly closer scrutiny revealed that the flags being waved were not Libyan . . . but Indian. The crowds themselves were also identifiably Indian. It appeared to be a blatant misuse of stock footage to fill a visual hole and generate a false impression.

When a few eagle-eyed souls complained to the BBC that it was putting out barefaced propaganda – not for the first time – the video was quietly withdrawn. A statement from BBC producers claimed it was a simple live feed error, whereby footage was accidentally broadcast through 'international agencies', showing a rally in India. But many were dubious, sensing instead an attempt to show the world that Gaddafi was about to fall, just before he did. Error or not, it made for a useful propaganda coup which might have been helpful with influencing this very outcome if it encouraged a final push from the Libyan rebels.

Given that the soon-identified Indian rallies (held in support of the anti-corruption campaigner Anna Harare) had taken place four days before their presentation as images from Tripoli, how would this footage have made its way onto BBC screens as 'live'? There are many procedures in place to prevent the broadcast of live images that might be violent or unsuitable for the time of day, so why was this 'live feed' not checked for accuracy and vetted before it was connected through? It should in any case quickly have been apparent to those in the control room that these were not scenes from Libya, had anyone glanced at the flags and the faces. More disturbingly, it is as likely that this recording was especially sequestered from the news archives for broadcast. But, as the Harare story was not featured in the programme that day, nor was it due to be, why would it have been retrieved to be ready for showing? No full response to address the detail of the concerns over this footage has ever been issued by the BBC, despite several attempts to extract one.[6]

The conspiracy view, unsurprisingly, has it that someone knew very well that some kind of visual material was needed to further the Libyan agenda (widely considered to be yet another NWO move, along with the Syrian and Iranian situations) and reached for the most conveniently available candidate, guessing that most viewers wouldn't notice the difference – as the majority didn't. It wouldn't be the first time such a thing had occurred: on the day of 9/11, a video purporting to show Palestinian Muslims celebrating the fall of the twin towers was widely circulated on the American CNN network, seemingly to inflame the hatred already being felt towards Islam (given that blame had been almost instantly apportioned by the media before the dust had even settled). Yet the scenes are claimed to have been recorded a few years earlier and said to be entirely unrelated to the 11 September attacks.

The India/Libya broadcast may not have been the first major public deception over Libya. The bomb which destroyed Pan-Am Flight 103 over Lockerbie in Scotland in 1988, killing 270 people on the plane and in the town below, was broadly perceived to have been ordered by Colonel Gaddafi's regime at the time, and a Libyan was eventually convicted for the crime in 2001. Yet even mainstream publications such as the British satirical magazine *Private Eye* have loudly called Libya's guilt into question, with much contrary evidence unaddressed by official inquiries. If Flight 103 was not blown up by the Libyans, though, then who was responsible? Naturally, all options from Palestinian militants, Mossad agents and elements from Iran or even South Africa have been suggested, but other people believe that it was arranged as just one more fold in the long, carefully staged road to the New World Order.

The WikiLeaks 'Revelations'

Returning to Iraq and propaganda issues, it was revelations concerning the behaviour of Western troops there that first drew public attention to the website known as WikiLeaks. More recently the personal crises of its somewhat mercurial founder, Julian Assange, and his battles against extradition to Sweden on charges of sexual misconduct – which he claims are trumped-up reprisals – have conveniently stolen much of the attention. This is unfortunate, as WikiLeaks was without question the first source to rightly call attention to misuses of military power in Iraq, before widening its remit to expose other atrocities.

WikiLeaks operates by providing an open database, free to access, where anonymous whistleblowers and inside sources can 'leak' confidential documents on subjects they consider are of great concern to the public. Just one year from the website's inception in 2006, it was said to have received over a million documents, and that number grew as the years passed and interest inevitably mounted.

When newspapers such as the *Guardian* and other global media outlets entered into agreements with WikiLeaks in 2010 to publicize some of the less sensitive, but still embarrassing information, especially in regard to US State Department diplomatic communications, the profile of the website and its incriminating data went stratospheric. Authorities were aghast, and arguments raged about the morality of the operation, with even members of the public concerned about the wider effects on national security and the potentially compromising position into which the information might place some of the informants named in the documents. Many of the more sensitive references *were* blanked out, but not all.

So was it all worth it? Were any major conspiracies revealed, as some truthseekers had hoped, by the unprecedented deluge of new, previously classified, information? Concern was certainly raised by the planned assassinations of government ministers in the 'rogue states', or by the detail of what really went on at the Guantánamo Bay US prison compound and suchlike. However, full outrage was reserved for the release of gunsight footage from a US Apache helicopter during an airstrike against a group of Baghdadi insurgents in 2007. The indiscriminate strafing of both armed and *un*armed civilians, with children nearby, shocked viewers, while the audio recorded a coldly efficient disregard for human life ('light 'em all up'). Records of other dubious military ventures, particularly in Afghanistan, also disappointed observers who had until that moment clung onto a cosier illusion of 'their boys' doing a tough but necessary job, whereas the truth revealed an unholy relish behind some of the killing. Few lessons, it seemed, had been learned from Vietnam, where the processing of men into unfeeling machines caused untold psychological damage to a whole generation of US soldiers.

Aside from the intent to cover up such unsavoury events, however, these didn't quite constitute evidence of a full-blown conspiracy for the hardcore seekers. So what else was present in the WikiLeaks material?

The diplomatic cables splashed across the world's media in 2010, displaying the content of emails and supposedly confidential transcripts of conversations or meetings, were in many ways a distraction from the more serious elements, and merely proved what everyone knew at heart – that politicians and their aides were endemically less than honest with their feelings about colleagues, or counterparts in other countries, and were as prone to sniping and gossip as most people. It wasn't comfortable for some of the high-profile characters implicated, but it was survivable. Other WikiLeaks information, from everything on climate change propaganda and banking irregularities to toxic waste dumping and membership of far-right organizations, caused commotions of different kinds, but it seemed to be resolutely mainstream in its subject matter.

Was this really all that WikiLeaks had to reveal, given the prevalence of computer hacking and the seemingly unending wellspring of documents it had access to? Where, asked the truthseeker community, was the detail on, say, 9/11 and other potential false-flag plots, or maybe UFOs and secret military technology? WikiLeaks was soon perceived by some conspiracy theorists as being just another component of distraction, taking the heat off the really big issues by focusing attention on the lesser ones that could be more easily absorbed and moved on from. Was WikiLeaks, in fact, a complete set-up from the start, or had it simply just not got near the important layers of *really* hidden information and was itself being manipulated to issue stories that couldn't be officially sanctioned but which were nonetheless helpful to have out there? There is some justification for these allegations, given some of the odd omissions which might at least have been referred to somewhere in the documents. But perhaps this misses the point: what WikiLeaks *did* do was once and for all reveal the reality of civilization's usual dealings to itself, this time in plain sight. Any remaining delusions that integrity and goodwill fuelled military or political campaigns were pretty much shattered by the disclosures, for those still concentrating.

If there was any truth to the view that WikiLeaks had been manipulated against its will, by 2011 it had clearly served its purpose and was under heavy fire from the authorities. The arrest the year before of Bradley Manning, the US army soldier accused of being responsible for some of the most damaging leaks with regard to Iraq and Afghanistan, seemed to mark a watershed in the effectiveness of the website. Although it had thus far managed to evade international law through loopholes and legal forethought, WikiLeaks's happy continuation was also compromised by banks and credit card companies which, under pressure from the USA, now refused to deal with it. Meanwhile the pending charges and personal attacks on Assange, with accusations of anti-Semitism thrown in for good measure, weakened WikiLeaks's perceived imperviousness, and its moment in the sun seemed to have passed. Assange fell out with some of the website's fellow founders and went solo, his threats to reveal even more damning evidence of political fallibility left dangling once he found refuge in the Ecuadorian embassy. Manning, meanwhile, was left to face a US court martial on various counts of treason and kept in solitary confinement, although his supporters fight on. The lasting legacy of WikiLeaks, however, was its further negative impact on the collective capacity to trust.

The MPs' Expenses Scandal

Although not a conspiracy in the conventional sense, but indisputably corruption, another major development which had a detrimental effect on trust in authority exploded in 2009, when the press gained access to the extravagant expense claims of a large number of British MPs (Members of Parliament). The subsequent fury across the country as revelations poured out over a period of weeks demonstrated, curiously, that a parliamentary system which allowed thousands of war victims to die in the face of a probable deception could be forgiven, but one that fraudulently took large amounts of public cash could not.

Some of the expenses, claimed for the likes of porn videos and duck houses, were laughable if reprehensible, but others were more serious, with ghost second homes and long-settled mortgages falsely claimed for, pilfered from the national purse. Parliamentary corruption was nothing new, previous scandals having involved financial incentives being given to MPs by lobbyists and other privileges exchanged for confidential information, but the sheer scale of the institutional criminality exposed by the expenses scandal left many citizens reeling. It is hard to find a British citizen today who would say they trusted an MP implicitly.

Once again, as a result of this exposé, the more alternative-minded of the new doubters found themselves being drawn to other areas of speculation, for where there is corruption, conspiracy is usually not far behind. Britain's 'Climategate' the same year, which exposed seemingly calculated withholdings of important data from within the Climatic Research Group – information which might challenge the dramatic and tax-aiding global warming hypothesis – didn't help. Suddenly, it was not such a leap to consider that MPs who would lie about something as basic as dinner expenses, or indiscriminately cover for disingenuous scientists, would very probably deceive on larger scales too.

Sure enough, full-blown conspiracy theories soon began to arise over the very timing of the expenses scandal, leading some to consider that the whistle had been blown for more reasons than may have met the eye. Not least, the endless media obsession with ducks and mortgages managed to eclipse the far more crucial issues around the European Parliamentary elections being held at the height of the scandal, thus avoiding important debates over the seemingly underhand extensions of the Treaty of Lisbon, for instance, which ushered in a more strictly federal Europe without the need to vote for one. In the same breath it undermined belief in the British constitution itself, leading some to call for greater unity with the EU as a corrective measure to all the parochial dishonesty (rather missing the point that corruption would seem to be as rife within the EU as anywhere else). The European project is seen by many truthseekers as one of the paths to the Orwellian super-states aspired to by the New World Order, with the significant troubles of the euro currency considered not an irregularity, but a factored-in component *designed* to crash at a chosen moment to make way for a more heavily regulated and federal system.

On one level, disillusionments such as that caused by the expenses scandal undoubtedly help people see the truth of how things really are: a healthy development if they encourage more considered thinking on how to better the world. Less good is the resulting cynicism that can also generate profound apathy, risking a stagnant slide towards a disempowered population reluctant to stand up for itself – perhaps that is the very idea, according to some. After all, why bother even trying to deal with a state riddled with layers of such entrenched corruption so obviously stacked against the individual? This dangerous mindset was further fostered by the peeling away of even more layers in 2011.

Murdoch: Rule by Proxy

When it emerged in 2011 that illegal phone hacking of celebrities, politicians and other prominent figures had extensively taken place at the UK tabloid the *News of the World*, run by media mogul Rupert Murdoch's News International (News Corporation, globally), there was a predictable reaction of public annoyance. When it became clear that everyday folk, including murder victims and their families, had also been targeted, irritation turned to horror. Notwithstanding the fact that many of the outraged were the same readers who had for years gleefully lapped up the ill-gotten gains of the hackings, there was still a sense that a line had been crossed.

The defence that had long held off further investigation of News International – that the hacking had been carried out by a tiny minority of journalists, already sacrificed to prosecution some years back – crumbled when it transpired that many more people than claimed must have been aware of the underhand methods by which numerous stories were sourced. When ex-*News of the World* editor Andy Coulson, followed by News International's chief executive Rebekah Brooks and other high-profile staff were arrested and bailed under the police inquiry that followed, an unhealthy and insidious underbelly of British public life began to surface. This was complicated with accusations that the police themselves had sold stories to the paper in the past.

Rupert Murdoch, with his son and business partner, James, was soon called to appear in front of a parliamentary committee, where, despite a protestor's foam pie, remorse was expressed but responsibility deferred. Murdoch shut down the *News of the World*, presumably hoping that the matter might be forgotten, but the furore continued, with other News International newpapers being drawn into the mire.

The subsequent Leveson Inquiry, a government-commissioned public inquiry into the 'culture, practices and ethics of the press', chaired by Lord Justice Leveson, which expanded its remit to investigate the journalistic habits of the entire media, interviewed not only the Murdochs, Coulson and Brooks again, but other editors, reporters and victims, some of them 'showbiz' stars. While undeniably fascinating, this circus was allowed to eclipse far more serious elements, which the public was duly distracted from in a manner that some thought suspicious.

The role of Andy Coulson, for one, was noticeably sidelined by the tales of celebrity angst, yet his part in the proceedings had clearly lifted a lid on something the establishment seemed keen to move on from. The fuss over the controversial 2010 appointment of Coulson as incoming Prime Minister David Cameron's communications director in the face of the brewing accusations (resulting in Coulson's resignation just months later) had been high profile, but it was the exposure of the close relations between News International and the government, like Tony Blair's before it, that really mattered. Yet this did not, in truth, receive the overwhelmingly persistent coverage it deserved.

The revelations that did briefly make the news made it clear that Blair in particular had many long-standing social ties with Rupert Murdoch (becoming godfather to one of his daughters in 2010, something kept very quiet at the time), suggesting that the mogul must have been surreptitiously influencing British governance for over a decade.[7] As for Cameron, in his first year of office alone, a remarkable 100 meetings or so had taken place between top News International executives and the prime minister or high-level cabinet ministers such as George Osborne (a regular Bilderberg attender – *see* pp. 231–2). Cameron himself already had a close social relationship with Charlie and Rebekah Brooks (2012's 'Horsegate' disclosures later revealed cosy riding weekends on a horse loaned to the Brookses by the police) and ensured that one of the first important meetings he had in the days following his accession to power was with the person that clearly mattered the most – Rupert Murdoch.[8] Accusations that a secret deal was made to grease the path for News Corporation's attempts to gain full ownership of the BSkyB television network (a bid which collapsed amidst the scandals) were denied, perhaps predictably, but the affair left an indelible taint which strongly suggested unhealthy government partiality.

What was unquestionably established by something that had begun as a simple phone-hacking investigation was that Britain, and almost certainly other countries where the News Corporation empire is strong (the USA, especially, where Murdoch's Fox News network is renowned for its right-wing rhetoric), had been suffering from rule by proxy for far too long, with the needs of voters coming second to the demands of the real beneficiaries. As the façade finally broke, even MPs and high-ranking police officials came forward to complain of implicit threats from the Murdoch press over the years, uncovering the culture of bullying and intimidation that had gripped the nation for maybe decades. A collective sigh of relief could be felt to ripple through the population at the fall of this unholy regime. Although people knew that nepotism and lobbying was probably a fixture of every government, to have it so starkly revealed was something new. Some victims had long railed against this situation, but had felt powerless, fearing reprisal exposures of their personal lives if they tried to call attention to it.

There is one truthseeker version of events which says that the revelations around the Murdoch empire were a deliberate move, designed especially to further a serious restriction on the freedom of the press, and thus free speech; but many others believe that simple hubris and an unstoppable avalanche of corruption's over-stacked cover-ups had finally resulted in the laying open of this subtle but unmistakable conspiracy.

Despite this hiccup, it remains that the media will always need the ear of governments, and the governments will always foster the support of the media, regardless of Cameron's sudden epiphany, which saw him and his colleagues rapidly distancing themselves from Murdoch's team, with new sniffs of disapproval in their direction. The danger of the revised situation is that the seemingly irresistible secret meetings between media executives and authorities may have been driven further underground, rather than becoming more overt. Similarly, the unexpected disclosure of the unhealthily intimate relationship between then British defence secretary Liam Fox and arms lobbyist Adam Werrity in 2011 – strongly suspected of influencing government defence contracts without any official remit – appeared merely to reveal how business is usually done rather than it being a one-off anomaly. Again, the revelation was necessary, but was likely to breed more secrecy rather than openness.

The complex web of corporate media ownership and the links with the arms industry, banking and governments is explored a little further in chapter 8, but enough underhand influence has been cited here to demonstrate why doubt in authority will unavoidably creep in when such a tangled mass of undeclared interests and interferences is revealed by the lifting of just the smallest stone.

The Sean Hoare Mystery

Another element which hurriedly and mysteriously absented itself from all the mainstream coverage of the phone-hacking scandal concerned the former *News of the World* journalist Sean Hoare in July 2011, found dead at his home just before he was due to give official testimony against his former boss, Andy Coulson. Hoare had been a typical News International hack for years, digging for spicy if sometimes factually incorrect stories of celebrity gossip, but his increasing predilection for drugs and alcohol (which Hoare blamed on encouragement from his own employers) led to his sacking in 2005. Bitter at his treatment, Hoare had become very vocal in his insistence, as expressed to *New York Times Magazine* in 2010, that he and other journalists at News International had been bullied into the culture of amoral snooping by the likes of Coulson, who, he said, had directly ordered him to hack mobile phones.

Hoare's drinking had undoubtedly worsened amidst all the media attention around his claims, but in his last few weeks he specifically warned friends of his fears that someone was out to kill him with a view to silencing his disclosures, and that he was receiving intimidation and threats. Bizarre it was, then, that when Hoare's body was discovered at his house on 18 July 2011, police described his death as 'unexplained', but not suspicious. This troubled some observers. If his passing remained unexplained, how could suspicious circumstances be ruled out?

Predictably, Hoare's demise was widely promoted as the reckoning of his own unfortunate addictions, with all the predictions of his own assassination brushed aside as the random mutterings of intoxicated paranoia. The results of the notably evasive police investigation into the cause of death remained unannounced for months, during which talk of either Hoare or his untimely end had quickly fallen – or been taken – away from the spotlight. When the verdict was finally (and quietly) delivered, unspecified 'natural causes', probably due to liver damage, were cited, with no further elaboration.

Needless to say, the hasty dropping of Hoare's claims as the central focus of inquiry, and the uncertain circumstances of his passing, left many people convinced that something suspicious was at work. But without the huge public fuss accorded to similar casualties such as Dr David Kelly, the wheels turned and the world soon moved on, the story removed from most people's consciousness.

The sceptics dutifully scoffed at the conspiracy view of Hoare's death, highlighting the police investigation and the wide media acceptance of his alcoholism as all the evidence needed to support the natural causes verdict. Yet, given that the police themselves were being accused of corruption – with Hoare having stated that police had actually passed on not only stories but also mobile phone tracking technology to News International staff – and that much of the media itself stood to lose credibility and risk prosecution in the wake of his and others' testimonies, these could hardly be seen as reliable criteria. Inevitably, conspiracy theorists have accused either Murdoch's empire, corrupt police, government intelligence, or all three, of having ordered Hoare's death. With toxicology and forensic reports available only from or through the very agencies under suspicion, truthseekers can perhaps be forgiven for remaining cynical.

Conspiracy Theorists at Heart

Herein lies a central issue. Authorities do lie. Deceptions do take place. Proven or very likely conspiracies are littered throughout history, as we have discovered. Somewhere deep inside, for all that it allows itself to be distracted, the public conscience knows this and now maintains a low-level but inherent distrust in official information. Especially when high-profile public figures are suddenly removed from this earthly realm at key moments or in questionable ways, polls show that we are nearly all, at heart, conspiracy theorists.

The Sean Hoare story was scrambled and moved on from just rapidly enough that it didn't sink into the collective mind enough to become a classic assassination legend, yet most people seemed at best dubious about it for the short time the event remained in view. Other individuals, however, with much greater publicity, have famously gone down in questionable circumstances, leaving the vast majority of observers suspecting probable conspiracy, as the next chapter explores.

IN SUMMARY . . .

Political Conspiracies: Arguments Against

Events such as Watergate or the MPs' expenses crisis may be political scandals on a level of nothing more than small-minded individuals lying or conducting espionage to preserve personal influence rather than wider agendas being at work – Historic achievements as significant as the Moon landings are simply too huge to have been faked, and those who believe the hoax theories are simply the politically disillusioned who have fallen into foolish paranoia – The Iraqi weapons of mass destruction stories, even if known to be uncertain at the time, were necessary possibilities which had to be acted on and in any case enabled the happy downfall of a tyrant – WikiLeaks revealed little more than minor squabbles and routine military necessities – Links between governments and News Corporation may be acceptable normal practice in a world where good relations between authorities and the media are essential, and the death of a crucial witness to the Murdoch revelations was nothing but a coincidence.

Political Conspiracies: Arguments For

Political scandal is nearly always shown in retrospect to have masked wider misdemeanours involving many more people than are exposed in the immediate revelations, which are quickly contained at the time – At least some of the Moon landings evidence can be shown to be unreliable in certain areas, whatever really happened, with one or two NASA photographs being provable fakes – Mounting a lunar hoax might not need to involve as many people as is sometimes claimed – The evidence of the Iraqi weapons of mass destruction was widely known to be false even at the time of the allied invasion, and documents and footage revealed by WikiLeaks unequivocally demonstrate that the truth of Western actions in the Middle East is habitually kept from the public – Democratic principles are almost certainly compromised by the hidden cronyism that has become endemic in the Western political system, and governments of recent times have been clearly exposed as being far too influenced by media lobbying – Deaths of important witnesses seem to occur with alarming regularity.

CONCLUSION

The political world is the interface between the quiet forces with the real power – whether legitimate corporate and financial players or conspiratorial manipulators – and the everyday business of running a civilization. Yet too often is it revealed to have fallen into corruption and falsification even at a surface level. As the 'scandals' that emerge into full public attention seem to occur so frequently, what faith can anyone really have in the complex machinations and dubious dealings that must be going on far beneath? Imagining that something as historic as the lunar programme could have been at least partially misrepresented becomes less of a stretch when the overall picture of endemic deception, abuses of power and rule by proxy is considered. The sheer audacity of the weapons of mass destruction scare that was used to justify action in Iraq, and the all-too-common manipulation of media conduits to spread propaganda, show that there is little that authorities won't consider doing when their agendas demand it.

CHAPTER 5

ASSASSINATION CONSPIRACIES

When public figures die in mysterious or controversial circumstances, it is inevitable that conspiracy theories will arise. Sometimes these mask simple grief and denial, a lack of acceptance that someone important is gone. But a number of assassination allegations require a little more consideration. In a world where ruthless minds appear to treat people as chess pieces to be played with or removed as necessary through false-flag attacks, there seems to be little reason to think they would hesitate to take out individuals as well. But achieving this without raising suspicion is not so easy, requiring, perhaps, the need to dress up murders as accidents or suicides. Two famous cases stand out in this regard, but even accepted assassination scenarios are rarely as straightforward as they appear.

I) JOHN F KENNEDY

An Iconic Murder

It is widely described as 'the mother of all conspiracy theories'; there can scarcely be a person on the planet who remains unaware of the controversies over the iconic death of US President

John F Kennedy at Dealey Plaza, Dallas, on 22 November 1963. The horror of the moment is imprinted on the collective memory (largely through the vital 8mm cine film taken by Abraham Zapruder), with Kennedy's head exploding and his pink-suited wife Jackie scrambling across the boot of the limousine.

Thus everyone accepts that JFK was the victim of bullets fired by someone; it's just that no one can quite agree on who fired them and why. For all the years of speculation, almost nothing has ever been universally settled about what exactly happened. As such, raking through every detail yet again is unlikely to pay dividends here, but a few points stand out as important for the purposes of these pages.

Analysis of the Shooting

There is little doubt that Lee Harvey Oswald, an ex-US Marine and one-time defector to the Soviet Union, was responsible for one of the shots which took out Kennedy, fired from an overlooking window of the Texas School Book Depository as the President's motorcade passed by.[1] Some witnesses say several shots were heard (six possible impulses are said to have been recorded on a controversial police 'Dictabelt' recording), but at least two other bullets are generally agreed to have been fired on the day. The question is, by whom? The official Warren Commission, which infamously dismissed any wider conspiracy beyond Oswald, concluded that he fired all the shots, and that one bullet missed while another sliced through both Kennedy and Governor John Connally (who survived), before a third inflicted the fatal wound to the President's brain.

Contrary to the commission's conclusions, however, the much-discussed evidence of shots also being heard from the fence at the top of the now-legendary 'grassy knoll' (a raised area to the side of Dealey Plaza) is not insubstantial. It is interesting to note that when *Science and Justice* journal, a publication of the British Forensic Science Society, analysed audio recordings of the assassination, they concluded a '96% certainty' that shots had been fired from there, although critics maintain that the sounds were merely acoustic rebounds. The official version, on the other hand, insists that Oswald, incensed by Kennedy's treatment of Cuba, among other grievances, acted alone. The problem lies in the numerous anomalies which present themselves in this scenario: from claims that one man couldn't possibly have fired three shots so quickly or precisely, to doubts over even which gun was used; many people remain doubtful. The first policemen on the scene unambiguously described Oswald's weapon as being a 7.65 Mauser, but by the time the Warren Commission reported, this had become a 6.5 Italian Mannlicher Carcano, seemingly to match a rifle he was known to have owned before the assassination. This has led to theories, aside from the grassy knoll candidates, that yet another gunman, using a different rifle, may have been in the same building as Oswald, but that evidence for this was suppressed to leave Oswald with the sole blame.

As immortalized in Oliver Stone's in itself not entirely accurate but still salient 1991 film *JFK*, great doubts also hover over the 'magic bullet', the first shot to hit the President. Even the usually conspiracy-deflating Wikipedia witheringly points out that this somehow managed to 'traverse fifteen layers of clothing, seven layers of skin, and approximately fifteen inches of tissue, struck a necktie knot, removed four inches of rib, and shattered a radius bone'. More incredibly still, the same bullet then somehow passed on into Governor Connally, to cause further injury to his chest and wrist before lodging in his thigh. Although it was the third projectile which did the fatal damage to Kennedy's skull, the arguments over the second one are important, because if this bullet did *not* behave in the manner described, then it follows that other shots must have been fired from different directions within the same split seconds. Those who refuse to countenance this cling to the magic bullet theory, but to most conspiracy theorists this smacks of a convenience with which to support the official 'lone gunman' verdict – a term which has now passed into popular culture as flagging up an establishment-approved orthodoxy being enforced in the face of considerable contrary evidence.

But if the theorists are right – and in the case of JFK, this means most of the world's population, according to polls – then one might assume that the additional gunmen must have been seen, if not identified, somewhere in the vicinity on the day. As it happens, there are indeed many reports of suspicious-looking figures hovering in unusual places at the time of the shooting. Although some of this might be retrospective paranoia (the passing of a presidential motorcade, with much advance promotion, would have brought out all sorts of curious onlookers), we have already seen that Frank Sturgis claimed that the purpose of the Watergate break-in was to steal incriminating photographs of US agents secretly stationed around Dealey Plaza (*see* p. 91), while reports of three mysterious 'tramps' (albeit clean-shaven and unconvincing ones) keeping an eye on things have also added to the conjecture.

Potential Perpetrators

Although he himself denied his presence (a stance supported by some later inquiries), one of the 'tramps' was widely reckoned to have been one E Howard Hunt, a CIA station chief whose name has been linked many times to JFK's shooting. Whether he was in Dallas that day or not, he was certainly the man who went on to arrange the failed Watergate burglary (for which he served 33 months in prison before being pardoned by President Gerald Ford, along with Nixon himself). Shortly before Hunt's death in 2007, his son claims that his father privately told him he *had* been part of a plot to assassinate Kennedy. This raises inevitable fears that Kennedy's death was orchestrated perhaps not by

Cuban exiles, Fidel Castro, the Mafia, the Soviets, a consortium of bankers or discontented Israelis, all of whom (and more) have been put forward as possible sponsors, but by forces much closer to home, with the theorists' stalwart Lyndon B Johnson often implicated as the prime suspect. In this view, the killing of JFK was essentially a *coup d'état*.

Sifting all the numerous choices, it is certainly the case that Kennedy's approach (and colourful lifestyle) had alienated many of those used to a more traditional presidential demeanour, and the efforts of him and his brother Robert F Kennedy to curtail the powers of both legal (if only just) institutions such as the Federal Reserve (*see* p. 231) and illegal ones such as the Mafia had undoubtedly ruffled some usually untouchable feathers. Cuban exiles, meanwhile, angry at the fumbled attempt to retake their country from Castro's revolutionaries in the 1961 Bay of Pigs incident, had made loud and public threats against Kennedy. The revolutionaries themselves would doubtless have also been happy to put an end to his term of office. At the other end of the spectrum, more elaborate claims point to Kennedy's desire to declassify UFO evidence as being yet another reason for various black-ops cabals to require his removal (*see* chapter 7). There was plainly no shortage of factions which stood to benefit from JFK's death. But the most likely sources seem to point to hands within US intelligence services as having been the tools behind the assassination's arrangement, whoever the paymasters were.

The inherent problem with Kennedy conspiracy theories is that there are now so many of them, some logical and interconnected, others more contradictory and extravagant, that it has become almost impossible as the decades have passed to extricate fully the key threads which might hint at the most probable truth. Maybe all of the accused played a role somewhere in the background, whether they knew they were working for the same ends or not. But identifying the truth is unlikely to get any easier until confidential documents are finally released from the archives.

Removal of Evidence and Witnesses?

Some claim that important pieces of JFK assassination evidence were tampered with from the start. The crucial Zapruder film, which, whilst not being the only footage taken of the moments around the shooting, is certainly the clearest, is not in itself entirely reliable. There have been several assertions that important frames have been removed from the publicly available versions, or that critical minutiae may in places have actually have been scratched from the original emulsion. The late and influential conspiracy theorist William Cooper claimed that some of this occurred to conceal detail showing that the driver of the limousine, William Greer, had himself fired one of the deadly bullets by quickly turning around with a gun from the front seat while the other shots were incoming. This is not widely agreed with, but it adds yet another layer of potential intrigue. Other visual evidence, such as autopsy photographs purporting to show the damage to the president's skull, has also been called into question, with loud contentions that the released images do *not* show the real injuries, but have been switched to cover up proof of the additional gunmen.

One useful witness who might have revealed more would, of course, have been Lee Harvey Oswald, but he was himself infamously – and expediently – shot dead just two days after his capture, at the hands of outraged nightclub owner Jack Ruby, supposedly striking a vengeful blow on behalf of the citizenry. But, just as some say that Kennedy himself had been left oddly vulnerable by an unusual lack of protective agents on the day of his shooting, so too has concern been raised at the seemingly lax security at the police headquarters from where Oswald was being brought out to be taken to the county jail. With a melee of jostling press reporters and cameramen waiting for him, this apparent carelessness allowed Ruby simply to step from the crowd and shoot Oswald in the stomach at point-blank range.

Far from being an incensed member of the public, it has been alleged that Ruby had personal connections to Oswald and was party to inside knowledge of the JFK assassination plot. It is worthy of note that Rose Cherami, a self-confessed drug addict who had worked as a stripper for Ruby, told police in advance of 22 November that she knew there were plans to kill Kennedy. She also claimed, in the aftermath of both shootings, that Ruby and Oswald had once had a gay relationship. Doubters poured scorn on her stories, but her sudden 'accidental' death under the wheels of a car two years later made some take them more seriously.

Ruby himself was quickly convicted of Oswald's murder and might have added important details of his own at a second impending appeal trial, having hinted that he knew far more than he had been allowed to say at the first. However, he apparently died of cancer in late 1966, before he had the chance. At a televised news conference in 1965, Ruby had said:

Everything pertaining to what's happening has never come to the surface. The world will never know the true facts of what occurred, my motives. The people who had so much to gain, and had such an ulterior motive for putting me in the position I'm in, will never let the true facts come above board to the world.

When a reporter then queried, 'Are these people in very high positions, Jack?', Ruby responded with a 'Yes.'

By this time, Ruby had clearly become a conspiracy theorist himself, believing that cancer cells had been deliberately injected into his body by prison doctors. Later, Ruby apparently told his psychiatrist, Werner Teuter, that JFK's killing was 'an act of overthrowing the government'. Ruby claimed to know 'who had President Kennedy killed', but feared for his own life, stating,

I am doomed. I do not want to die. But I am not insane. I was framed to kill Oswald.

As with so many other events where answers to awkward questions might be too readily available from named witnesses (see below), it should be recorded here that an above-average number of other key witnesses in connection with the killing of Kennedy appear to have met strange demises.[2] The further death of Robert F Kennedy, dying shortly after being gunned down in a Los Angeles hotel in 1968, created yet another tier of conspiratorial allegations.

The Warren Commission

Set up just weeks after JFK's assassination to provide a full investigation into the event and those following it, the Warren Commission predictably concluded that both Oswald and Ruby were the sole players. Its final report, delivered just ten months after Dealey Plaza's darkest hour, was heavily criticized even at the time for its sloppiness and inconsistent analysis, with all interviews held in suspiciously closed sessions. Remarkably, only one transcript out of the 94 witness testimonies was actually read by every member of the commission, when it might have been assumed that each would have wanted to see all of them in order to make a valid judgement. Overall, the Warren Report felt less than convincing and failed to inspire confidence in anyone but the staunchest patriots. Its verdict was unsurprising to some minds, given that it had been set up by the very man that they, rightly or wrongly, believed may even have been responsible for the shooting – President Johnson.

When the Watergate scandal brought public trust crashing down further, the public scepticism about the Warren Report accelerated massively and became damaging. This may explain why a further inquiry, using new evidence, was mounted by the House Select Committee on Assassinations (HSCA) in the late 1970s. Its final report in 1979, while backing up some of the Warren Commission's findings as regards bullets and wounds, did make some attempt to take on board the other theories which had been bubbling under, and accepted the likelihood that another gunman had been involved, although the main responsibility was still left with Oswald. The HSCA's main concession, therefore, was to acknowledge that a wider conspiracy had 'probably' been at work, although it failed to follow up any of the implications of this conclusion, seemingly in the hope that history would soon confine the whole business to the eternal grey box of unsolved mysteries and move on – a strategy that mostly appears to have worked.

Important Lessons

Here, perhaps, is the greatest lesson to be learned from the shooting of JFK. There *are* still people who insist on the lone gunman theory and dismiss all other speculation as poison from the treasonous fringe, but the overwhelming mass of observers suspect that something more insidious was at work. This conspiracy theory, for once, resides firmly in the mainstream. Yet the vast mythology that has grown up around the 'curse of the Kennedys', with all its affairs and scandals, Cuban missiles, Marilyn Monroe and the Mafia, has swallowed up the magic bullet, grassy knoll and mysterious tramps with it, allowing the more serious inferences to go unaddressed. This is of concern, because if a secret cabal capable of removing the leader of the world's greatest superpower was at work even then, what might it be doing today? For all the fingers pointed at the likes of Johnson and the CIA, lurking in the background is always the idea that, beyond the selfish egos of individuals, the wider New World Order plan lies.

If the vast majority of people believe that JFK's death was a conspiracy, but feel that too much time has passed and too much confusion been stirred into the mix for it really to matter any more, as would seem to be the case, then it stands to reason that similar tactics might well be employed on a regular basis. There is probably an art to obfuscating just long enough that the murkier points of an atrocity become confined to an unreachable past. By such strategies, murder becomes nostalgia. Something similar is possibly being attempted over 9/11, creating an urgency among truthseekers to keep the many questions about that more recent atrocity fresh and alive while it is still in full living memory.

A crucial point remains: especially with the Kennedy case, certain events turn most of us into conspiracy theorists. The question is, can those theories produce enough proven evidence in time to prevent such crimes from occurring again? Already, even a more recent assassination theory, this time involving a member of the British Royal Family, has begun to fade into a hazy realm of myth.

II) DIANA, PRINCESS OF WALES

Mass Mourning

Those who hold to the Kennedy lone gunman hypothesis might argue that without proven evidence of others being involved it cannot be described as a conspiracy. Only when the presence of supplementary plotters or assassins is assumed does it cross into that category. What no one doubts, however, is that the President *was* unlawfully killed. Yet, when even establishing this becomes an uphill struggle in the face of official denial, it is curious to observe that the public doesn't lose its natural propensity towards conspiracy thinking.

Of all recent history's major upsets, the death of Diana, Princess of Wales in a car crash at the Pont de l'Alma underpass shortly after midnight in Paris on 31 August 1997 had the most direct impact on the people of Britain, and many beyond. Scenes of characteristically restrained but still acute mass hysteria followed the announcement, and an atmosphere of intense national mourning, not seen since the death of Queen Victoria nearly a century before, gripped the nation. This culminated in the televised funeral, which saw streets across the nation empty and an eerie silence descend, outpourings of grief being expressed even by usually stoic individuals. Just briefly, the 'stiff upper lip' slipped, as something very profound was touched in the collective – a phenomenon which has been oft-debated in the years since.

It was easy to forget, during all of this, that Diana had not been so well regarded in the years leading to her end. In the glory days of her doomed marriage to Prince Charles, heir to the throne, something of her innocent and apparently caring nature had seemed to speak to the people, bringing a new human quality to an often-remote Royal Family. Diana's popularity consequently soared to almost surreal heights, creating expectations that no public figure could live up to indefinitely. But, sure enough, since the break-up of the marriage, her criticism of the royals, tales of multiple affairs, illegally taped phone calls to lovers ('Squidgygate') and very public personal revelations made in books and interviews, actively encouraged by Diana herself, had sullied her image. Yet something in her very fragility, together with the admissions of everyday failings, still ensured that a streak of sympathy towards the Princess remained. With the shocking news of her death, the view of Diana as a superstar martyr to the modern world increased a hundredfold, enhanced by the accusations that 'paparazzi' photographers may have contributed to the crash by pursuing her vehicle. The gaping hole left in the public psyche by the sudden absence of the 'People's Princess' starkly illustrated just how many collective fantasies had been projected onto Diana, making her loss feel an all the more bitter blow to people who had, almost without realizing it, vicariously lived through this poster-girl for the masses.

Murder Polls

So was it, then, a deep state of psychological denial and anger that compelled people almost immediately to seek external responsibility for Diana's death? Or did this occur because there was actual evidence to suggest that the devastating crash, which killed Diana, her lover Dodi Al-Fayed and the driver of the car, Henri Paul, may have been contrived – an assassination made to look like an accident? Polls taken in 2007, ten years after the event, showed that a remarkable proportion of British people believed that Diana was murdered. Some reports alleged a 90 per cent adherence to this view, while more moderate polls said one in three, but either way the results were telling. For all the official inquiries which have since said otherwise, little has changed in this regard. The strength of views lessens somewhat beyond Britain's borders, but those within them would not appear to care what outsiders think.[3] The combined gut of Diana's own people knows its own mind in this regard, and this hugely significant statistic must make belief in her assassination one of the most subscribed-to conspiracy theories of all time in any one country, even more so than with Kennedy in the USA.

Do statistics make a belief right, though? The verdicts of at least three French and UK inquests or judicial inquiries are clear on what happened: the driver, Henri Paul, was three times over the French alcohol limit for driving and consequently lost control of the car as it sought to speed away from over-eager photographers. This scenario seems acceptably probable at first glance, but, as we have seen, things are frequently not that straightforward, and the Diana case, in the details around both the crash and its aftermath, does present a number of anomalies that deserve some thought.

Assassination Evidence?

The main piece of evidence for the official verdicts – the blood test carried out on Henri Paul – has come under heavy criticism from several quarters, with many claims that the sample was either accidentally or deliberately switched with that of a suicide victim brought into the hospital that same night. While acknowledging that some confusion had at one point crept in, the authorities have insisted that later checks made against Paul's DNA and eye fluid confirm the high level of alcohol in his system that night. On the other hand, one of the blood samples apparently showed levels of carbon monoxide that should have rendered Paul more than unfit for duty that night, yet nobody described him as seeming unwell or behaving oddly, which again calls either the sample or the analysis procedure into question.

Indeed, one of the main problems which presents itself over Paul's condition is the observation that at no point in either CCTV footage or in the recollection of most witnesses did he show the slightest signs of inebriation. The bar bill shows he had apparently had just two drinks at the Ritz Hotel before leaving with Diana, Dodi and bodyguard Trevor Rees-Jones, but seemed sober and calm. It is curious to note that Lord Stevens, leading the UK's 2006 Operation Paget inquest into Diana's death, directly informed Paul's parents, in a meeting with them, that their son had *not* been drunk, yet just five weeks later his own report stated the exact opposite, with no reason given for the sudden turnaround. The parents maintain that evidence showed no excessive drinking had taken place. The fact that Paul (who had just qualified as a private pilot) had no history of heavy drinking and that the Fayed family had employed him for 11 years without a single disciplinary blip suggest that driving under the influence would have been out of character.

Questions have been raised about Paul's true identity. He was not one of Diana's usual drivers, and had known links to the French security services, if fairly low-level ones. Some sources have indicated that he may also have been working with MI6, which doesn't have a good track record on moral actions, having reportedly mounted a number of shady assassination attempts against leading political figures, including a failed one on Libya's former ruler Colonel Gaddafi.[4] This has led the less restricted fringes to consider more Manchurian candidate theories, whereby Paul might have been subjected to a suicidal mind-control programme. This is perhaps not so impossible, given the successful demonstrations of similar techniques by celebrity hypnotists such as Derren Brown. Paul was also found to have been in possession of a small fortune in his bank accounts, with no clear explanation of where the funds came from. It seems unlikely he was paid to kill himself, but, hypnotism aside, it is not entirely improbable that he could have been manipulated into participating in some kind of chase set-up which he never suspected might include his own death.

The details of the accident itself have been the subject of much confusion, some of which has already passed into modern legend. Tales of a bright flash seen just as Diana's Mercedes entered the Pont de l'Alma tunnel, and reports of a white Fiat Uno, which, paint samples demonstrate, did clip the limousine (or the other way around) have fuelled the speculation that the crash was deliberately engineered. Dazzling people with bright lights is a technique known to be used in combat. It has been suggested that the light may have been shone either from the Fiat or another car, blinding Henri Paul, while the brief collision sent the Mercedes hurtling into a roof support pillar before spinning and rebounding to a halt.

Critics of the blinding scenario contend that reports of the flash are tenuous and contradictory. They also point out that the fatal driving manoeuvres leading to the crash had already begun before Diana's car entered the tunnel, and that timing the claimed calculated events and positions so precisely at high speed would be very difficult. This said, running cars off roads into fatal crashes *is* a long-established assassination technique among various intelligence agencies, notably the CIA.

The Fiat itself has never been properly identified, although Dodi's father, entrepreneur and then owner of Harrods, Mohamed Al-Fayed, asserts that it belonged to a French photographer known as Jean-Paul James Andanson. Given the much-boasted capability of modern police forces to track down stolen vehicles, and the preponderance of security cameras across Parisian streets, it is indeed strange that the French authorities, despite investigating over 4,000 white Fiat Unos, never managed, officially, to identify the mystery car. Indeed, no salient CCTV footage was apparently available to cast light on any aspect of the crash, with the tunnel cameras not being operated at that time of the night.

When inquiries showed that Andanson had – he claimed, at least – not used his own white Fiat Uno for several years before the events at the Pont de l'Alma, cynicism about the role of the other vehicle crept in. However, when he was then found dead in a burned-out BMW in 2000, just as accusations were mounting, suspicions were raised again as yet another potentially important figure in an ongoing intrigue met an untimely and peculiar end. In the vehicle, Andanson's head was found detached from his body – an extremely unusual effect from a fire – and there was a small round hole in his skull (although no gun was found anywhere in the vicinity, nor indeed car keys); yet neither of these puzzles were in any way seen as anomalous by authorities. A verdict of suicide by self-incineration was recorded. The failure of this curious episode to come under scrutiny at any of the following inquests ensured, unsurprisingly, that truthseekers decided to hold their own views on the matter.

Aftermath of the Accident

The condition of Diana in the crashed Mercedes immediately following the impact has also been called into question. As a morbid reminder of the importance of road safety, none of its occupants had been wearing seatbelts; only Rees-Jones survived, albeit with substantial head injuries, while Dodi Al-Fayed and Paul appeared to have died almost instantly. Reports vary as to the condition of Diana herself. As paparazzi photographers, almost incredibly, continued to take pictures, some witnesses say she was alive but unspeaking, bleeding from the ears and nose. However, the first doctor to tend to her (one who happened to be passing by) stated she had no visible injuries and was murmuring in shock. Either way, it is generally agreed that Diana was alive when removed from the car around 35 minutes on, but that she went into cardiac arrest shortly after, dying a few hours later.

One story which has not received the coverage it may deserve, perhaps because others fear for their lives, is that at least one of the French surgeons at the Pitié-Salpêtrière Hospital, where Diana was tended to, privately claimed that expectations for her survival were apparently good when she was brought in. However, when a British medical team arrived at the hospital, local staff were relieved and ordered from the room – and Diana was unexpectedly pronounced dead by the replacement doctors shortly thereafter. This has led some to speculate that someone was quietly making sure the Princess would never recover. It is rumoured that the surgeon was planning to reveal this in a book, but that he himself then died in a car accident, his wife disappearing soon afterwards. Conspiracy paranoia? Maybe. But it is clear, from some of the foggier elements present in the overall details of the Diana case, why so many people continue to have doubts about the official verdicts.

Premonitions and a Wider Plot?

Maybe all of the conspiracy allegations could be dismissed were it not for the fact that the Princess herself had provably feared for her life, to the point of giving a chillingly accurate prediction of her own fate. In a letter written to her former butler Paul Burrell in October 1996, Diana, who had made references elsewhere to dark forces afoot within the royal establishment, wrote:

> *This particular phase in my life is the most dangerous – my husband is planning 'an accident' in my car, brake failure and serious head injury in order to make the path clear for him to marry.*

Interestingly, this disturbingly candid distress call goes on to name Tiggy Legge-Bourke, controversial nanny to Princes William and Harry, as Prince Charles's intended new wife – not the expected Camilla Parker-Bowles (now the Duchess of Cornwall), who is referred to in the letter as 'a decoy'. Whether Diana was confused here, or whether it was felt, with the wide publication of this communication after her death, that it would have been too damning to go ahead with a marriage to Legge-Bourke, is unknown. But it is very plain that the Princess had been tipped off by someone, somewhere, that a plot was being mounted against her. The Legge-Bourke allegations are another fascinating seam of the Diana conspiracy theories; there was certainly an acknowledged rivalry between the two of them, with Diana apparently jealous at Legge-Bourke's closeness to both Charles and her sons following the break-up of their marriage.

Neither did Legge-Bourke and Camilla Parker-Bowles have much love for each other, according to varied sources. With this in mind, some believe there was also a failed plot to kill Camilla, just weeks before Diana's death. Evidence for this is provided by the mysterious car crash Camilla experienced in June 1997 on a country road, where she fled the scene after hitting another car at high speed. She said she had run away for 'security' reasons. It has been suggested that perhaps her brakes 'failed', or that she had herself been driven into the other vehicle by some means and that she ran from the scene in case someone intended to finish her off. It is curious that the other victim of the incident, who was left trapped in her car, tipped into a ditch by the impact, never pressed charges against Parker-Bowles, nor did the police pursue the case, perhaps in the hope that it would be quickly forgotten, as indeed it was.[5]

In this scenario, having bungled an attempt to remove one pawn from the board, but later having succeeded with Diana, could it be that Camilla was spared because *two* fatal accidents in connection with Charles would seem too obvious? Whatever really occurred with Legge-Bourke, Camilla plainly got the upper hand in the end, or at least everyone was firmly ordered to play new parts in a hastily rewritten script to avoid a wider scandal. Who was writing that script, though, and why? Maybe, as Diana wrote in her letter, they were 'all being used by the man [Charles] in every sense of the word'. Others, however, believe that higher powers may have stepped in to intervene without even Charles's knowledge or consent. It should be noted that Diana believed the 1987 motorcycle death of Barry Mannakee, her bodyguard and possibly a lover during her marriage, was also staged.

As for the content of Diana's letter to Burrell, backed up by very candid statements made to her solicitor Lord Mishcon, if it was just a coincidence that her life ended in the way she had envisaged, then it was a major one. Typically, the mainstream has allowed this surely crucial letter to fall into the background, not helped by the later antics of Burrell himself, who was accused of perjury at the subsequent inquests and went on to seek fame for light entertainment purposes, demeaning him in the eyes of an already hostile press. Despite this, it is accepted that the letter is genuine, but it is too often sidelined as being the ramblings of a stressed and emotional woman. But then it could be somewhat stressful to hear that one's own murder is being planned, as Apollo 1's Virgil Grissom, journalist Sean Hoare and weapons inspector Dr David Kelly – all of whom seemed to have similar intimations of their own fates – might have attested.

Why Kill Diana?

All this begs the question that *if* Diana's death was deliberately arranged, as so many British people believe, then why?

As it happens, there has been an array of not implausible reasons put forward to explain why several factions may well have been queuing up to find ways to marginalize Diana (some believe MI6 was behind the release of the damaging 'Squidgy' tapes, for instance). Maybe the Princess wouldn't have lived for long even without the underpass incident. There have been all manner of theories put forward to account for the need to remove her entirely, but the main hypotheses usually boil down to one or a combination of the following, all with their own strengths and weaknesses:

- Diana was soon to be engaged (or already was) to Dodi Al-Fayed, and the Royal Family wanted to avoid a genealogical connection to a Muslim family. This view has been robustly promoted by Mohamed Al-Fayed, but friends and witnesses have cast doubt on this, with some pointing out that their relationship was fairly new, and maybe not that harmonious, with Diana having only recently broken up from a serious two-year relationship with another Muslim, Pakistani heart surgeon Hasnat Khan. The Royal Family had apparently shown no public disapproval of Diana's connection with Khan, so why would Fayed present a problem? Others, of course, contend that what the Royal Family says and what it really thinks are two completely different things.
- Diana was pregnant with Dodi Al-Fayed's baby and, similarly, the Royal Family could not tolerate a Muslim bloodline entering the lineage, this time in a rather permanent way. Although this is a view widely subscribed to, official test results on Diana's body ruled pregnancy out.

Truthseekers hardly consider the word of officialdom to be failsafe, however.

- Prince Charles wanted Diana removed to grease the path to remarrying without adverse publicity, as intimated by the Princess in her letter to Burrell. There is no question that Diana's absence did help Charles gain more acceptance of his eventual marriage to Parker-Bowles, although the Legge-Bourke conundrum remains unresolved in this picture. That this is the view Diana clearly subscribed to must obviously be taken into serious account, yet some of the less hardcore theorists find it hard to believe that the likes of Charles would support such a scheme. Those who see the Royals as blood-drinking reptiles naturally differ in this view – see below.

- The Queen's husband, Prince Philip, took matters into his own hands over and above Charles's authority, and plotted Diana's death for some of the above reasons or more, believing her revelations were bringing the Royal Family into disrepute. This view was heavily promoted by Mohamed Al-Fayed in his courtroom attempts to convict the 'killers' of his son and Diana, but was, perhaps predictably, rejected by the British courts.

- Diana's growing campaign against the use of landmines and other questionable military devices was becoming a threat to influential arms manufacturers concerned about the effect of her work on their reputation. Diana's close relationship with Dodi Al-Fayed could have created an embarrassing problem too close at hand for some, given that Dodi's mother had been Samira Khashoggi – sister to the Saudi billionaire arms dealer Adnan Khashoggi. Diana's campaign had certainly been successful in galvanizing public support and was gaining ground at the time of her death.

- The New World Order was also concerned about Diana's growing prominence, given her inside knowledge of the British Royal Family and its links to various intelligence agencies, things which the Princess had begun to allude to in her candid interviews and published letters. In this view, NWO operatives took her out before further damage could be done, adding secret society symbolism into the mix to make for something of a ritualistic death. Similar claims have been made over Dealey Plaza, where JFK was shot – that site has several occult inferences in its layout, as does the whole of Paris, which is rich in Masonic relics and subliminal patterns. The fact that Diana's car crash took place directly beneath the 'Flame of Liberty' monument above the underpass, a potent mystical symbol, has been seen as significant. It is also a place claimed to have once have been the site of a burial chamber of Merovingian kings and/or a Roman temple to the goddess . . . Diana.
- Diana was a direct descendant of Jesus and Mary Magdalene, and/or carried the bloodline of Merovingian kings and the Stuart dynasty, rivals to the House of Windsor. As such, she risked becoming a saintly figure who might reveal too much hidden history and unsettle the established power-bases.
- The Royal Family is in truth a mask for a race of dominating extra-terrestrials (*see* chapter 7) and they did not want certain bloodlines mixing with the ET genes.

The list could continue, covering everything from the theory that Diana was executed on the orders of a jealous Hillary Clinton, who had heard that the Princess was due to be forcibly 'married' to her own husband Bill in a secret occult ceremony, to the notion that Diana didn't really die at all and that the whole event was a set-up to enable her to live a secret life as a recluse, presumably in the same quiet paradise where Hitler, Elvis and Jim Morrison all shipped up at one time or another (*see* p. 26).

Some of the above possibilities appear, at first glance anyway, to be more reasonable than others. But in a world where big lies are told so often, is anyone in a firm enough position to really be able to make fun of one above another?

Diluting Credibility

One difficulty that presents itself in terms of Diana conspiracy theories being taken seriously is the nature of those promoting them. It is perhaps unfortunate that the not entirely unreasonable ideas concerning royal resistance to Muslim bloodlines have come to be indelibly linked with the claims of Mohamed Al-Fayed, who, unfairly or not, is rarely portrayed by the media as a credible figure. His exuberant and outspoken manner has perhaps allowed genuine grief at the loss of his son to translate into often-unguarded and unverifiable accusations. Fayed's insistence that Prince Philip gave orders to stage the crash – an allegation unlikely to be well received in a country which has never much favoured republicanism – has enabled the press to sideline him as an eccentric. By association, the subsequent ridicule has been used to denigrate the potential significance of the undeniably odd anomalies around Diana's death. Fayed is far from the only person to be concerned about the truth, as the polls demonstrate, but more sober questioners have too often been eclipsed by the gaudier aspects of the circus around it.

This effect was not helped by the *Daily Express*, which kept numerous Diana conspiracy stories on its front covers for years. Each was promoted as another nail in the coffin of the official account, only for none of them to come to anything in the final inquiries, whereafter the sensational claims, often with good points buried within them, were quietly dropped, never to be discussed again. Some truthseekers believe this was in itself a coordinated strategy of a long-established kind. Sensing from the public mood that the mainstream was not going to be able to avoid discussing conspiracies this time around, maybe the powers-that-be consequently *chose* to saturate the population with multiple theories, some sensible, others wild, until all of them sank from view under the weight of their own confusion. History records that this tactic generally works; the public sigh, turn the page and put the kettle on, knowing that something isn't right, but having neither the time nor the energy to pursue it further.

Thus the Diana theories have already become, like the Kennedy conspiracies before them, just another part of a dark and extraordinary saga, a story doubtless set to become one of the Grimm-like fairytales of future centuries. Yet, if the conspiracy view is correct, and the official conclusion wrong, the fact is that the people who helped take the Princess's life are probably still alive and influencing our world today.

Certainly, several years on, the public's propensity for believing that public executions were still continuing, albeit in a different guise to that of times past, was showing no signs of diminishing.

III) DR DAVID KELLY

The Iraq Gambit

As we saw in the previous chapter, spring 2003's devastating allied invasion of Iraq took place largely on the strength of an intelligence dossier which claimed that the country's leader, Saddam Hussein, was preparing weapons of mass destruction that could be deployed against the world within 45 minutes. The war resulted in thousands dead and much greater influence for Western powers in the Middle East – but none of the alleged weapons was found. This was no surprise to the diplomats and insiders who had tried to call attention to their absence before the guns started firing.

Prominent among these was the former microbiologist and UN weapons inspector Dr David Kelly.

With impressive credentials, having worked for the British Ministry of Defence in such places as the controversial secret research laboratories at Porton Down, Kelly was an important and informed observer of potential weaponry accumulation, chemical, biological and conventional. Perhaps someone should have listened to his quiet concern, therefore, that the war against Iraq was being rushed into without serious forethought or evidence, but it was blatant that the decision had already been made and so the wheels of war rolled on regardless. Even as early as February 2003, Kelly, who had himself contributed information to the crucial dossier published just six months before, was voicing the fact that there had been 'a lot of pressure' put on its compilers to make a more robust case for war than was truly honest.

When the initial wave of the invasion ended and the smoke cleared to reveal no weapons of mass destruction, by May 2003 Kelly could contain his views no more and expressed them – as an off-the-record source – to the BBC radio journalist Andrew Gilligan. Sensing an important story, Gilligan used this information, along with other views he had gathered, to make the (then) sensational claims on the Radio 4 *Today* programme that the dossier had been deliberately 'sexed up'. Kelly's name was not mentioned in the report, but his anonymity would not last long.[6]

Official Fury

The response to the BBC story from Tony Blair's government, led from the front by press secretary Alastair Campbell, was one of blind fury, perhaps at an injustice, but more likely because it touched a raw nerve in an area where it knew it was weak. Gilligan's report was slammed as a 'lie' and, in an unusually touchy move, an apology was demanded from the BBC. With the press baying to know who the main informant was, the Ministry of Defence and Blair's aides soon, albeit by subtle but inexorable means, allowed it to become clear that Kelly was the man at the core. This highly irregular move (the state normally protects its own staff) appeared to be a vengeful act designed to load as much shame on one man as possible, seemingly in an attempt to distract from the information itself by demolishing the source's reputation. When government spokesmen began referring to Kelly as a 'Walter Mitty'-like character (James Thurber's fictional Mitty being a day-dreaming fantasist), the denigration of a man who, until only a few weeks before, had been regarded as one of the best in his field had firmly descended into cheap personal attacks.

Besieged by journalists and government intimidation, Kelly, a gentle and private man, was understandably taken aback by the furore which had suddenly erupted around him. Called to give account of himself before Parliament's Foreign Affairs Committee on 11 July 2003, Kelly was harshly grilled in an apparently punitive public interrogation, an experience that was undoubtedly stressful and difficult.

All of that might explain why, just a week later, on 18 July, Kelly's body was found in woodlands near his home at Harrowdown Hill, Oxfordshire. He had apparently died from a self-inflicted gash to one wrist and had several (nearly) empty packets of co-proxamol painkillers on him; it appeared that the pressure had become too much for Kelly, resulting in a sad, suicidal exit. The ingratiating expressions of grief from the likes of Blair and Campbell, as patronizing as they were, reinforced the emphasis that a man had ended his life in tragic circumstances of his own making. But had he?

Public Doubts

With memories of Diana's traumatic departure and all its unanswered questions still lingering, the British public was perhaps quicker to think twice about David Kelly than it once might have been. Almost immediately, suspicions were raised among the general populace, even before all the questionable details were revealed. Kelly's demise seemed too conveniently timed (with investigations into the WMD debacle looming), somehow too *obvious*. In the days following his death, it wasn't too hard to find someone expressing this in conversation. Once, maybe, such alarmist talk would have seemed like fringe eccentricity, but not in the wake of recent history's deceptions and disappointments. Again, polls are revealing here, with one 2010 survey on Kelly revealing that by then only 'one in five' people still believed he had committed suicide.[7] As with Diana, such a statistic speaks either of a blanket mistrust in authority, or of the weaknesses of the government-sponsored investigation.

With echoes of the Warren Commission, the Hutton Inquiry that delivered the suicide verdict on Kelly has been heavily criticized for its failure to interview key witnesses or to address particular points of concern. The hasty setting-up of the inquiry has itself been the subject of some scrutiny. Kelly's death was reported to Tony Blair while he was on a flight to Japan, yet Lord Hutton had already been appointed to lead an investigation even before the plane touched down, as if everything had been pre-prepared in anticipation of such a tragic event. Hutton was not generally considered the best man for such a position, never having chaired any such inquiry before, raising reasonable assumptions that he was more likely selected for his record of defending the British government against accusations of irregularities (as a former senior barrister in Northern Ireland), rather than as someone who might take the authorities to task.

Suspicious Circumstances

As it happens, the whole timing of Kelly's death was serendipitous for the Blair administration, with parliament having just adjourned for the summer on the very day that Kelly went for his final walk in the woods, sparing the government humiliating televised scenes in the Commons. Even more serendipitous was the fact that the Thames Valley Police investigation into Kelly's death, Operation Mason, was, according to police records, apparently opened nine hours *before* its own subject's disappearance was reported – an incongruity that has never been satisfactorily explained. Again, it suggests signs of pre-planning for an event that someone knew was coming. The name of the police operation has also raised eyebrows among truthseekers concerned with the influence of secret societies in such matters.

The behaviour of the police after Kelly's absence was first reported by his wife Janice is no more explicable, with a mysterious 45ft radio antenna (size claims vary) being erected in the Kelly family garden on their arrival. No reason has ever been given to explain this procedure, unheard of in a missing persons case. Some believe the aerial may have been installed to enable the police to communicate directly with Blair's plane, which would have interesting implications, especially since at this point, as far as anyone officially knew, Kelly could still have been found alive and well at any time. Janice herself was unceremoniously evicted from her own house and forced to stand in the garden at night while police searched the house with a sniffer dog (even looking into the airing cupboard at one point, as if Kelly might have been hiding there); yet it was already clear that Kelly was definitively missing, hence his wife's call to the emergency services. Bizarrely, wallpaper was even stripped from their sitting room wall that night – a highly unusual forensic test to make when searching for someone. A helicopter that came down over the nearby woods where Kelly's body was found the next day is another unexplained mystery of Operation Mason, the purpose of which has never been declared, leading even the *Daily Mail* to ask whether the craft might have 'either deposited or collected somebody or something' at the site.[8]

With the eventual discovery of Kelly's corpse by daylight, things became more, not less, confused; both the placement and condition of his body have become the most contentious aspects of all in what has become one of the more pondered potential assassination scenarios of modern times.

Louise Holmes and Paul Chapman, the two local search party volunteers who first happened upon Kelly's dead body, both testified that it was sitting slumped against a tree. However, by the time the police arrived and recorded their 'official' finding of Kelly, he was flat on his back, entirely separate from the tree. By this time a blunt gardening knife, a watch and a partially drunk bottle of mineral water were also very visibly part of the scene – none of which was originally present, according to Holmes and Chapman. This has led conspiracy observers to wonder whether either the occupants of the unexplained helicopter or the police themselves had somehow redressed a murder scene to give it more of a suicide 'look'.

The water, of course, could explain how Kelly was able to down 29 of the 30 co-proxamol tablets (the odd remaining tablet left in the packet has stimulated more suspicions, as if it was left specifically to make for an easy identification of the drug), while the knife, one which Kelly had owned for many years, might account for the gash to the ulnar artery on his left wrist. Yet herein lie some of the main problems with the official suicide verdict.

The Hutton Inquiry insists that the main cause of death was a mixture of blood loss and the effects of the overdose. However, all those who witnessed Kelly's body at Harrowdown Hill, whether in its first or second position, reported that only a small amount of blood was visible. Critics of the conspiracy theories contend that much of it might have soaked into the ground by the time the body was found, but a major point of dispute surrounds the ability of the small ulnar artery to vent such a fatal loss of blood in the first place, particularly in cold night air, which generally closes wounds more quickly than would be required to be fatal.

One of the first major challenges to the suicide verdict came from a consortium of three independent doctors, making their doubts about Kelly known through a letter to the *Guardian* newspaper. In 2009, other medical experts joined them in campaigning for a new inquiry, much of their concern based on the observations regarding the inability of the ulnar incision to have been a main cause of death. It has been countered that Kelly had a heart condition that gave him unusually narrowed vessels in the arteries, making him more susceptible to a smaller blood loss than might usually be fatal, but other factors here have kept the doubters vocal.

Gruesome though it is to consider, those who choose to commit suicide by cutting their wrists usually carve vertical lines down the main arteries along the inside of the forearm, causing a huge loss of blood. Kelly, a doctor of microbiology, would very likely have been aware of this. The ulnar, on the other hand, is a very tough artery to cut and would have been especially painful and difficult to saw through, especially with the blunt concave-edged knife found by police at the scene. Whatever Kelly's state of mind may have been, he had no history of self-harming which might suggest he would choose such an agonizing method, one which had far less guarantee of success. There were no other reported British suicides in 2003 that used such an awkward 'technique'. Moreover, a friend, Mai Pederson, informed the police inquiry that Kelly had a long-term weakness in his right arm that meant he struggled to cut even steak at mealtimes. Why, then, would Kelly choose such an especially hard way to exit the world?

The co-proxamol tablets are problematic in themselves. Not only was the amount found in Kelly's blood just a third of what should have been necessary to have killed him (according to the official inquiry), but only a fifth of one tablet was actually found left in his stomach, the rest presumably having been vomited out – or never swallowed in the first place. A quirk in the personality of Dr Kelly throws doubt on the fact that he would select such a way to go; it was well-known among his close acquaintances that he found it difficult to swallow even a small number of tablets in normal circumstances.

The standard official response to this – that Kelly was not in his normal frame of mind and therefore took his life in a more peculiar way than might be expected – makes the wide assumption that Kelly was depressed enough to be in this state in the first place. Testimony from friends and family suggest no signs of this being the case. Unquestionably, Kelly was stressed by the unexpected spotlight that had been thrown on him, but even his sister, Sarah Pape, a consultant plastic surgeon, when telling the Hutton Inquiry of her final chats with her brother, described his demeanour thus:

> [He was] tired, but otherwise it really was a very normal conversation. Believe me, I have lain awake many nights since, going over in my mind whether I missed anything significant. In my line of work I do deal with people who may have suicidal thoughts and I ought to be able to spot those, even in a telephone conversation. But I have gone over and over in my mind the two conversations we had and he certainly did not betray to me any impression that he was anything other than tired. He certainly did not convey to me that he was feeling depressed; and absolutely nothing that would have alerted me to the fact that he might have been considering suicide.[9]

Indeed, Kelly seemed to have many pleasures still to live for at the time of his death. Things were looking up: the worst of the parliamentary inquiries seemed to be over; his daughter's wedding was approaching, something he was reportedly much looking forward to; and his own cherished work as a weapons inspector in Iraq was about to resume despite all the fuss, with a new trip scheduled.

The cynical might point out that it is almost as if whoever might have planned a faked suicide for Kelly didn't bother to do their homework in a number of areas, given the weakness of his cutting arm, his aversion to swallowing tablets and his increasingly cheerful state of mind in the days before his death. It is almost as if the planners were given the wrong script to work from if they wanted to create a scenario that wouldn't fall prey to endless conspiracy theories. They had also chosen a man who was a practising follower of the Bahá'í faith – a religion that firmly denounces suicide.

How and Why?

If Kelly was killed, then how this might have been achieved can only be speculation in the absence of – officially, at least – any other obvious causes of death from the post-mortem. Poison or asphyxiation would presumably have shown in the post-mortem, although it has long been believed that shadowy intelligences may have electromagnetic devices that can induce heart attacks. Hardcore conspiracists say both former Foreign Secretary Robin Cook and Labour leader John Smith may have fallen victim to this technique when each became obstructive to the unstoppable ambitions of the Blair camp. Why this dubiously useful weapon would not be used for the quiet removal of all targeted figureheads, however, has never been properly reasoned, unless such repeated action would begin to look too obvious. Others point out that more subtle forms of death may simply never have been looked for in the face of an apparently obvious suicide.

It is curious to note that David Kelly appears to be yet another victim who seemed to have a premonition of his own ultimate fate, albeit more ambiguously this time. Kelly had reportedly made assurances to Iraqi officials that no military action would be taken against the country if they complied with UN weapons inspections, but he feared there might be a threat to his life if such action did go ahead, once telling a British ambassador, David Broucher, that if Iraq were invaded then he would 'probably be found dead in the woods'.

The British government were predictably happy to allow this reported statement to sound as if Kelly might always have been someone capable of taking his own life, although this would seem an uncharacteristically weak retreat for such a reportedly stolid personality. Was it in truth that Kelly knew his own people might need to remove his awkward presence in such a situation – as the majority of conspiracy theorists believe? Or was it, as a number of moderates have suggested, that either Iraqis angry at Kelly's apparent betrayal, or exiled dissidents resentful at anything that was seen to exonerate Hussein's regime, may have been the ones taking their revenge, in which case Kelly may simply have been pondering a not implausible outcome from that direction? Whichever, the all-too-precise nature of his own prophecy is an element which has resonance with other problematic fatalities of recent history.

Procedural Anomalies

Despite the areas of concern around the circumstances of his death, the vocal minority that reject all notions of conspiracy about David Kelly refuse to see any insurmountable anomalies. But what about the *procedural* anomalies that followed? Among several important areas ignored or sidelined by the Hutton Inquiry, the issue of the coroner's death certificate has itself been a cause of discontent. Part of the very reason for the inquiry was to define the causes of Kelly's death, so why, then, was a death certificate suddenly issued by the local registrar, on the orders of the coroner, just a week into the hearings, directly stating the cause as haemorrhaging from an incision in the left wrist? This highly irregular move, which pre-empted the inquiry and rendered much of its purpose irrelevant, suggests that pressure was being applied from the start to get the matter cleared up quickly, irrespective of the evidence. It was eventually revealed by probing parliamentary questions raised by Norman Baker, MP, that, shortly before the inquiry opened, two covert meetings took place between the coroner and Home Office staff with their own official pathologists. These questionable engagements may throw light on where the causes of death, so prophetically listed on the certificate, were ascertained. In fact, a number of protocols around the issue of death certificates were contravened in the case of David Kelly.

An MP Fights for Truth

If one of the weaknesses that kept questions about the death of Diana from being taken seriously in the mainstream was the perceived idiosyncrasies of their most high-profile advocate, Mohamed Al-Fayed, then the public issues raised around David Kelly were greatly strengthened by the championing of its cause by Norman Baker, MP for Lewes, East Sussex. Baker, who had won political awards for his persistent battling in areas where most members of the House would not dare to tread, was vocal in his refusal to accept the official line on the Kelly affair. His determination to get to the bottom of the case led him to step down from the Liberal Democrat frontbench for a while to conduct thorough research and incisive investigation – more than the Hutton Inquiry did, for the most part.

Baker's conclusions were published in the bestselling 2007 book *The Strange Death of David Kelly* and have been hugely influential in taking this particular conspiracy theory far beyond the usual alternative fringe. This has not prevented Baker from being the subject of sceptical criticism, but in his beliefs that Kelly was almost certainly murdered, the public is overwhelmingly on his side. Baker claims he received a cyber-attack which wiped his hard drive on one occasion, suggesting that others also felt his investigations were getting close to the bone. There is no question that Baker's persistent research has helped turn up much of the information discussed here, forcing the release of evidence that might never have surfaced without his status as an MP.[10]

The Hutton Timelock

The world may have to wait a while for further important information on Dr David Kelly to become available. With the delivery of his final report, Lord Hutton decreed that full publication of vital documents, medical reports and forensic evidence must be withheld for an astonishing 70 years – claiming it was in the interests of not putting Kelly's family under further stress.

The justifiable outcry at this very suspicious announcement stimulated more consortiums of medical experts and concerned public figures to apply further pressure, resulting in a slight concessionary turnaround in October 2010, when the full text of Hutton's post-mortem report *was* released to quieten the critics. This, naturally enough, simply restated the official verdict in a little more detail, and many felt it fell far short of the comprehensive evidence that was needed for the true picture to emerge, especially as it had been so clearly influenced by the questionable death certificate issued before the inquiry had even concluded. Somewhere towards the end of this century, perhaps we will be allowed to hear more, but in the absence of further concessions the view that Kelly was pushed, rather than fell, is likely to persist.

Critics of the conspiracy view point to a number of Kelly's friends or contacts who, seemingly more hurt by the idea of murder than suicide, refuse to countenance alternative theories of the situation, stating that he *could* have been capable of taking his own life. Truthseekers, however, see these views as overly defensive, concealing grief with denial. Similarly, the general silence that has descended over Kelly's family, who will not discuss assassination theories, nor seemingly anything these days, when they might well be in possession of some important information (especially Kelly's wife), have led some to suggest that intimidation, persuasion or even financial settlements may have bought their silence. Disgusting nonsense? Maybe, but if so it is a nonsense that many believe.

Mass Assassinations

Assassinations and consistent reports of strange deaths among awkward witnesses concerned with everything from the Apollo missions to the deaths of JFK and Diana suggest that little conscience may be applied by those who consider life to be cheap.

There are several examples where whole groups of people appear to fall victim to a 'removal' programme. *The Progressive Review*'s webpage, 'Arkansas Sudden Death Syndrome', for instance, lists an incredible 50 or so statistically strange fatalities among those who have had business or personal connections with the US political heavyweights Bill and Hillary Clinton over the years.[11] The causes range from murder, accidents and many suicides, to a man who apparently drank himself to death with domestic mouthwash. There is no available evidence that the Clintons themselves had anything to do with these unfortunate demises, but if it isn't a bizarre statistical blip (as similar patterns around the likes of JFK and 9/11 witnesses would suggest it isn't), then somebody, somewhere, would appear not to like the people around them very much.

Such examples tend, on the whole, to remain solely in the realm of minority awareness, whatever their true significance. What, though, of mass deaths that are so large, so monumentally significant and so much in the public eye that the questions around them become simply impossible to ignore? We must come, at last, then, to the conspiracy theories of 9/11.

IN SUMMARY . . .

Assassination Conspiracies: Arguments Against

The killing of JFK is too long ago and too confused in its detail to be able to draw any useful conclusions today – If it was such an obvious conspiracy, why didn't later governments expose it? – The drink-driver verdict on the Diana car crash has been backed up by too many inquiries to be false, and all other speculation is simply convoluted paranoia or based on circumstantial evidence – Dr David Kelly's family will not discuss assassination theories and so must believe the official verdict; therefore everyone else should too – Norman Baker, MP, is prone to believing in conspiracies and is not to be taken seriously.

Assassination Conspiracies: Arguments For

The vast majority of people believe that more than one assassin was involved in killing JFK, as even later official inquiries agree, and therefore the shooting was by definition the result of a complex conspiracy that deserves a new and serious investigation – Later governments may have harboured some of those behind the actual assassination – The official hearings over Diana's death did not look at a number of important areas that, on inspection, make it more likely that the driver's blood test was unreliable and that other factors must also have come into play – The anomalies over Kelly's death are too strong to ignore, and family and witnesses may have been persuaded into silence – Norman Baker had no history of investigating conspiracies, but was moved to pursue Kelly's case solely on the blatant irregularities around it – Too many key people die in mysterious circumstances too often for their sometimes bizarre deaths to be coincidences.

CONCLUSION

Even today, the West sponsors multiple open assassinations of 'terrorist' leaders in Middle Eastern states, but assassination has also been a staple tool of regimes and underground forces against its own figureheads throughout history, as chapter 2's citing of Roman conspiracies makes clear. Acting so obviously today would never be tolerated, so the setting-up of patsies or the feigning of certain situations would therefore become necessary for any who would spirit away key informants or inconvenient inspirations, while covering their tracks in the process. When lives are seen as expendable, the taking down of just one more irritant would be unlikely to worry the beneficiaries.

It is hard not to be suspicious when, time and again, unexplained elements, seemingly anticipatory events or curious cover-ups muddle what should be straightforward evidence of accidents or genuine suicides. Even indisputable assassinations are too often not what they at first appear to be, with subsequent inquiries evasive or suspiciously sloppy. It is unsurprising then, that the public chooses to keep its own mind on what it thinks really goes on.

CHAPTER 6

9/11 AND RELATED CONSPIRACIES

*If the shooting of JFK was the 'mother of all conspiracy theories',
then 9/11 must be the son. The widespread doubt which has been
expressed about the official story is very much the culmination of
the many mass disillusionments from the last few decades. The often
highly charged debates which have grown up around what at first
seemed an irrefutable occurrence neatly distil most conspiracy theory
staples under one umbrella. All the classic elements are present: the
allegations of a state-sponsored false-flag attack to create a mandate
for oppressive control and desired conflicts; problematic forensic
evidence; contradictions and holes in the official version of events;
clear evidence of obfuscation in official reports; and events which seem
to contravene both common sense and the laws of physics – according
to the theorists. A number of other thematically related events, such as
the London 7/7 bombings, have attracted similar scrutiny.*

I) 9/11

A False-Flag Event?

The criteria listed in the paragraph above are only the very basics
of the claims that the truth has not been told about the notorious

attacks which took place on 11 September 2001. It stands to reason that they are savagely denied by those affronted at the very idea that there *is* even an alternative view on the official version of events. The orthodoxy, as indelibly enforced in the mainstream, holds that Osama bin Laden and the al-Qaeda network arranged for the hijacks of four jet liners, which, now piloted by terrorists, were flown into the World Trade Center (WTC), the Pentagon and woods in Pennsylvania respectively, killing around 3,000 people. This narrative has already passed into dark legend, and, as such, needs little reiteration here. Yet, deep in the collective gut, it is hard to deny that there is a disquiet about what really happened on 9/11.

The widespread doubt that has grown by the year is evidenced by the polls conducted for 9/11's tenth anniversary, which exposed the remarkable reality that something approaching half the global population had doubts about the official story. In the UK, the ICM poll service 'found that more people agree than disagree that the official account of what happened on 9/11 might turn out to be wrong in important respects'. Indeed, only 8 per cent of respondents 'strongly agreed' with what they had been told to believe.[1] The conspiracy view has once again become mainstream without anyone quite realizing it, yet this striking lack of faith is repeatedly misrepresented or ignored by the media, and attacked by Western politicians. Questioning 9/11 is often blocked by the stance that doing so is 'disrespectful' to the victims and their families. Truthseekers counter that it is more disrespectful not to re-examine every detail of the episode, in the hope that uncovering the real truth might help prevent future atrocities.

It should be noted that the use of the term 'conspiracy' in this context refers to those views which refute the official position; it is a long-noted irony that, for all the establishment's apparent distaste towards such thinking, the bin Laden/al-Qaeda version is in itself the precise technical definition of a conspiracy theory, albeit one which postulates covert *external* forces working against the West rather than ones stemming from within it. The difference is that for all the rapidity with which the public were fed the external-conspiracy scenario, to this day – despite the impressions given – no definitive proof for it has ever been presented. Not that this stopped news broadcasts from blaming al-Qaeda within minutes of the attacks, before any claimed intelligence was even released.

If broad doubt over the deaths of Diana and David Kelly seemed rooted in an immediate instinctual knowing, the alternative 9/11 'inside-job' theories took a little longer to percolate, if only because the events themselves initially seemed so overwhelmingly terrifying that lingering shock and reflex patriotism helped reinforce a mass conditioning which obscured any deeper contemplation. Within a year or two, however, with the emotions subsiding, concerns that had at first been only whispered began to be heard more loudly. The rise in the use of the internet as the primary information tool around the same time also played its part, enabling minority views to be expressed in uncensored forums.

By 2005, the 9/11 'truth movement' was in full swing, with campaigns being mounted, websites proliferating and polished documentaries being burned onto DVD in impressive numbers, distributed by an eager throng of well-meaning individuals, by now firmly convinced they had been lied to. The passion was predominantly fired by the fact that the events of 9/11 *still mattered*, even years on, because of the resulting 'War on Terror', with its associated withdrawal of fundamental freedoms that affected everyone. The demoralizing and seemingly ill-organized wars launched by the West against Afghanistan and Iraq were further reminders of the fateful day's legacy. An oft-verbalized desire from various leaders to 'move on' from now 'historical' events still continues to be resisted by those who believe that the original attacks were staged not by Middle Eastern terrorists, but by covert forces within Western intelligence services and probably beyond.

The inside-job hypothesis is the central accusation of the 9/11 truth movement. If it could be demonstrated beyond doubt that the attacks were either wholly engineered, partially manipulated or even simply allowed, then the entire basis of many of today's global power games, which threaten the peace of the world, would be crucially undermined. The fervour that shines in the eyes of those who fight for the 'truth' of 9/11 is undeniably impressive. But is it justified?

Again, the full basis for the wide conviction that 9/11 was a classic false-flag conspiracy can be explored elsewhere in countless sources that will keep readers occupied for months, but the essential aspects are broadly summed up here.[2]

The Hijackings

The officially accepted scenario of 9/11 sounds simple enough: hijackers, under assumed names, boarded each of the relevant planes and then took control of the flights by attacking or threatening the cabin and cockpit crew with concealed 'boxcutter' blades. Thus under al-Qaeda control, the planes were flown into their targets.

Yet many unexplained facets present themselves here, from the seemingly illogical movements of the hijackers themselves on the way to the airports (Boston, Newark and Washington, DC) to the fact that the assumed names they apparently used have never been identified from the passenger lists, definitive versions of which have not been released either. It has to be taken on trust that the authorities know who they were. Additionally, the terrorists seen in the security footage purporting to show them passing through customs do not match the descriptions given by staff on the day, while the timecodes shown in the videos are contradictory and inconsistent, suggesting that judicious editing may have taken place.

Oddly, passenger numbers on the hijacked flights were uncommonly low that day, with one of the usually busy commuter planes (Flight 93) flown at just 19 per cent of its normal capacity. Some have speculated that numbers were deliberately kept low that day to make the hijacks easier, with potential passenger resistance minimized.

What we know of how the hijackings actually took place has come almost entirely from accounts given by frightened passengers or cabin crew who managed to call their loved ones using their cell phones (mobiles). Yet how some of these calls took place at all has been the subject of much controversy. For example, CNN anchorwoman Barbara Olson was on Flight 77 (which we are told hit the Pentagon), and great emphasis has been placed on information gleaned from two conversations between her and her husband Ted (US solicitor general at the time), whom she reportedly managed to reach before the fatal impact. However, when the FBI sequestered the relevant phone network records, they in fact showed that just a single cell call, not two, was attempted – and that it failed to connect. When presented with this conundrum, Ted Olson said the call must have been made from a commercial 'seatback' phone. But American Airlines has confirmed that Flight 77 did not have such a facility. So how did the Olson conversation take place?

In fact, despite the legends that have been built up around the 9/11 phone calls, only a limited number of the recordings have ever been released to the public, and some of the transcripts that *have* been reported are more than a little peculiar ('Mom, this is Mark Bingham,' says a Flight 93 passenger, oddly giving his surname to his own mother at the start of a very stilted conversation). Given the abilities of modern technology to recreate synthesized voices, a large number of people believe that at least some of the famous calls may have been faked, duping friends and relatives.

If this sounds too bizarre, it should be noted that when the Canadian science writer A K Dewdney, puzzled by the 9/11 calls, decided to hire a plane to test the capability of cell phones at different altitudes, he found it impossible to get a signal at any height over 8,000 feet. Only in more recent times has technology been introduced to allow cell calls on some flights, but this was not the case in 2001. Messages from the hijacked planes may have been possible as they flew low over New York, but this does not explain how so many claimed connections were made from Flight 93, which was flying between 34,000 and 40,000 feet for most of its ill-fated journey (coming down in Pennsylvania without hitting its target). Hollywood films and TV movies have been based on the accounts apparently derived from those calls, yet Flight 93's altitude brings their veracity into significant question. When confronted with Dewdney's findings, the authorities changed their story, claiming that seatback handsets had been used instead, saying that perhaps only two of the calls had been made from cell phones – but even these should not have worked, and the availability of seatback facilities on Flight 93 has never been established.

Nevertheless, if the orthodox version of the hijackings is accepted, there are still many unexplained aspects. There are strict procedures in place to prevent easy entry to a cockpit, and crew are trained never to let assailants in, no matter what may be occurring elsewhere in the plane – so how were the terrorists allowed to pass through, so fast that no one had time to raise the alarm to air traffic control? Planes are fitted with emergency Mayday buttons that can be operated at a touch, yet not one pilot in the four planes managed to operate theirs. Interestingly, Flight 77's 'black box' data recorder shows that the cockpit doors were never opened during its final voyage, creating yet another puzzle.[3]

The fact that Flight 77's data recorder was the only one allegedly recovered from the 9/11 crashes has raised suspicions too, as boxes are specifically designed to withstand almost anything and are nearly always found following disasters. Rescue workers have claimed that the others *were* retrieved, but the authorities continue to deny this. Likewise, reportedly only Flights 77 and 93 had their cockpit voice recorders recovered, as if to ensure rather conveniently that some kind of evidence was available to confirm that the planes which have had the most doubt cast on their presence or trajectory (see below) *were* actually there.

It has been suggested that, whether hijackers were onboard or not, the planes might have been forcibly taken over using remote control systems, perhaps negating the need for the cockpits to be accessed. This might make sense of some of the remarkably accurate flying skills seen on 9/11, when even staff from the flight schools that inadvertently trained some of the alleged terrorists have expressed the view that their pupils were barely able to fly light aircraft (a point particularly pertinent to the Pentagon impact – *see* pp. 180–1). Defenders of the official story scoff at the idea of remote control, but given that the US now mounts many of its air assaults using 'drone' technology operated from far away, it is hard to see why this should not be considered. Curiously, just a few months before 9/11, the short-lived *X-Files* spin-off TV series *The Lone Gunmen* featured an astoundingly prescient episode whereby a jet airliner is hijacked using remote control – and sent to plough into the World Trade Center. Thus the idea of commandeering an aeroplane by such means, and the fact that the WTC might be a target for jet liners being used as missiles (something US National Security Advisor Condoleezza Rice claimed 'no one could have imagined') was already firmly lodged in the collective at the time, albeit expressed in fiction.

9/11 Foreknowledge

Even outside the world of fiction, it is now widely acknowledged that strident warnings had in fact been given by intelligence services that such attacks were in the offing. Quiet awareness of this had plainly been disseminated among certain members of the business community, given that there was an astonishing 1,200 per cent increase in trading activities in the week before 9/11, with particular focus on American Airlines and United Airlines – the companies which would be most affected when their planes were violated just days later. Traders were essentially betting that their stocks would 'go short' when there seemed no open reason at the time for anyone to think this. Trading in other companies which would be affected seemed equally prophetic. Meanwhile, San Francisco's mayor, Willie Brown, was sent mysterious warnings to 'be cautious' about flying to New York on 11 September; civil rights campaigner Dick Gregory was told by a 'friend' not to be in New York that day and new World Trade Center owner Larry Silverstein took out a major destruction insurance policy just weeks before the attacks.

Something in the ether was unmistakably making itself known, but all of this was somehow ignored by the incumbent George W Bush administration, leading many to wonder if 9/11 was 'allowed' to happen, as opposed to being directly organized by an inside cabal. However, claims by ex-CIA and FBI operatives of a consistent refusal to apprehend known extremists who were suspected of planning such attacks speak as much of an overt setting-up. A truck bomb that caused deaths and injuries at the WTC in 1993 may have been an earlier attempt at the same strategy – an event that ex-FBI whistleblower Emad Salem says was supposedly set up by the FBI as a sting operation against a jihadist terror group, but ended up inexplicably going ahead using real explosives instead of dummies. So, if the core arrangement of 9/11 did originate from covert Western intelligence services, or even if remote control was somehow applied to the doomed planes, it does not necessarily follow that al-Qaeda patsies were not also actively involved somewhere down the line, Perhaps they believed that they *were* acting alone, but were unwittingly played by distant forces, generating enough evidence to allow them to take the whole blame, in the same way that the Gunpowder Plot conspirators may have been set up in 1605 (*see* chapter 2).

Engineered Confusion?

Whatever or whoever was piloting the planes, conspiracy believers point to the consistent failure of the authorities to track the rogue flights as another contentious area. For the first time in hijacking history, someone in each plane managed to switch off the transponders (automatic beacon signals), which we are told made the flights untraceable. Yet NORAD (North American Aerospace Defense Command) and other agencies entrusted with the vital task of protecting US airspace often boast of their ability to track any flying object, however small, using radar and other equipment. So why were transponders necessary to find the planes? In its defence, NORAD uses the bizarre 'coincidence' that a number of high-level security exercises were taking place that day (Operation Vigilant Guardian, among others) – ones that posited precisely the same scenario of hijacked planes hitting important buildings. The fact that this did actually occur the very same day undoubtedly caused enormous confusion ('Is this real world, or exercise?' says one hapless air traffic controller when informed of the hijackings, heard in released recordings). Such an unlikely coincidence has left many convinced that the exercises were an intentional part of the plot, the planners knowing how useful such operations would be in sowing uncertainty and offering good excuses for inaction. Even under the hypothesis that al-Qaeda was directly responsible for the attacks, their operatives should have been unaware of these arrangements, given their top secret status – unless they were tipped off by insiders.

Until 9/11, planes even suspected of being hijacked were routinely intercepted within minutes of abnormal behaviour or radio silence, but on this day no fighters were scrambled until far too late, and then inexplicably flew at speeds too slow to make any difference. The main defence for the relative inaction is that no one had time to find and intercept the planes before the damage could be done, but glaring inconsistencies in the testimony of high-level staff strongly indicate that this was not the case. The officially published air traffic control transcripts, for instance, have been verifiably re-edited in recent years, seemingly to obscure who knew what and when, while Vice-President Dick Cheney, Secretary of Defense Donald Rumsfeld and General Richard Myers – key decision-makers in such crises – all say they were either not present or informed enough in time to act decisively. This is notably contradicted by testimony from White House Security Chief Richard Clarke and Secretary of Transportation Norman Mineta, amongst other staff, who have firmly stated that their colleagues were present at least 30 minutes before they claim – an important chronological difference in such a tight sequence of developments.

Mineta even reports being present during an episode that morning which suggests that Cheney was deliberately allowing a rogue plane to approach the Pentagon. When an operative seemed to questioned the wisdom of this, asking whether the (unspecified) 'orders' still stood, Cheney snapped at him: 'Of course the orders still stand – have you heard anything to the contrary?' The Pentagon was struck soon after. Defenders of the official version say this is open to misinterpretation, but those who believe that Cheney was a main player in the 9/11 conspiracy hold this episode to be an important piece of evidence, implicating him in a 'stand down' scenario. The omission of this conversation from the final 9/11 Commission report suggests that the authorities may also have recognized its damning connotations.

As for who was really flying the planes at these moments, there are many unsolved issues surrounding the hijackers, with some of those named having issued statements to claim they are still alive today. Aside from the almost too obvious evidence supposedly left in cars (copies of the Koran, incriminating documents, plans, etc.), one of the criteria used to identify the terrorists was the miraculous survival of some of their passports, which somehow survived huge fireballs to flutter down to the ground almost intact, when everything else was pulverized to dust. Indeed, it is the nature of the destruction following the hijacks that has been the greatest point of focus in the conspiracy world.

The Pentagon

Before looking at the mysteries surrounding the destruction of the *three* towers which fell at the WTC, which generally receive the most scrutiny, it should be noted that one of the first anomalies to be identified by truthseekers was the markedly limited damage at the Pentagon. We are told that a 228-passenger Boeing 757 ploughed into one side of the US military's headquarters, yet the visible hole in the early images of the impact site (before the roof collapsed) appears to be little more than 20 feet in diameter, with some cursory damage either side. With a total wingspan of around 125 feet, and a tail 44 feet high, how had a craft of that size entered such a small space without causing wider devastation? The photos show no debris around the entry point, and workmen's cable spools, present when the plane came in, stand seemingly unaffected. Windows on the floor just above the hole are unbroken. The questions arising from this remarkably clean strike from such a large object loaded with fuel have never been satisfactorily answered.

The authorities contend that the plane entered the building at such a speed (around 500mph) that most of the debris ended up inside the structure and was therefore not readily visible, adding that the wings either folded back as they struck, or somehow vaporized with the force. Putting aside the problematic physics of vaporizing wings, the fact is that several witnesses inside the Pentagon have remarked at how little of the plane seemed to have survived – few seats, bodies or suitcases were immediately apparent. The rare shots of debris that do purport to be from Flight 77 display objects such as engine foils which are too small to be from a large jet liner; some have identified them instead as being from an A3 Sky Warrior, an obscure US fighter plane. This and the oddly penetrative clean strike qualities of some of the restrained damage (as compared with the huge explosions seen at the twin towers) lead some to wonder what really did hit the Pentagon on 9/11.

A number of eyewitnesses on the day described seeing a much slighter projectile enter the building; a missile or a small plane rather than a 757. A large plane *would* appear to have come down low over the building just before the explosion, perhaps leading people to assume this was responsible, but many believe it was a decoy for the real perpetrator, which may have flown in beneath it. It might be assumed that CCTV would clear up any confusion, but the very few frames ever released from what must be a multiplicity of available images fail to show anything other than a vague blur that leaves the questions hanging.

If it was Flight 77 that hit the Pentagon, even more puzzles arise. How, for instance, did the hijacker Hani Hanjour manage to execute what has been described by pilots as one of the greatest feats in aviation history, when his own flight trainers claim he could barely handle a tiny Cessna? If the official claim is correct, the Boeing 757 dropped several thousand feet in less than two minutes without stalling or breaking up in mid-air, performed a perfect last-minute tight turn, skimmed roadside light poles without being diverted sideways, and handily struck the one part of the Pentagon that was under renovation at the time and comparatively unstaffed. This can be seen as oddly serendipitous when heading straight into the natural bullseye of the structure would appear to have been so much easier and potentially more destructive.

A Theory for Flight 93

A question thrown up by the conspiracy view is that if it were not Flight 77 that hit the Pentagon on 9/11, then what happened to that plane and its passengers? There have been a number of ideas proposed to account for this. There are a number of plane-switching theories in circulation (some of which incorporate more extravagant claims that what looked like planes were, in fact, projected holograms) which posit the notion that the actual hijacked flights – if they ever were really hijacked and didn't just quietly divert somewhere – may have secretly landed and disembarked, their occupants perhaps never knowing what was really going on. Some say the abnormally low passenger numbers on all the flights (*see* p. 174) enabled their collective occupants to be packed onto Flight 93, which was then sent off to be discreetly shot down over Pennsylvania. There are certainly many reports of aerial explosions just before the plane came down, and the miles-wide debris field and anomalous sooty smudge we are told was Flight 93's main impact site (with almost no plane parts found) suggest that much of it may well have been destroyed in the air.

The US military deny shooting down Flight 93, even as a protective measure, and adhere to the heroic tale of the passengers storming the cockpit and bringing the plane down before it could reach its target ('Let's roll'), but, as we have seen, the cell phone calls that are supposed to have given us much of this version of events may not be wholly reliable.

The World Trade Center

Of all the memories seared into people's minds, the images of the World Trade Center's famous twin towers exploding with aeroplane impacts or crumbling down into dust are without doubt the most powerful of 9/11. The psychological shock generated by these globally televised nightmares is held by most conspiracy theorists to have been one of the key tools in the conditioning of the human race to submit to the mandate of the New World Order. Yet the same images are also held to contain some of the most important pieces of evidence to show that 9/11 was deliberately – and literally – engineered.

The bottom line of the official post-mortem on the WTC is that crucial fireproofing is said to have been removed from the steel girders by the impacts of the aeroplanes, allowing the heat of the subsequent infernos to weaken the structures to the point of eventual collapse, falling floor by floor within seconds. On immediate inspection, this would seem to be a reasonable hypothesis from what we see in the footage. However, an unusually large number of professional architects, engineers and physicists, far outside the usual conspiracy boundaries, have challenged this verdict.

This is not the place for a prolonged scientific analysis (many other sources provide the evidence in detail), but the main assertion of the truth movement is that the fire and damage could not by themselves have been enough to bring the buildings down so quickly or so totally. Until 9/11, no steel-framed modern building had ever collapsed due to fire, yet on this one day it occurred an incredible three times.

The photos and videos of Flights 11 and 175 hitting their respective towers in orange balls of flame show clearly that much of the aviation fuel, held to be one of the biggest contributors to the 'infernos', in fact ignited into the air on impact, burning out very quickly to leave a thick black smouldering suggestive of relatively low temperature fires. Steel is generally accepted to lose its strength at a heat of around 2,800°F, but even the official reports suggest that the highest temperatures which could have been reached in the towers could not have exceeded 1,800°F. The removal of the fireproofing is usually cited as the problem here, but this is only a theory, with no available evidence to prove it beyond a few inconclusive tests which crudely involved firing bullets at metal plates on plywood boxes. Even allowing for the fireproofing arguments, critics believe that the towers should never have come down in the way we see, at virtually freefall speed without unevenness or hesitation, if a process of natural collapse was at work.

How else, then, might the WTC have come down? Most challengers assert that explosives of some kind must have been used, pre-planted in the buildings in the weeks before 9/11 to ensure that the towers fell with maximum spectacle. If so, this would suggest the activity of agents with greater access to the buildings than Middle Eastern terrorists would have been able to achieve. It goes without saying that defenders of the official version robustly attack this stance, but the evidence is hard to dismiss completely when closely examined.

Several observable aspects are usually proffered as proof of explosives. In the footage of each tower falling, filmed from multiple angles, small 'squib'-like blasts can be seen pushing out in places up and down the height of the structures, sometimes far below the violent collapses occurring at the top. Often rejected as being merely the result of air-pressure waves passing through the buildings and pushing out office debris, it has been convincingly countered that such waves would not reach as far down as the levels at which these squibs are seen, given that the top floors are freefalling as fast as anything can travel for much of their descent; the speed of the falls is one of the main reasons why a process of natural collapse is so widely challenged. Demolition experts have remarked on the near-identical resemblance of the 9/11 squibs to those created by demolition charges used to bring down old structures.

Other evidence that explosives may have been placed in the towers is provided by firemen, rescue workers and WTC staff, many of whom described unexplained blasts going off inside even while the structures were still standing. The first of these appears to have taken place in the basement 30 seconds or so *before* the first plane hit, according to janitorial staff in the North Tower. Testimonies supporting internal explosions are numerous and convincing, yet the official 9/11 Commission report managed to conclude that no significant accounts were recorded. Firemen have claimed since that they have been ordered to keep quiet or risk redundancy, while interviews with them specifically reporting explosions in the towers, widely televised at the time, have been almost universally edited out of later programmes or repeats.

Luckily, the internet preserves many of the original accounts. One telling description, backed up by many other reports, was given by WTC office worker Teresa Veliz, recounting her experiences while being evacuated from the North Tower:

> *There were explosions going off everywhere. I was convinced that there were bombs planted all over the place and someone was sitting at a control panel pushing detonator buttons . . . There was another explosion. And another. I didn't know where to run.*

Perhaps the most obvious explosions of all can be seen in the footage of the main 'collapses'; many people have observed that the tops of the towers, rather than simply falling down, in truth effectively *explode* outwards, spreading debris so far that rubble and human remains were being found several blocks away even years later. The fact that one tower is seen to topple ominously towards the street at one point, before mysteriously correcting itself, suggests that material below it is simply dissolving into the air, rather than collapsing as such. Architect Richard Gage has demonstrated that one of the key principles of the official story – that the descending tops of the towers acted as 'piledrivers' crushing the floors below them – cannot be correct, as the videos clearly show that everything at the top effectively disintegrates as it falls, with nothing left to provide such a downward force.

Some of those who claim the presence of explosives point to the discovery of what would appear to be micro-particles of 'nano-thermate' in dust sampled from the WTC remains, as researched by physicists such as Dr Neils Harrit and Professor Steven Jones (*see* p. 15).[4] Critics have said the particles are nothing but paint, but this was examined and ruled out in the early stages of analysis. Nano-thermate, on the other hand, can be used to generate rapid explosions and high-temperature fires, and is commonly deployed in the demolition industry. One tell-tale sign for it might be melted steel – precisely what can be seen in footage taken shortly before the fall of one of the towers, running down in sparkling torrents from a corner of the building. Arguing about damaged fireproofing and temperatures which might or might not have weakened steel slightly is one thing; accepting that those temperatures went on to reach extreme heights which actually *melted* it is a far greater stretch. But molten steel was verifiably found by clearance workers in large amounts even weeks after the attacks, and aerial thermo-imaging revealed tremendous temperatures that could not possibly have resulted from a simple collapse.

Some theorists reject even the nano-thermate arguments, with researchers such as Dr Judy Wood believing that some kind of experimental high-energy technology may have been used (*see* pp. 13, 16), while others point to micro-nuclear devices as a pos-sibility. Certainly, not much was left from a supposed structural failure. Recovery workers remarked on the almost inexplicable absence of telephones, filing cabinets or any other solid objects which might reasonably have been expected to be found in the debris. Instead, all of it seemed to have turned to a fine white toxic dust (which many New Yorkers breathed in, to their long-term detriment), powerfully suggesting something at work capable of generating incredibly high temperatures.

Whichever way it is looked at, the evidence that there was more to the fall of the twin towers than met the eye is hard to ignore. Office workers in the WTC buildings reported unexplained mini-vans off-loading equipment, and nameless maintenance staff being ushered into the towers in the weeks before 9/11. The weekend before the main event, there were reports of an unusual security 'power-down', which saw cameras being switched off and electricity cuts instigated across parts of the buildings while some kind of unspecified 'cabling upgrade' was performed. Was this a mask for a more sinister kind of upgrade? If so, who was carrying it out? Presuming that al-Qaeda was not so organized as to be laying demolition charges in one of the most important complexes in the world without raising suspi-cion, the conspiracy view has it that paid operatives of whoever was really behind 9/11 were more probably at work – and had all the security clearances they needed. Some have pointed to the fact that the firm Securicom, which was in charge of the WTC's security, was co-owned by Marvin Bush – brother of President George W Bush – making for another less-than-reassuring coincidence.

As for what the President himself knew, although some truthseekers have accused him of being one of the perpetrators of 9/11, others believe he was not a major player and may not have been told what was really going on until later that day. One theory has it that Bush was forced to go along with an inside-job plot by shadow authorities, with an implicit threat to his safety if he didn't. As the President had fled into the skies aboard the aeroplane Air Force One shortly after the attacks, he would have been particularly vulnerable to a staged accident or another 'terrorist' strike, as a message using code words that al-Qaeda shouldn't have known ('Angel is next' – Angel being Air Force One, we now know), allegedly received by the US authorities that day, would suggest.

Bush has certainly not been straight about his own experiences on 9/11, and seems to have tried to cover some tracks. This is evidenced by his later claims that he had actually watched TV footage of the first plane crash before he famously went into a schoolroom to read a story to children in the face of a national crisis. But footage of that first impact was not available for broadcast on 11 September itself (the video still trapped in a camera owned by the French documentary-makers Jules and Gédéon Naudet, who were filming NYC firemen that day), so how it was that Bush saw it, or why he simply *said* that that he saw it, is yet another of the many mysteries of 9/11.

WTC 7

Of all the enigmas, conspiracy theorists usually point to the fall of Building Seven (WTC 7) at the World Trade Center complex as being the smoking gun which exposes what they see as the obvious contrivance of all the events. WTC 7 was set back some way from the twin towers, with Buildings Five and Six in between. At around 5.20pm, after several hours of mayhem following the loss of the twin towers, it hardly registered with the public when WTC 7 gracefully collapsed into its own footprint to become just another casualty of the day. As everyone had already been successfully evacuated, what did it matter? Yet the peculiarity of the fall of WTC 7 is that it was never struck by an aeroplane, and exhibited only a few relatively modest fires throughout the day.

The impacts and more extensive blazes at the twin towers could be seen as reasonable justification for their demise if not thought about too much, but with no such caveats available for WTC 7, as time went by, people began to ponder its sudden collapse. Soon intense speculation grew that this building had also been demolished using explosives – particularly suggested by its swift (again, in freefall for at least two seconds) and regimented descent, as remarked on by several demolition experts. If the twin towers were designed to go with maximum spectacle, this block was seemingly wired to descend without calling attention to itself. But if so, why go to the trouble of bringing it down at all?

It has been considered that the events of 9/11 may have been coordinated from WTC 7 (some have suggested it as the source of the remote control transmissions), and that the offices within it might have contained incriminating evidence that demanded removal lest restoration workers make awkward discoveries later. Others may also have exploited the opportunities the day provided (which would still imply detailed foreknowledge of the attacks), as it was of great convenience to the accused that a large number of important documents concerning the unfolding Enron company corruption scandal were being stored in the building at the time – all of them lost. A number of other crucial files and precious commodities *were* reportedly removed from WTC 7 by happy chance in the days before 9/11, but not these ones.

The authorities decry all this, stating that far more fire, spread by falling debris from the neighbouring towers, was present in the building than was visible, and that this contributed to a 'new phenomenon' whereby 'global collapse' was initiated by heat expanding the steel beams. Yet it took seven years for the official report of the National Institute of Standards and Technology (NIST) to come up with this supposedly scientific explanation, and its details are disturbingly flawed. Without plane impacts, no fire-proofing could have been removed, thus taking away much of the rationale which could at least be put forward for the twin towers' collapse. The report also fails to take into account the vital observation that concrete expands at much the same rate as steel, thus flawing its own theory that the heated expansion of the beams caused them to break away from the concrete, snapping the shear studs holding the building together. Perhaps most damningly, assessments of the fires which the NIST says caused the high temperatures in WTC 7 were based not on the unexceptional blazes visible in images or reported by eyewitnesses, but on *presumed* fires of much greater intensity factored into computer models. In other words, the models were programmed to create virtual fires which might, in the most extreme conditions, have brought such a structure down, but these did not reflect the ones that were there in reality. Researchers of 9/11 such as David Ray Griffin have severely challenged the NIST's findings, effectively accusing it of committing scientific fraud.[5]

If simple fire *did* bring down a 47-storey steel-frame building – one that contained a number of important offices for the CIA, the US Secret Service, the mayor's Emergency Command Center, the US Department of Defense and the Internal Revenue Service – then it is a mystery how such a poor design could ever have been accepted, and even more of a mystery as to why many other similarly constructed buildings have not been abandoned in cities across the world as a result. Oddly, no fire in a modern tower block since – and there have been several, often burning far longer – has ever resulted in a total collapse.

The accusations that WTC 7 was demolished are supported by the fact that there seemed to be a wide expectation of its fall even several hours before it came down – at a time when no one should have considered that such a thing was possible. If it supposedly took the NIST seven years to work out why such an unprecedented event happened at all, why would anyone have remotely anticipated it on the day? Yet officials were giving out warnings about WTC 7's dangerous state even by lunchtime, and fire crews were making very specific statements that 'this building is coming down' shortly before it did. BBC News even managed to report that the block had come down *23 minutes before its actual fall*, making it likely that a prepared media statement had already been issued – but a little too early. These clues point strikingly to a scheduled taking-down of WTC 7.

WTC owner Larry Silverstein's infamous remark about Building Seven in a subsequent TV interview, that the authorities had decided to 'pull it', appeared to speak of a direct demolition ('pull it' being a recognized demolition term), but this was later somewhat unconvincingly rescinded to explain that he was just referring to 'pulling' the firemen out. Perhaps there had been a brief consideration of admitting to demolishing WTC 7, albeit on safety grounds, before someone realized the implications of this. After all, professionals usually take days or weeks to lace buildings with charges, so how could it have been neatly set to blow within hours, and in the immediate vicinity of the biggest disaster ever seen in New York? This might have suggested that WTC 7 was pre-charged, therefore – an unheard of and insane policy – and would have thrown an interesting light on the explosives claims concerning the twin towers.

Once again, reports of blasts taking place within WTC 7 in the hours before its collapse are rife, with especially strong testimony coming from city housing authority worker Barry Jennings, who claimed that he and another colleague were present in the building early in the day when a huge explosion took out the stairs below them. Official channels have tried to imply this was due to the fall of one of the twin towers nearby, but Jennings stated it happened well before this; the timing of TV news interviews with him, filmed shortly after he escaped from the building, support his chronology. Indeed, Jennings said that when they arrived for duty at the Emergency Management Command Center in WTC 7, at around 9.03am, it was already deserted – yet official records say the office was not abandoned until 9.30am, providing yet more contradictory oddness.

Barry Jennings might have had more to say, and was beginning to become vocal with his claims that bombs were present within WTC 7, but he died from unknown causes in 2008 aged only 53 – just as the NIST report negating his claims was issued. As ever, there have been a number of other mysterious deaths associated with important 9/11 eyewitnesses, taking us back into familiar conspiracy territory.[6]

Who Were the Perpetrators?

It can be seen even from this very brief précis of the issues surrounding 9/11 that there are many important questions still to be answered by official channels. Of all the most widely subscribed-to conspiracy theories, 9/11 as an inside job is incontestably the one supported by the most observable anomalies. This does not mean that every proposed alternative permutation is true, but then most of the points promoted to support the official story are equally uncertain. What is clear is that the full picture of what really happened on 11 September 2001 has not yet been told. The 'omissions and distortions' (as Griffin accurately describes them) present in the final 9/11 Commission report published in 2004 make it, in most truthseekers' eyes, about as reliable as the much-derided Warren Commission verdict on JFK. The fact that the 9/11 Commission was headed by people with close ties to the

Bush administration, and that it avoided even mentioning glaring issues such as the fall of WTC 7 in its final analysis, virtually guaranteed conspiracy speculation from the start.

But if al-Qaeda did not act alone – or acted at all – then who did help stage 9/11 so successfully? We have already seen that, rightly or wrongly, many fingers have been pointed at Vice-President Dick Cheney. He and several other prominent 'neoconservatives' on the US political right, including Donald Rumsfeld and Paul Wolfowitz, were all names associated with the Project for the New American Century (PNAC), a think tank that produced a telling document almost exactly one year before 9/11. Entitled 'Rebuilding America's Defenses', it was a blueprint for a more powerful and imperialistic USA, setting out the conditions that would need to be created to enable the country to maintain its status as a leading world power. Its now most famous line stands out:

> *The process of transformation, even if it brings revolutionary change, is likely to be a long one, absent some catastrophic and catalysing event – like a new Pearl Harbor.*

Just a year later, many of those who compiled the PNAC document were running the country, following the controversial election which saw George W Bush only just winning after bitter rows over voting irregularities, and the US had its 'new Pearl Harbor', a term specifically referred to by the President in the wake of 9/11. Given many of the conspiracy accusations directed towards the 1941 Pearl Harbor incident (*see* chapter 3), maybe this was not such a wise allusion to make. But it might have been an accurate one.

From the enormous focus often placed on the PNAC document, observers might presume that most challengers of the official story hold neoconservatives to have been entirely responsible for 9/11, but some think this may in itself may be a sideshow. Perhaps inevitably, one pool of doubters implicates Israel as being another major player, accused of aiding the plot to help generate the very backlash against the Muslim world that followed. Dealing with supposedly unbiased claims of 'dancing Israelis' seen celebrating the burning towers, and assertions that Mossad agents were operating in and around the events of 9/11, is a difficult balancing act for conspiracy theorists, risking giving fuel to the knee-jerk reactionism of anti-Zionist camps. The fact that some have strayed into this territory at all has allowed journalists such as David Aaronovitch (*see* p. 13) to slam the entire truth movement as being an anti-Semitic exercise, but this is both untrue and unfair. In the absence of definitive answers, all possibilities are bound to be considered. Overall, however, no matter which faction may have played a part in what, 9/11 is primarily seen as the keystone in the New World Order plans for global domination – something explored more fully in chapter 8.

Regardless of whoever did instigate the attacks, or at the very least allow them, what is beyond question is that 9/11 brought with it many useful tools for those who believe in rule by force, and without a doubt the neocons got their 'catalysing event' to bring about the desired transformation of America. The 'War on Terror', launched in response to the attacks, snatched away many essential freedoms previously taken for granted in the West, and hugely accelerated the rise of the surveillance society, all in the name of our protection. The introduction of worryingly flexible anti-terror legislation across the world, including the US Bill of Rights-violating 'Patriot Act', opened dangerous windows for those who might develop totalitarian tendencies. The hunt for Osama bin Laden, meanwhile, named as the primary culprit even before any loosely assembled evidence was presented, provided the mandate to invade Afghanistan and carry out all that followed, while that same mandate was extended far beyond its brief to encompass action in Iraq and other nations, as we have seen.

The captured Khalid Sheikh Mohammed and the other claimed 'masterminds' behind 9/11 may have been involved, but there is a pervading feeling that copious waterboarding, combined with plea-bargaining and a desire for martyrdom, might have led them to say anything. As for bin Laden, whether the man finally shot down in his underwear in a Pakistani residential compound in 2011 was really him is almost irrelevant. Many doubt it. Numerous reports suggest he had actually died some years before, either from natural causes or quiet assassination, and much cynicism has been expressed over the very poor-quality video and audio recordings purporting to come from him in the decade after 9/11. In a 2007 television interview, Benazir Bhutto, leader of the Pakistani People's Party, appeared to allude directly to the fact that bin Laden was already dead. Sceptics claim that she simply 'misspoke' and was referring to someone else, but just weeks later she was dead herself, killed by a suicide bomber.[7]

Any useful information that interrogating bin Laden might have gleaned for the world was thrown away by his apparently senseless killing, and conclusive proof that the man executed in Pakistan *was* bin Laden was apparently dispensed with when the US Navy compassionately threw his body into the sea on the way home. Curiously, some 22 Navy SEALs from the same unit that assassinated the al-Qaeda leader never made it home themselves, dying when their helicopter was shot down less than three months later.

It is perhaps the case that too many patterns can sometimes be drawn by too many researchers with time on their hands, but it is not hard to see why conspiracy theories arise so easily in the face of such circumstances, especially in a world where lies are told so often. As one of the masters of lies, the Nazi minister of propaganda, Joseph Goebbels, once famously remarked:

> *If you tell a lie big enough and keep repeating it, people will eventually come to believe it. The lie can be maintained only for such time as the state can shield the people from the political, economic and/or military consequences of the lie. It thus becomes vitally important for the state to use all of its powers to*

repress dissent, for the truth is the mortal enemy of the lie, and thus by extension, the truth is the greatest enemy of the State.

II) OTHER MODERN FALSE-FLAG EVENTS?

The Oklahoma Bombing

While, for the conspiracy world, 9/11 has become the most archetypal of all probable false-flag atrocities, it is far from being the only major candidate. We have already seen how, just over the last century or so, there appear to have been a number of events which follow the pattern (the *Lusitania* and *Liberty* incidents stand out in particular). There may even have been a direct US precedent to what happened on 11 September with the deadly truck bomb that took out the Alfred P Murrah Federal Building at Oklahoma City on 19 April 1995, killing 168 people and injuring hundreds more.

Although a single bomber, Timothy McVeigh, was convicted and executed for the crime – supposedly a revenge attack for the 77 people who died at the hands of the FBI in the Waco siege at David Koresh's religious cult compound in 1993 – the evidence strongly suggests that more than one blast must have taken place to have caused such damage and that, again, perhaps explosives had been pre-placed in the building by hands unknown. The anti-terror legislation that followed this attack seems to have helped pave the way for the more sweeping measures that 9/11 would consolidate.

Russian Manipulations?

Modern false-flag contenders are not constrained to American shores, with Russian intelligence services having been accused of perpetrating a number of such incidents, most strikingly the huge explosions which took out a number of apartment blocks in the cities of Moscow, Buynaksk and Volgodonsk in September 1999, killing 293 residents and injuring over a thousand. The blasts were blamed by the authorities on Chechen terrorists, but others soon turned their suspicions towards the Russian Federal Security Service (or FSB, a direct descendant of the KGB), which was alleged to have carried out the bombings itself in an attempt to provide a reason for a full-scale incursion into Chechnya. It also helped elevate the reputation of the FSB's former director, one Vladimir Putin – who went on to lead the country in one guise or another for many years. Although this theory was predictably given great publicity by Chechen politicians, it did also gain support in the Western media, especially by journalist John Sweeney in the *Observer* newspaper.

The allegations have been forcefully denied by Russian authorities, but odd notes were nevertheless struck by the circumstances and timing of the apartment attacks. Three months before the explosions, the Swedish journalist Jan Blomgren had already published a piece claiming that the Kremlin was planning 'a series of terror bombings in Moscow that could be blamed on the Chechens', suggesting that advance information was seeping through from somewhere.[8] Then, on 13 September 1999, following the Moscow blasts, a speaker in the Russian Duma, Gennadiy Seleznyov, announced this:

I have just received a report. According to information from Rostov-on-Don, an apartment building in the city of Volgodonsk was blown up last night.

This statement was miraculously prescient; the Volgodonsk apartments were not bombed until three days after this statement was made.

When Volgodonsk was indeed then hit, explanations were demanded, but Seleznyov refused to answer, to the point of turning off his microphone in the Duma chamber – a strange response to pertinent requests. Two years on, Seleznyov eventually stated that he had been referring to another attack in Volgodonsk and that the dates had simply been mixed up. Given that this other incident had been a small and unsuccessful grenade incident, it is hard to see how it could have been described in the terms he used. Unsurprisingly, many were left unconvinced by this less-than-satisfactory clarification. The resonance of this with the BBC announcing the fall of WTC 7 in advance of its actual collapse has not gone unnoticed, suggesting that a pre-scripted statement may once again have been issued somewhat earlier than intended, implicating Russian intelligence services in knowing full well what was due to happen.

More charges of conspiracy were aimed at Russia when, on 10 April 2010, a plane carrying the Polish president Lech Kaczyński, together with many senior members of his government and the president of the National Bank of Poland, crashed in fog near Russia's Smolensk airport. There were no survivors. The contingent had been on its way to Warsaw to commemorate the 70th anniversary of the Katyn massacre, where Soviet secret police executed thousands of Polish citizens in 1940, and feelings were still running high on both sides. Perhaps this is why, despite the poor flying conditions and the verdicts of pilot error, accusations were rampant that Russia had somehow staged the crash in some kind of attempt to weaken the political resolve of its neighbour. Rumours (based on unproven audio recordings) of survivors being shot at the site of the accident were rife, and weaknesses in the subsequent Russian investigation, including discrepancies in the claimed autopsies, have led to allegations of a cover-up by Russia and calls for an independent international inquiry.[9]

In this case, such theorizing could be born of grief, historical resentments and the need to find someone to blame for a terrible occurrence, although it might also be observed that placing so many important officials on one vehicle is probably not a very wise thing to do. It does seem to be a mistake made just a little too often, as was seen in the 1994 Chinook helicopter crash (first blamed on the pilots, then 'faulty software') at Scotland's Mull of Kintyre, which managed to eradicate 25 important counter-terrorist officers from Northern Ireland, or at the later shooting down of the aforementioned helicopter (also a Chinook), which took the lives of several of bin Laden's claimed assassins.[10]

7/7

For the majority of conspiracy theorists, Britain itself was the target of a significant false-flag terror attack on 7 July 2005 ('7/7'). The official account has it that four home-grown Muslim extremists blew themselves up in London on a bus and three underground trains that morning, taking 52 passengers with them and injuring many more. These devastating attacks so shocked the nation, for all its memories of IRA action in previous decades, that questioning it is still a taboo in many forums, generating disgust and anger. But, like 9/11 before it, doubts have crept in over the years, leading many truthseekers to ponder a number of anomalies.

Among the concerns, the following items are the most conspicuous:

- The lack of any clearly identifiable CCTV images of the bombers.
- Timecode and timeline discrepancies in the released security footage.
- Notable contradictions and inconsistencies in the official account's version of which trains the bombers took and precisely where the explosions took place. The train they were initially claimed to be on was actually cancelled that morning, for example, forcing a later revision of the official narrative to account for this.

- The supposed terrorists had long been under surveillance by intelligence forces, and may even have been recruited by them to take part in mysterious 'exercises'.
- Similar 'exercises' were taking place the very day of 7/7, which postulated a scenario of bombs going off at the *very stations* where three of them were then apparently detonated (as related that morning by security adviser Peter Power on BBC Radio 5 Live).
- Images from the trains appear to show damage coming from *beneath* the carriages.
- Peculiarly specific damage to the bus which blew up at Tavistock Square (which one witness claims was deliberately diverted from its normal route by obstructive cars).

Other problematic areas have also been cited, but it can be seen from these points alone that even this seemingly straightforward terrorist case is rife with unexplained incongruities that were guaranteed to set conspiracy theories running.

Certainly, the claim about exercises 'coincidentally' occurring at the vital 7/7 flashpoints stretches credulity, especially when compared to the almost identical situation with the drills on 9/11 (*see* p. 178). Claimed links between the bombers and the British security services, who, it is now confirmed, knew of their extremist leanings and had been monitoring them for some time, have led to speculation that they were encouraged and allowed to carry out the attacks, set up as patsies (as may have occurred with the 1993 bombing of the World Trade Center – *see* p. 53). Others believe they may have been duped into participating in an exercise that had them carrying live explosives without their knowledge, which were then set off by remote control. Yet the reports (and images) of damage apparently having come up from below the carriages, rather than in them, have led some to wonder whether the explosions were entirely, or partly, the result of bombs planted on the tracks rather than backpack blasts. One survivor from the Aldgate train said:

The policeman said 'mind that hole, that's where the bomb was'. The metal was pushed upwards as if the bomb was underneath the train. They seem to think the bomb was left in a bag, but I don't remember anybody being where the bomb was, or any bag.[11]

The memories of several other survivors concerning the bombers or what they were wearing seem very hazy, with many contradictory descriptions having been given. A number of other accounts suggest a complete absence of the men that the official versions insist were there, but most of these reports have been ignored by the authorities.

All these 'disgraceful' conspiracy theories might be cleared up easily with definitive proof and unequivocal security footage, but what has been presented to support the orthodox account of 7/7 thus far is inconclusive, with only one bomber actually being identifiable by his face in the available images. This has not stopped official inquiries from drawing firm conclusions based on evidence that would not normally be considered admissible in court, with an absolute presumption of the accused men's guilt seemingly having been established before investigations even began – just as with 9/11.

The 7/7 situation is admittedly far less clear-cut than 9/11, and different in as much as there is so little visual material available for analysis. This has enabled the concerns to be more easily sidelined in the public eye, but the ongoing truth campaigns speak of a determination in some quarters not to let the issue go.

Drawing Threads Together

What nearly all of these modern false-flag allegations have in common is that they are considered by truthseekers to be part of a pattern which lays down a solid path for the machinations of the New World Order. Other possibilities are usually added to this list, including the 2004 Madrid train bombings in Spain, the Bali bombings of 2002 and various failed attacks from shoe or underwear bombers on planes, together with all manner of exposed 'al-Qaeda-linked' plots around the world, which seem designed to heighten fear and hatred towards the Muslim world and increase oppressive social controls in the name of safety. Indeed, there is substantial evidence that the threat from the catch-all al-Qaeda quarter may well have been exaggerated for effect, as we shall see in chapter 8.

Before we explore the New World Order threads in more detail, there is one more strand of conspiracy theory that also needs to be taken into account, one which has taken a back seat so far in this text: the wide belief that, in addition to geopolitical manoeuvring and social engineering, more paranormal elements may drive the motivations of those pulling the strings.

IN SUMMARY . . .

9/11 and Related Conspiracies: Arguments Against

9/11 is too big to have been attempted as a false-flag event, involving too many people and risking exposure for the perpetrators – Who would do such a thing 'to their own people'? – The anomalies in the official timelines, records and forensics of the attacks are nothing more than inevitable confusion in the 'fog of war' – The collapses of the towers were natural and fully consistent with the laws of physics, albeit constituting unusual occurrences or a 'new phenomenon' – Government-sponsored scientists are more qualified to comment on what occurred than so-called physicists from the 'fringe' – It is disrespectful to the victims of 9/11 to challenge the details of what occurred – Questioning 9/11 is unpatriotic, even treasonous – The media firmly support the official version of events and thus the 'truth movement' cannot be right, or it would have gathered more mainstream support – Evidence for other claimed false-flag events is equally tenuous and should never be taken seriously.

9/11 and Related Conspiracies: Arguments For

It would not take that many inside operatives to grease the path to successful attacks, sowing enough confusion to cover their tracks – Some argue the perpetrators ARE being exposed and the power-hungry rarely have scruples about killing their own people – The anomalies of 9/11 are simply too many and too extraordinary to be written off as coincidences – The 'new phenomenon' explanations for the falls of the towers rely either on guesswork or demonstrably distorted hypothetical models which do not take into account the real conditions on the day, or misrepresent the physical attributes of the buildings – The scientists challenging the official story are as qualified, sometimes more, than those paid to put the government view – More disrespect is shown towards the victims of 9/11 by not investigating precisely what happened, ignorance risking other such events being staged – The attacks are more likely to have been treasonous than those seeking the truth about them – The media is complicit with the cover-ups around 9/11, whether through institutional scepticism or intimidation – The discrepancies around other false-flag possibilities display similar patterns to 9/11 and are unlikely to all be imagination.

CONCLUSION

Of all the many conspiracy claims, 9/11 has the most layers of evidence, suggesting that whatever the ultimate truth of the attacks, the official version fails to address legitimate concerns which hint at other agendas being played out. The increasing public doubt over 9/11, backed up by the unusual but telling support of a significant number of high-calibre professionals and academics, speaks of a meaningful disquiet that deserves some proper attention.

With the establishment showing every sign of wanting to sweep the whole thing under the carpet of history – as with JFK, the USS *Liberty*, the Tonkin ruse and various other incriminating events which have fallen into a hazy mythological past – the 9/11 truth movement feels an urgency to preserve the issues in the public eye. As the tapestry of contemporary global conflicts and liberty issues is still firmly rooted in the attacks of 2001, and with related incidents showing signs of similar manipulation, there is at least the opportunity to keep the flame of enquiry burning. For if 9/11 was even a partial false-flag attack, the world we are living in today is based on one of the greatest deceptions ever perpetrated, and it must surely be opened up for true investigation so that healing can take place and a more positive way forward can be forged for our civilization.

CHAPTER 7

EXTRA-TERRESTRIAL CONSPIRACIES

Behind the endless speculation around the more obvious geopolitical manoeuvres which attract the attention of conspiracy theorists, there is a deeper suspicion from some quarters that more esoteric agendas influence the motivations of the alleged puppeteers. Accusations are rife that knowledge of paranormal activity is being withheld from the public, especially concerning extra-terrestrial visitations and the true origins of our civilization. Could it be that Earth was infiltrated long ago and seeded with a ruling class that is far from human?

I) EXTRA-TERRESTRIAL ROOTS

The Distraction of Debunking

Of all conspiracy theories, some of the most controversial – and scorned – are the beliefs that knowledge of mystical powers and an awareness of the presence of extra-terrestrial visitors have long been kept secret. It is certainly the case, as we shall see, that those in the higher echelons of influence would appear to have far more interest in 'paranormal' and occult areas than has ever been admitted to. Could an important stratum of our history have been hidden from us, but privately embraced by those in command? Some truthseekers believe so, and hold that the routine debunking and public marginalization of such subjects has in truth been a massive exercise of intentional distraction.

Ancient Astronauts

In 1968, two milestones in popular culture independently picked up on a theme which would have unexpected consequences for a particular strand of conspiracy theory decades later: Stanley Kubrick's seminal and visionary film *2001: A Space Odyssey* (co-written with Arthur C Clarke) depicted other-worldly artefacts influencing humankind's evolution in the deep past, stimulating profound discussions in the new counterculture and conventional society alike. Erich von Däniken's bestselling book *Chariots of the Gods*, meanwhile, also speculated on visitations from 'ancient astronauts' in earlier ages, but went for documentary evidence based on prehistoric carvings and artefacts which might depict flying craft, spacesuited creatures and other potential alien activity. The academic backlash to this reading of history has been savage since, but it quite caught the public imagination at the time and never entirely fell from view. The many mysteries still surrounding the construction and purpose of the likes of the Nazca line complexes in Peru, or the pyramids in Egypt, have left some still convinced that they were created courtesy of extra-terrestrial intervention.

The furore caused by the discovery of a humanoid stone 'face' on Mars by NASA's Viking mission of 1976, greatly fuelled by the subsequent conjecture of Richard C Hoagland, reignited the appetite for ancient astronaut theories, creating a whole industry of new conspiracy theories around them. NASA's denial that anything was there other than an amusing piece of simulacra was met by rebuttals that alongside the face sat a number of unexplained artefacts on the Martian plains of Cydonia, including pyramids and apparently artificial constructions, geometrically aligned in ways that could not be easily explained away. The resonance of these alignments with the layout of the Neolithic Avebury complex in the English county of Wiltshire (where the majority of Britain's fiercely debated and mysterious crop circles appear) deepened the speculation.[1]

When much clearer images from later NASA probes appeared to reveal the Cydonia 'monuments' as little more than disappointing collections of rocks, with perhaps faint resemblances to faces and objects, aficionados refused to budge, alleging photo manipulation or pointing to the possible effects of erosion in having softened the edges of the artefacts. Claims of further structures being visible on Mars, and even the Moon, gleaned from new and crisper images, continue to be made by the year.[2] Beyond more obvious possibilities, one line of thinking to explain the suspected faking of the Moon landing photos (*see* chapter 4) has it that NASA was simply unable to show the astonishing reality of what was found there and had to prepare its own, less shocking, evidence while official channels quietly carried out their own investigations.

Other discoveries have suggested the possibility of even the contemporary presence of alien activity around Mars. In 1988, Russia launched two probes to explore Phobos, one of the curious asteroid-like Martian moons. The *Phobos 1* probe was lost en route, but when *Phobos 2* managed to arrive safely in 1989, all was well until it attempted to approach Phobos itself. Following the capturing of one final intriguing image, all transmissions from the probe ceased. The probe's final view appears to show either a long cylindrical object parked near Phobos or some kind of light beam. Later analysis of some of *Phobos 2*'s earlier shots of Mars showed a long 'spindle-shaped' shadow on the surface, perhaps cast by the 'cylinder'. Was the probe intercepted by some kind of intelligence? No one has ever satisfactorily explained what happened to *Phobos 2*, but the above-average failure rate of probes to Mars (eight lost to date) from Russian, US and international missions has suggested to some a presence there that sometimes prefers to be left alone, sparking claims of cover-ups.[3]

Beyond von Däniken, another important adherent to the ancient astronaut theory was the late Zecharia Sitchin. His controversial interpretations of Sumerian and other Mesopotamian legends, which tell of the arrival on Earth of god-like beings in ancient times, have greatly influenced conspiracy theories concerning extra-terrestrial bloodlines. The Anunnaki – considered by some to be the same race recorded as the Nephilim in the biblical book of Genesis – were believed by Sitchin to have been alien visitors who came from the planet Nibiru. According to his account of the ancient texts – much criticized by mainstream historians – the Anunnaki genetically engineered the human race from primordial hominids as a slave species, before retreating from Earth when Nibiru began its long elliptical journey back out to the far reaches of the solar system. However, the extra-terrestrial bloodline that was left, seeded among a certain branch of humankind, ensured that a ruling elite would continually resurface from time to time throughout history to reassert its dominance over other humans in preparation for the eventual return of Nibiru.

For all the criticism Sitchin's version of events has received, numerous other myths and legends around the world do appear to tell tales of godlike beings descending from the skies to intervene with humankind's development. Chapter 6 of Genesis, which describes them as the 'sons of God' is quite blatant in its description of the interbreeding that took place:

> *The sons of God, looking at the daughters of men, saw they were pleasing, so they married as many as they chose . . . The Nephilim were on the earth at that time (and even afterwards) when the sons of God resorted to the daughters of man, and had children by them. These are the heroes of days gone by, the famous men.*[4]

The theme of our genetic evolution being interrupted and altered has continued even into modern popular culture; *2001: A Space Odyssey* is prominent amongst the examples.

As for the return of Nibiru (or 'Planet X'), some theorists believe this is due to occur sometime soon, warning of potentially catastrophic effects to our planet as the wanderer re-enters the inner part of our solar system. Evidence for this has been shaky to date (and sometimes faked – *see* p. 28), but multiple assertions of astronomical cover-ups have been made to account for the silence on what would surely be a sensational development were a new planetary body incontrovertibly known to be heading our way.

It has been suggested that the upsurge of UFO sightings and other apparently extra-terrestrial phenomena in recent decades may herald an advance wave of the returning Anunnaki, and that the dark-eyed 'grey' beings often reported from claimed alien encounters are the cloned 'helper' drones alluded to in Sitchin's translations. A brief summary of some of the evidence in this area may be helpful.

II) UFOS

Objects in the Sky

Tales of unexplained aerial objects would seem to go back *ad infinitum*, littering religious and historical texts throughout time (the biblical Book of Ezekiel's description of 'wheels within wheels', for instance). They are generally attributed to hallucinogenic experiences or primitive interpretations of astronomical phen-omena, but others believe that some of the reports are too specific to be dismissed so lightly. The sky was always looked to as the theatre of the gods, as the development of astrology and its progeny, astronomy, attests, so it could be argued that anything seen there might once have been taken as evidence of external intervention. But some accounts seem very similar to what we would today refer to as UFOs. Even tales of folk being carried off into the fairy realms, encountering goblins and other elemental creatures, seem to have resonance with modern alien abduction stories, now so numerous that some brave explorers of psychology accept them as a serious phenomenon, whatever their true origin (as we saw with Professor John Mack – *see* p. 15).

Before the rash of UFO sightings that seemed to proliferate from the mid-1940s onwards, the previous century had already seen a number of 'flaps' concerning unidentified aerial objects. In the mid-1880s, a spate of mystery airships were reported in California, at a time when airship technology was only just in its infancy. It has been suggested that these may have been early prototypes being tested in secret (as some believe 'alien craft' seen today may be covert military technology), but closer links with the more usual view of UFOs are forged by stories which describe behaviour far beyond the capability of airships. Accompanying claims of witnesses interacting with non-human occupants of the craft also suggest extra-terrestrial connotations. Indeed, 1896 saw the first-ever account of an attempted alien abduction, when three 7ft-tall creatures were reported to have tried to drag a local colonel onboard a featureless metallic 'airship' with pointed ends.[5] The general airship scare eventually died down for a while, put down to hoaxes or paranoia – something initially supported by the resurfacing of reports when German Zeppelins started operation around the First World War. Yet not all the stories could be so easily explained.

Other aerial phenomena of the early 20th century have been reinterpreted as UFO activity in more recent times. The claimed apparitions of the Virgin Mary at Fatima in Portugal in 1917, for instance, which saw three shepherd children famously receive messages of prophecy from a glowing female being, are backed up by remarkable eyewitness accounts given by thousands of people of a huge orb (presumed at the time to be the Sun) performing extraordinary acrobatics in the skies above the crowds. The unusual amount of supportive testimony (photos exist which even purport to show the orb) and the fact that the Vatican took it seriously enough to classify it as an official miracle is impressive, while the descriptions of the whirling, seemingly laws-of-physics-defying movements of the object have reminded modern observers of behaviour reported in many claimed UFO sightings. The reported instant drying of rain puddles and wet clothes at the closest pass of the orb is another aspect which has been reported in other 'close encounters'.[6]

Towards the end of the Second World War, bomber crews and airmen from a number of countries reported the presence of 'foo fighters', inexplicable glowing spheres which would follow aeroplanes, never interfering, but seemingly curious. Their ability to swerve rapidly away at any angle was beyond either natural phenomena or any available technology, although it was feared at the time that they might be secret devices of the enemy.

Roswell and Other Claimed Close Encounters

The most famous alleged occurrence in the decade which appeared to see such a major rise in UFO reports was the now-fabled Roswell incident. On 7 July 1947 the New Mexico newspaper the *Roswell Daily Record* reported, incredibly, that the Roswell Army Air Field base had successfully retrieved a crashed flying saucer. The immediate fuss was swept under the carpet, however, by the presentation of weather balloon debris to journalists the next day, who were told that this was all that came down in the nearby desert.

But decades later, information from ex-military personnel and other whistleblowers began to make clear that *something* strange must have occurred at Roswell, especially when Major

Jesse Marcel (who had fronted the weather balloon story) came forward to deny the official version. Marcel stated that what he and other personnel had witnessed could only, in their view, have come from an extra-terrestrial craft. More elaborate claims from other Roswell locals told of alien bodies (the 'grey' variety reported by many claimed contactees) having been brought into the local hospital, adding spice to the story and spiralling it into UFO legend – some would say, myth. Shifting cover stories (the balloon became a device for detecting Soviet atomic tests, and the bodies were explained away as crash-test dummies) only added to the intrigue.

Getting to the truth of what really occurred at Roswell, given the many claims and counter-claims, is now difficult at this distance, with even some ufologists doubting the extra-terrestrial elements of the story. However, a large number of conspiracy theorists do believe that an important encounter did take place and that the craft was retrieved and taken to a hangar at the now in itself legendary Area 51 (or 'Dreamland'), a Nevada desert testing site for confidential US military projects. It has been suggested that the reverse-engineering of captured UFOs has secretly been the source for several of civilization's recent technological advances, while mysterious 'men in black' are said to turn up at the scenes of alleged encounters to gather further data and contain public knowledge.

There have been many other stories of military units encountering extra-terrestrials, but getting to the bottom of any of them becomes harder as the years go by, with layers of concealment and debunking clouding any chance of reaching an irrefutable conclusion. The Rendlesham Forest incident of 1980, for instance, in which US soldiers guarding a UK military base in Suffolk claim to have witnessed a conical UFO at close quarters in nearby woodlands, has been assailed by varied and sometimes weak means (disregarded as being a lighthouse seen through fog, covert hallucinogenic experiments, etc.), yet the actual accounts seem too particular for some of the more mundane explanations to ring true.

Meanwhile, civilians have reported many variations on lights, saucers, discs, triangular craft and cylinders over the years, with thousands claiming personal encounters with the occupants. Although the greys are the most commonly reported variety, other beings have been described, including tall 'Nordic'-looking humanoids and insectoid or reptilian creatures (*see below*). In view of the treatment that professional witnesses have received, it is perhaps unsurprising that the public's stories have been handled even more shoddily for the most part. Yet recurring themes of bizarre operations, alien 'implants' and remarkably accurate visions of the future having been conveyed by the apparent ETs are so dominant that, if nothing else, the abduction phenomenon surely demands attention as a major psychological crisis of our times. But even Carl Jung met ridicule when he tried to tackle the subject with this sensible approach in his perceptive 1959 book *Flying Saucers: A Modern Myth of Things Seen in the Sky.*

Official Responses

When authorities do appear to investigate UFOs, impressive data is often sidelined or simply ignored, as was demonstrated by the USAF's Project Blue Book, which gathered information on over 12,000 sightings between 1952 and 1969. It wrote most of them off – probably correctly – as having mundane causes, but admitted that a not-insubstantial 22 per cent of cases 'remained unsolved'. Yet no more was said about this surely significant number of apparently non-mundane encounters. Most official inquiries have followed much the same pattern, for all the impressive roll calls of ex-military personnel, astronauts (including Apollo 14's Ed Mitchell) and commercial airline pilots who have come forward with their own testimony, either personally or through conduits such as Steven Greer's ambitious Disclosure Project, which has gathered considerable positive evidence for the UFO phenomenon.[7]

The US government came down heavily on British computer expert Gary McKinnon when he hacked into American military and NASA files between 2001 and 2002, seeking proof of UFO cover-ups. This sparked more than a decade of attempted extradition procedures unlike any before them, suggesting a particular touchiness in this area. Controversial figures such as Nick Pope, who claims to have worked for a UK Ministry of Defence department which investigated UFOs, have stated that the authorities have far more interest in such phenomena than is ever declared. Pope himself has been accused of being a government 'plant', but his contention would make sense of some of the alleged cover-ups surrounding elements of ufological folklore such as 'Majestic 12' (a secret investigation project said to have been set up in the wake of Roswell) or the 'NSC 5412/2 Special Group'. It may be that all these rumoured organizations are confusion tactics in themselves, introduced into the conspiracy world to mask the real operations, while the media's debunking and regular claims that 'ufology is dead' – in the face of actually increased sightings – could be viewed as the workings of a complex double-bluff, sowing interest and uncertainty all at the same time.

Whichever way it is looked at, the presence of some kind of unknown force operating in our airspace, while not entirely denied, is barely discussed by authorities and quickly brushed aside. Yet sometimes there may be glimpses of more honest opinions. According to Steven Spielberg, following a special screening of his 1982 movie *ET*, an unsmiling President Ronald Reagan is reputed to have said: 'There are a number of people in this room who know that everything on that screen is absolutely true.' Spielberg has written this off as a joke, but others believe Reagan, a firm believer in mysticism and astrology, was making a rare declaration of the truth in this area.[8]

John F Kennedy clearly took UFOs seriously (as did presidents Gerald Ford and Jimmy Carter). On 12 November 1963, Kennedy ordered a full declassification of relevant CIA documents to NASA with a view to sharing UFO information with the Soviets. Two weeks later, he was dead; this might be a coincidence, of course, although in the conspiracy world little is seen as coincidence.[9]

Origins and Purpose?

As for precisely why extra-terrestrials might be here, opinions vary enormously. If real, are they, as numerous sci-fi movies would have it, scouting us out for a planned invasion, or are they here simply to gather knowledge and genetic material for some kind of galactic archive? Claims of UFOs leaving behind mutilated cattle with specific organs cleanly removed are rife and may indicate some kind of organic extraction programme, but people also claim to have had physical material taken from them during encounters. Are the visitors benevolent forces, wanting to save humankind from its own excesses, or are they using us to take DNA and maybe save themselves from some kind of evolutionary crisis? (Some say they could, in fact, be humans from the future.) Are they here instead to inspire us subtly to a new stage of enlightenment, creating the more advanced crop circles (aerial phenomena are often witnessed over the host fields) and transmitting psychic messages? Or are they advance parties from Nibiru, assessing the situation for the return of their masters? Could all of these possibilities be occurring? In essence, are they here to police us or to fleece us?

Where extra-terrestrials might come from is another unresolved issue. If they have developed some kind of instantaneous method of interstellar propulsion, they might be from anywhere (some abductees say greys come from the star system Zeta Reticuli).

Those unable to accept 'warp drive' theories have suggested that the visitors may have long ago colonized the interior of our own Moon (or the interior of a hollow Earth) and have been essentially native for centuries, manipulating the human race from behind the scenes. UFOs have also been seen coming up from the sea.

The mainstream implication of all the persistent debunking and academic sneering, on the other hand, is that the belief in visiting aliens is all a kind of collective madness – a huge psychological projection from the inner recesses of mass consciousness, creating fictions that eventually take on a kind of hallucinogenic reality for the impressionable. That attitude is perhaps not quite fair, especially when it comes from a media that has played a major part in having introduced them into the global psyche in the first place.

Fake Aliens?

The idea of ETs as a collective psychogenic thought-form has helped grow yet another branch of conspiracy thinking. It has been suggested that the New World Order might try to use the *concept* of an alien threat as a huge psy-ops experiment, designed to encourage further the creation of a one world government (*see* chapter 8). In this view, some, if not all, of the ufological evidence (including the debunking, as part of the psychological conditioning) may have been deliberately introduced into our culture to build us up slowly for the day when 'aliens' – but in reality fake ones – are finally seen to arrive.

If a mass visitation of ET vessels were to materialize in plain sight, this could indeed present a dilemma in a world prone to complex deceptions. Could we trust our usual senses in that situation? Concerns over the potential capabilities of holographic projection technology (often described as 'Project Blue Beam') have led to the development of the 'fake alien invasion' theory, in which fears have been expressed that the ruling elite might beam images into the sky to falsify an extra-terrestrial presence. Why might this be necessary, though? The answer may once again lie in the words of President Reagan, who, in a 1987 address to the United Nations General Assembly, stated:

> In our obsession with antagonisms of the moment, we often forget how much unites all the members of humanity. Perhaps we need some outside, universal threat to make us recognize this common bond. I occasionally think how quickly our differences worldwide would vanish if we were facing an alien threat from outside this world.[10]

Some believe this idea might have been taken literally by the NWO and that plans to implement such a 'common bond' by false means could be well advanced. All of which means that if ET craft are ever seen coming through the clouds *en masse*, transmitting either threats or welcomes, there is going to be a stratum of humanity which will eye them with deep suspicion. The future might well bring other similar dilemmas, with talk of faked second comings of Christ also occurring in an attempt to 'fulfil' biblical prophecies (*see* p. 228).

Real Powers

For those who believe that extra-terrestrials are very real, perhaps worse than a falsified presence is the notion that several governments might actually be working in cahoots with different alien factions, some good, some bad, manipulating us into situations for uncertain purposes of their own. UFOs would certainly appear to have some genuinely impressive powers, as the several accounts of unexplained craft neutralizing nuclear missile silos would attest. One prominent case was brought forward by USAF Colonel Robert Salas, who claims he was present at the Malmstrom base in Montana when a hovering saucer-shaped object appeared to cause a mass shutdown in 1967.[11] The implications of such reported capacities are plainly significant, if not a little worrying, especially when considered alongside what has become known as 'the reptilian agenda'.

III) THE REPTILIAN AGENDA

Roots of the Belief

Of all modern conspiracy theories, the 'reptilian agenda' has been one of the most divisive, even among the truthseeker community. Stemming from belief in the Anunnaki bloodlines, researchers such as televsion-presenter-turned-alternative-icon David Icke have narrowed down the identity of the extra-terrestrial elements, which may long ago have manipulated humanity's genes, to being reptilian in nature. Popularized through Icke's many influential books and striking lectures, the belief that these hybrid creatures have shape-shifting abilities and that their bloodline is still dominant today has led to the assertion that some of the key players in the ruling elite or 'Illuminati' may in truth be anything but human – with the British Royal Family branded as the leading carriers of the alien DNA.[12]

The novel visions called to mind by this theory, of the Queen or Prince Charles morphing from human to reptile and back again, have proved too much even for some dyed-in-the-wool conspiracy observers. They have accused the idea's proponents of having brought the entire truthseeking world, which struggles for credibility at the best of times, into serious disrepute. While some are willing privately to consider the concept, they can feel nonetheless that the derision generated by speaking openly of it in connection with other theories can only hinder the flow of important information about more readily demonstrable 'real-world' outrages. Others go further and have condemned the reptilian agenda's supporters as being establishment 'shills', sources either bought or fooled into promoting damaging nonsense with a view to bringing down the reputation of the entire conspiracy worldview. Needless to say, the shill accusations have also flown in reverse.

Tales of shape-shifting, blood-drinking aliens on the throne have without doubt been used by the mainstream to discredit plausible alternative views on other serious issues, all too easily smeared by association – but the reptile adherents remain unrepentant. So where does their undeniably heartfelt conviction come from?

Believers cite a surfeit of serpent imagery in ancient texts, not least the tale of the Garden of Eden, as being coded signs of the true nature of those who have long been in command, while mythologies of dragons and other reptilian beasts, frequently used as emblems by powerful families and monarchies, reinforce this view. The extreme fascination with dinosaurs in archaeology and lizard men in modern science fiction has also been seen as a sign of the subliminal presence of the secret reptilian masters. Subliminal to most, that is, except to victims such as Arizona Wilder and Stewart Swerdlow, just two of a select group who claim to have actually witnessed prominent politicians and members of the Royal Family shift into their reptile forms within seconds.

If becoming a reptile now and then does not sound like a great crime, it is the nature of what such figures reportedly *do* in that state which creates so much of the controversy. If testimony is to be believed, sexual abuse of both adults and children, frenzied occult blood-drinking rituals and human sacrifice are regularly carried out at places such as the Queen's Balmoral Castle residence in Scotland, and at other locations around the world, largely in secret chambers beneath the ground. Some of the accounts, fully available in books and websites, make for uncomfortable reading and don't give much hope for the human race, especially if the tales of entire underground cities devoted to human slave camps and 'larders', where millions of missing children from around the world are supposed to be held, are true.[13]

If the Royal Family were ever proven to be cold-blooded reptiles, this might at least make sense of the Diana assassination theories which directly implicate them, particularly if the royals were jealously guarding the purest form of the Anunnaki bloodline from outside influence (*see* pp. 151–3).

Criticisms and Defences

Some of the outraged scorn towards the reptile accusations is probably rooted in reflex protectiveness. Accepting that the likes of Tony Blair, George W Bush, Henry Kissinger, Dick Cheney, assorted Rothschilds and Rockefellers (who are the usual named suspects) and all manner of former ministers and presidents might be coldly lizard-like in their essential nature is not such a stretch for some observers. However, believing that the late Queen Mother, a seemingly gentle soul held in deep affection by the British public, was in fact one of the most voracious and savage members of her race, as supposed eyewitnesses have claimed, is rather more of a leap, causing not just amazement but actual offence to all but the staunchest republicans.

Less sensitive opponents have criticized the reptilian agenda more on points of logic, querying how bloodlines could be maintained so closely over the aeons, given the genealogical ebbs, flows and sometimes complete breaks in lineages known to have occurred throughout history. Believers counter that the reptile genes are re-identified and reactivated by esoteric means, and that carriers can come to an inner knowing of their true being which compels them to seek out other members of their race, who are usually most dominant in the ruling classes. By this process, and with the ancient wisdoms concealed from the masses through occultism and the upper echelons of secret societies, the hypothesis runs that extra-terrestrials took over our planet long ago and have ruled from the shadows. Those who tie this in with the expected return of Nibiru think that the reptiles have been holding the fort, keeping humankind enslaved in one way or another in readiness for the return of the gods. It is admittedly curious that in the Sumerian legends the gods came down precisely where modern-day Iraq is now. In this view, there has perhaps been yet another agenda to all the struggles over that country. As the reptilian gene appears to be more prevalent in Western leaders, has increased influence in Iraq become necessary to prepare secretly for the return of their masters?

Some have tried to attack the reptile theory on grounds of racism, asserting that talk of an infiltrating minority (especially the component which might be supporting extremist Zionist agendas, which several US neoconservatives have been accused of) is a thinly veiled metaphor for anti-Semitic sentiments; for lizards, read Jews. However, having accompanied him on a lecture tour for a Channel 4 programme, even journalist Jon Ronson (*see* p. 243), a staunch defender of his Judaic roots, satisfied himself that when Icke and his supporters talked of reptiles, that they really *did* mean the extra-terrestrial variety.[14]

Another major criticism has been aimed at the manner in which some of the claimed eyewitnesses have recovered 'memories' of their participation in reptile ceremonies (experiences supposedly brainwashed out of them). This has either involved hypnotic regression, or the information has come from a natural and more gradual resurfacing of images buried in their heads. Many psychologists have deep reservations about the dangers of relying on regression techniques; 'False Memory Syndrome' (FMS), in which childhood traumas manifest as symbolic but essentially fictional recollections, is considered to have been the source of several infamous claims of ritual child abuse later proven to have been unfounded on further investigation. FMS can also result from auto-suggestion on the part of an unscrupulous or inexperienced therapist, and similar concerns have been raised when regression has been used to recover memories of claimed alien abductions. Defenders inevitably counter that allegations of FMS are in themselves too often used to cover up information that authorities would prefer remained unexposed.

A Mask for Genuine Abuses?

The concern over FMS does not mean that child abuse is never carried out in an organized fashion, as the horrors of several exposed paedophile rings have demonstrated in recent years. Indeed, some researchers believe that the apparent lizard men memories may be psychological masks for genuine incidents of abuse, enhanced into fantasy settings as a kind of self-protection. Others have asserted that the introduction of the reptilian theories has been a specific psy-ops programme intended to deflect attention away from real child abuse rings involving participants with senior roles in authority. By associating such claims with apparently deranged people who believe in blood-drinking aliens, what would otherwise be very serious matters can instead be trivialized and sidelined in the media.

It is without question that the case around Hollie Greig, for instance, a Down's syndrome woman who claims she was routinely abused as a youth by a paedophile ring in Scotland, has been both helped and hindered by the wide support offered to her by the 'alternative' community. Hollie's mother alleges that doctors, judges and other high-ranking local officials were involved, but has met enormous resistance in her campaign for justice. Concerned that her case was being repeatedly dismissed by the Scottish authorities without serious consideration (something entirely ignored by the media, usually quick to pick up on child abuse), a number of genuinely compassionate conspiracy believers have championed her cause. This association, together with Hollie's Down's symptoms, has sometimes been used, if unfairly, to denigrate her plausibility. Yet there seems to be a disproportionate defensiveness in the response of the authorities, which in February 2012 saw Robert Green, one of the leading campaigners, jailed for several months, essentially for giving out information about Hollie's case – an act labelled 'a breach of the peace'. This forceful use of the legal system in a (failed) attempt to quieten the accusations ultimately resulted in yet more conspiracy theories and a strengthened campaign in support of both Robert and Hollie.[15]

Anxiety over the abuse of children in the truthseeker community, therefore, in whatever context, has at least helped highlight a very real problem. Given that a ritualistic ceremony attended by the leading lights of politics and industry each year at Bohemian Grove (*see* chapter 8) involves sacrificing the effigy of a child, such events cannot help but make some wonder if there is at least a grain of truth to elements of the alleged reptilian agenda, on a symbolic level if nothing else.

The Same Agenda?

The extra-terrestrial theories, then, are perhaps not so divorced from the nature of the other conspiracies discussed throughout this book as at first they might seem. In a way they metaphorically constellate the view that our world may be governed by personalities whose behaviour and lack of empathy often appears alien to the majority of humanity. But if the root of the New World Order *is* truly alien, does it really make much difference to what we have to deal with on a day-to-day basis?

For a majority of truthseekers, the NWO vision is the central hub of most conspiracy theories, pulling together many seemingly disparate theories into one unified pattern. Having alluded to it numerous times throughout these pages, we shall now more fully explore the New World Order's vital role in conspiracy folklore.

IN SUMMARY . . .

Extra-Terrestrial Conspiracies: Arguments Against

Talk of 'ancient astronauts' and alien bloodlines has been widely discredited by archaeologists, who have perfectly grounded explanations for glyphs, records and myths which are claimed to record alien activity – Too many sightings of UFOs are merely misreported mundane phenomena born from hysteria and cannot be taken seriously – Tales of the Roswell incident are based on nothing but hearsay and are even challenged within the ufological world – Claimed 'abductees' may simply be fantasists, psychologically traumatized individuals or unfortunates suffering from some kind of collective hallucination – The reptilian agenda is so patently ludicrous, based on the word of even more disturbed individuals or misguided 'wackos', that it is not even worth consideration – Bringing child abuse into the reptile theories is cheap sensationalism designed to give a false credibility to something already outrageous and offensive.

Extra-Terrestrial Conspiracies: Arguments For

So many ancient cultures record stories of beings from the heavens visiting our world and interbreeding with humankind that they cannot just be symbolic and must record something tangible that occurred long ago – Bloodlines are without doubt jealously maintained among monarchies and noble dynasties, something which could have more meaning than meets the eye – Reports of UFOs are made too often by qualified professionals and reliable military personnel to all be imagination or mundane phenomena, and it is clear that overt cover-ups are maintained – Whistleblowers from Roswell seem convinced that what crashed there was not human in origin and should therefore be taken seriously – Too many abductions are reported for all of them to be lies, and if some occur through a collective psychological experience, surely this is an important phenomenon worth study in itself? – The reptilian agenda sounds outlandish on the surface, but a significant number of people believe in it and it may embody at least some important truths – Child abuse is so serious that if it takes extra-terrestrial theories to bring it to the surface, then the association should not be entirely rejected.

CONCLUSION

The evidence that visitors or infiltrators from other worlds, both friendly and hostile, may be routinely interacting with us is not easy to discount completely in the light of the evidence. Information on UFOs and other unexplained activity *is* very clearly covered up – literally, in the case of documents which have been force-released under Freedom of Information requests, with much of their crucial content blacked out in the name of 'national security'.

For those unable to accept the more paranormal connotations of global agendas, however, perhaps there comes a point where it matters not whether the perpetrators of abuses and controls are human or extra-terrestrial. If the actions are the same, then the counteractions must be so too. Ultimately, the population of the world has to deal with its rulers, whatever their real form might be, and the assertions made about the kind of consciousness that might be driving the New World Order agenda remain relevant either way.

CHAPTER 8

NEW WORLD ORDER CONSPIRACIES

Behind virtually every conspiracy theory of modern times lies the thread that each component may serve a wider purpose: that of laying the foundations for a 'New World Order'. The belief that a shadowy ruling elite is gradually implementing a politically, economically and socially unified planet to its own blueprint by any means necessary has become a central pillar for most truthseekers, who see it as a plot to dominate through suppression of freewill and subjugation through fear. Derided by sceptics as the ultimate expression of misguided paranoia, the NWO theories have nonetheless made many people take a serious look at how their world is governed.

I) ONE WORLD GOVERNMENT

New Freedoms, Old Bonds

In 1913's *The New Freedom*, a collection of speeches and essays, future US president Woodrow Wilson wrote the following curious words:

> *Some of the biggest men in the United States, in the field of commerce and manufacture, are afraid of somebody, are afraid of something. They know that there is a power somewhere so organized, so subtle, so watchful, so interlocked, so complete, so pervasive, that they had better not speak above their breath when they speak in condemnation of it.*

While academics have other interpretations, this passage is seen by conspiracy theorists as an acknowledgement of the covert elite alluded to many times throughout the book you hold now. Perhaps ironically, Wilson's proposed 'new freedoms' wouldn't last long once he was in office, and he would go on to help found the Federal Reserve and a number of other institutions now traditionally eyed with suspicion. Nonetheless, this may be an overt reference to the all-pervading forces that are said to be putting the blocks into place for the New World Order. This staple of conspiracy doctrine is widely perceived as the underlying thread that binds together many of the plots, assassinations and political deceptions which keep researchers busy.

'New World Order' is not a term invented by truthseekers, but one widely employed by politicians envisaging a state of global unity, stability and prosperity. With certain countries policing it, of course. Such talk has inevitably become the target of intense scrutiny by those who fear that what the NWO is really moving towards is a 'one world government', a geopolitical super-entity to end all independent sovereignty and place great power into very few hands – hands that already have blood on them.

Origins of the New World Order

It could be argued that the Roman Empire and other ancient models (*see* chapter 2) were attempts to implement an enforced unification long ago. Run by a central body using a network of puppet provinces across the known world, it is a history surely not lost on today's planners. The genesis of the modern NWO, though, may have been seeded by the European secret societies of the 18th century. Those who believe occult agendas lie behind the project traditionally cite a short-lived Bavarian order, the Illuminati, as being one of its starting points. Although officially suppressed by 1785, the order is widely believed to have survived underground, infiltrating governments, financial systems and religious institutions, quietly implementing rule from the shadows through every group from Jesuits to Zionists. The many fictional representations of the Illuminati have probably blurred the reality and imbued whatever passes for them today with an unlikely omnipotence, but the name has stuck as a catch-all term for the perceived ruling elite.

The Illuminati, combined with higher degree Freemasons accused of contributing to the NWO agenda, are considered to have adopted (if as an affectation) their intrinsic mysticism and occult symbols from archaic cultures, predominantly Egyptian. Much of this knowledge is itself believed to have been preserved through the ages by the Rosicrucians, Knights Templar, Knights Hospitallers and other mysterious orders, jealously guarding important wisdoms for the exclusive use of the elite. This claimed influence from aeons past has fed directly into the extra-terrestrial bloodline theories discussed in chapter 7.

For all its supposed Bavarian influences, the true NWO blueprint is considered by scholars such as Terry Boardman to have begun with the ruling classes of Britain and America in the 19th century.[1] But the influence of secret societies on the founding of the USA in 1776 is widely believed to have been profound. It has led extremist Christians to accuse America of having been formed on Satanic principles with a view to fulfilling the biblical prophecy of the Antichrist, whose coming has supposedly been nurtured in the centuries since.

Conversely, others believe that underpinning US politics is a conviction that it is America's duty to help bring about the New Jerusalem spoken of in St John's Book of Revelation. Problematically, the prophecy cannot manifest (neither can the much-desired 'Rapture', where the devout hope for bodily ascension into heaven) until the cataclysmic battle of Armageddon has taken place. To some, this explains why world peace has not resulted from America's policies, if bringing about the apocalypse is its real agenda. Warlords convinced they are doing God's work (as George W Bush told Palestinian officials he was, when asked why he invaded Iraq in 2003) worry some people.[2] Certainly the influence of evangelical 'End-Time' preachers like Ted Haggard on presidents such as Bush has been powerful, and other leading politicians have shown similar leanings, with Hillary Clinton said to be a member of the End-Time movement 'The Family'. If certain citizens of America see themselves as being God's new 'chosen' people, taking on or sharing the mantle of the Israelites, this could be a factor in their country's proactive role in setting up a New World Order, using it as a vehicle for their own beliefs.

The other major founder of the NWO vision, Britain, may have similar convictions in its own 'chosen' status (with Tony Blair also having taken advice from Haggard). With many legends claiming that the Holy Grail was brought to British shores, it could be that biblical threads from long ago are once again being used for nationalistic ends. Perhaps it seemed natural that Britain, with its own burgeoning empire and as one of America's parent nations, should join forces with its progeny to reignite the dreams of an all-powerful political union to lead the world. By the 1870s, high-society links between Britain and America were blossoming, and the creation of the Pilgrim's Society in 1902, and the Round Table soon after, cemented bonds further, with an aim of uniting the moneyed classes across the Atlantic.

The Project Grows

Some reject the idea that religion underpins the NWO agenda, seeing it as a smokescreen for more earthly concerns of money, power and ideology. Indeed, when one of Britain's leading politicians Arthur Balfour wrote to America's President Theodore Roosevelt in 1909, esotericism seemed not to be in his mind, lobbying instead for what Terry Boardman aptly describes as:

> *A global Anglo-Saxon confederation that would police the world with the navies of the two countries and through their invincible domination bring eternal peace and prosperity.*

Over the years, similar proposals would follow Balfour's invitation, which some would say was duly, if quietly, implemented. Meanwhile, more public calls for a New World Order were made by leading academics such as H G Wells and Bertrand Russell, if founded in more Utopian ideals – that is, if Utopianism includes an open avocation of eugenics, which is another plan still feared to be lurking in the background.

However, if an Anglo-US alliance was the original core of the NWO, the two World Wars – considered by some to have been contrived for its very purpose (*see* pp. 68, 75) – saw a rebalancing of the driving forces behind it. After 1945, a blitzed and economically weak Britain was suddenly, to appearances at least, now a secondary force to the thriving USA. Along with a number of new countries aspiring to NWO ideals, America forged ahead with alliances and campaigns of its own, while the controversial 1948 foundation of the State of Israel refocused attention back onto the original promised land. However, the continued importance of institutions such as the financial City of London (effectively an independent state within the UK) and the British monarchy, reptilian or not, meant that certain powerful threads remained. Even now the USA goes out of its way to court British support for its actions, which is perhaps an odd thing for a superpower to do. It may be that the oft-mentioned 'special relationship' is more meaningful than at first appears, as Anunnaki bloodline researchers certainly believe.

Critics of NWO theories maintain that, by conspiracy theorists' own arguments, the contention that events such as the *Lusitania* sinking and the attack on Pearl Harbor had to be engineered to bring the USA into both World Wars (*see* chapter 3) is a sign of transatlantic division, not background union. Likewise, the traditional US unwillingness to comply with policies of the UN and NATO (founded in 1945 and 1949, respectively) that don't suit it could also be seen as evidence that America would resist absorption into a one world government. Conspiracy defenders, however, claim these 'reluctances' are part of the sleight of hand, feigning one stance but implementing another, albeit with a little petty hustling to ensure the New World Order continues to be led by one of its primary founders.

Likewise, sceptics who attack truthseekers' beliefs that the EU is one of the roads towards the Orwellian superstates allegedly envisaged by the NWO often do so on the basis that the euro has proved to be a contradictorily unstable currency. This is countered by the assertion that it was always *planned* to be unstable. Realizing that an overtly federal system would never be accepted in one go, it is surmised that the NWO drew the European nations into an initial stage of unification, well knowing that more federal 'protective' measures could gradually be brought in whenever the euro tottered. A new, far more centralized currency might be waiting in the wings when it is finally deemed necessary by the NWO.

Similarly, it is alleged that the dollar has been intentionally destabilized by contrived market crashes, as in 2008. These are said to be steps to pave the way for an eventual 'amero' currency to unite the USA, Canada and Mexico under a strict federal system, an idea scorned by cynics, yet widely believed. Certainly, fierce criticisms of the US financial system, with long-standing doubts over the very legality of the all-powerful Federal Reserve, continue to stir new conspiracy theories, particularly among right-wing activists. Some private US militias and survivalists have been arming themselves for the day they fear a final NWO coup will close the banks and bring martial law to the streets of America (*see* p. 246).

The Seats of Real Power

For all the speculation on the NWO, it may no longer matter which *countries* are involved, as real power already appears to be cross-border and lies far beyond the grasp of any democratic principles. It is asserted that the key decisions which affect our lives, in the West at least, were long ago farmed out to a series of high-level think tanks and quangos. These are attended by known politicians, royalty, media moguls and corporate leaders, but their meetings are closed to the public and the resulting resolutions passed down to selected parliaments to give an illusory sense of democracy.

The prime examples are usually said to include the Bilderberg Group, the Trilateral Commission, the Council on Foreign Relations, the World Economic Forum, the Tavistock Institute, the Club of Rome and other bodies. Meanwhile, mainstream 'initiatives' such as Common Purpose provide courses for both government and corporate employees to instil seemingly federal ideals into the community. Sceptics claim conspiracy theorists accord too much power to such entities, but both their existence and tendrils of influence cannot be denied, and even journalists have begun to question their morality – which says something. The Bilderbergers (named after the Netherlands hotel which hosted their first meeting in 1954) have come under particular fire. Their meetings are no longer even secret, although the full content of their discussions remains undisclosed. Yet most news agencies fail to report them, suggesting more media complicity in what amounts to a monumental cover-up. Just one exception, Charlie Skelton of the *Guardian* newspaper, did expose the importance of the Bilderbergers in June 2011:

> *In 2008, when George Osborne, as a private individual, hangs out in Corfu with a Russian oligarch (Oleg Deripaska), Nat Rothschild and Peter Mandelson, the British press has a field day with the gossip . . . But in 2011, when Osborne spends four days, in his official role as chancellor of the exchequer, cooped up with Lord Mandelson, a Russian oligarch (Alexei Mordashov), and the former vice-chairman of Rothschild Europe (Franco Bernabè) – along with the president of the World Bank, the president of the European Central Bank, the Greek minister of finance, the Queen of Spain, the chairman of Royal Dutch Shell, the governor of the Belgium National Bank, the chairman of Goldman Sachs International, and the chief executive of Marks and Spencer . . . this isn't news . . . I beg to differ.*[3]

As this unusually frank media report demonstrates, those who attend these groups are some of the very names generally cited (and often reviled) as being behind the New World Order. Representatives from the Rothschild and Rockefeller dynasties, along with leading bankers and industrialists, often rub shoulders with the prominent diplomats and politicians of the day, as seen from the above reference to Britain's George Osborne and Lord Mandelson. Their interest in fomenting centralized initiatives is not denied, with David Rockefeller (one-time chairman of the Council on Foreign Relations and founder of the Trilateral Commission) openly declaring in his 2002 *Memoirs*:

> *Some even believe we are part of a secret cabal working against the best interests of the United States, characterizing*

my family and me as 'internationalists' and of conspiring with others around the world to build a more integrated global political and economic structure – one world, if you will. If that's the charge, I stand guilty, and I am proud of it.

The problem is that while players like Rockefeller may promote such intentions as wise philanthropy, truthseekers see darker agendas. A case can be made, of course, that some form of international unity is more likely to bring peace and prosperity than fragmentation, but agreeing *which* form is another matter. The best of intentions can play into the hands of regimes more concerned with their own interests than humankind's. Trust has to be earned by those who would be seen to work for the greater good, and trust in the current aspirants, particularly those from financial institutions, is in very short supply these days.

Since the 2008 financial crash that took homes, pensions and reputations, the banking world is now seen as little more than a criminal cabal by most everyday observers – as one which uses hedge funds, derivatives, extortionate interest and irresponsible speculation to fuel executive jamborees at the expense of real lives. When problems arise, governments bail out banks with public money, but bonuses continue even as those at the bottom suffer deprivation. Lobbyists from the financial and corporate world, arms manufacturers and media divisions clearly come first in the priorities of ministers who supposedly represent the people; thus public resentment builds. As Alessio Rastani, an independent financial trader, put it so succinctly on the BBC News channel:

The governments don't rule the world. Goldman Sachs rules the world.[4]

Entrusting some of these same people with the future of civilization does not look too promising to much of the population. Conspiracy theories are bound to thrive in such an environment and those in the ivory towers might like to think about coming down to sniff the air from time to time before feeling hurt by public mistrust.

Puppet Leaders

Although awareness of the NWO and the specific groups which wield real power may be largely limited to conspiracy realms, most people sense that the politicians they vote for – if they now bother to vote at all – make little difference to the decisions ultimately made. There is an inherent understanding, certainly among the British populace, that everyday needs are largely neglected, and that the scandals which regularly lift lids on the reality of power are merely the tip of a very large iceberg. People know that governments are under the sway of anonymous suits in the background and that elections are sometimes influenced by nefarious means. This was keenly illustrated by the thorny resolution to the neck-and-neck stand-off between Al Gore and George W Bush in the 2000 US presidential election. The voting was openly seen to be riddled with irregularities (Bush was finally awarded victory with fewer 'popular' votes than Gore after a highly controversial recount in Florida), yet it seemed not to sink in that this was perhaps just a rare public revelation of normal procedure.

To be up for election at all, especially in the USA, would seem to require large amounts of money and membership of the right secret society, with orders such as Phi Beta Kappa and Skull and Bones being particularly dominant among candidates. The latter is firmly embedded at Yale University, Connecticut, and has produced several presidents and other politicians, including various members of the Bush dynasty, not least George W Bush.[5] Interestingly, only two presidents, Abraham Lincoln and John F Kennedy, are said not to have belonged to any Masonic order – and both were assassinated. Truthseekers consider that all US presidents are pre-selected by NWO influences for their own ends, with any nominal differences between candidates manipulated to resolution by tweaks of party funding, slanted voting procedures or the odd dirty trick.

Barack Obama very publicly fell victim to a conspiracy theory when he was attacked by rival political factions for being unable to prove he was born in an American state – a legal requirement for a president. Although some of the motivation may have been racist or at least anti-Muslim (Obama's father was Muslim), the challenges went very mainstream. For all the claims that Obama's birth was registered in Hawaii, no full certificate was forthcoming before his election in November 2008. An image of a short-form certificate published that June failed to quell the controversy, and loud suspicions were voiced that Obama was, in fact, born in Kenya, and thus a false president. More embarrassment ensued when he fumbled his presidential vows and had to retake them the next day to 'avoid conspiracy theories'. When an electronic facsimile of Obama's long-form birth certificate was finally produced in April 2011, discrepancies involving software 'image layers' convinced many that the certificate was a desktop-published fake. Defenders claimed the anomalies might have resulted from the scanning process, but the presence of any anomalies was undeniably awkward and the fact that it had taken several years to comply with the simple request of publishing a certificate did his reputation no favours.

For all the apparent welcome that Obama was given as a refreshing change to the circus of the George W Bush years, few truthseekers shed tears for him, pointing out that in his first year of office alone he had ordered more drone attacks and assassinations of Middle Eastern 'rebel leaders' than Bush had managed in two terms. Obama's signing away of further citizen rights and his broken promise to close the Guantánamo prison compound soon damaged his supposedly 'softer' credentials, serving as yet more evidence that leaders are carefully chosen to prevent real change, not create it. Through the NWO lens, the face, personality or skin colour of puppet kings matter not when the same board of governors remain in charge. Things seem to work much the same in most nations.

Hardcore theorists therefore dismissed the flurry around Obama's birth certificate as being nothing more than a distraction, with the cosmetic differences between Republicans and Democrats meaning little in the grander scheme. They saw greater reasons for apprehension over the individual sponsors who had groomed Obama for power for some years, specifically Zbigniew Brzezinski, the well-known political 'hawk'. Brzezinski worked closely with presidents Jimmy Carter and George Bush Senior and stands accused of effectively creating al-Qaeda by financing the Afghan Mujahideen 'freedom fighters' to fight the Soviet occupation in the 1980s. Many of these became the Taliban before turning against the West in the guise of al-Qaeda – which some say may have been the idea all along.

Asia and the Middle East

In 1998 Zbigniew Brzezinski authored a book entitled *The Grand Chessboard*, considered an appropriate title by truthseekers who believe we are all seen as little more than pieces on it.[6] The chessboard that concerned Brzezinski was central Asia and the Middle East, and in his chapters he outlined hopes and fears for the region from the US perspective of needing stronger influence there if America's superpower status was not to be threatened and crucial access to considerable oil and gas reserves was to be maintained. The book has something in common with the 'Rebuilding America's Defenses' document (see p. 192), which appeared to presage 9/11, expressing resonant sentiments about seeing off foreign threats while capitalizing on the perception of an outside threat of some kind. Brzezinski writes:

As America becomes an increasingly multi-cultural society, it may find it more difficult to fashion a consensus on foreign policy issues, except in the circumstance of a truly massive and widely perceived direct external threat.

That the very al-Qaeda Brzezinski was responsible for soon became the kind of external threat postulated, courtesy of the official 9/11 story, looks suspicious to some. Brzezinski may not have been involved with 9/11 (and he outwardly opposed the 2003 invasion of Iraq), but it seems his words were certainly taken to heart. Ongoing actions which affect the fates of many of the countries Brzezinski cited as being necessary targets for increased American influence (Afghanistan, Iran, Pakistan, Turkmenistan, Uzbekistan, etc.) appear to echo many of his recommendations, especially as regards fears over oil pipelines benefiting China and Russia, which seem – outwardly at least – not to be major players in the current NWO. The dramatic situations in Egypt, Iraq, Libya and Syria in the years following the 2010–11 'Arab uprisings' and the continuing tensions with Israel are generally considered as part of the same pattern and alleged by conspiracy theorists to have fallen prey to Western manipulation as part of the unfolding NWO plan.

In fact, David Icke has long said that a contrived war between China and the West is part of the projected itinerary, whether that nation knows it or not. It is also hard to imagine Islamic states giving in easily to a unification with infidels, so any NWO intentions over unwilling countries would presumably have to begin with an enforced subjugation. A manufactured third world war might be a necessary step towards this. The hypothesis that a new 'world religion' might be imposed afterwards to smooth over some of the inevitable lingering spiritual divisions has also been pondered. Some believe the suspected Judaeo-Christian End-Time policies (*see* p. 228) are merely being used by that lobby to gain support before they are eventually overthrown for the true mandate, providing further fuel for the Antichrist theories.

The al-Qaeda Myth?

Brzezinski's vision for the world in *The Grand Chessboard* concerns some, because it appears to echo some of the key elements in George Orwell's novel *Nineteen Eighty-Four*. This has alerted truthseekers to the totalitarian tendencies which may lie behind the entire NWO project.

In *Nineteen Eighty-Four*, the rigidly oppressed world of Oceania (essentially a unified America and Europe) is kept in daily fear of Immanuel Goldstein, an intangible terrorist threat invented or hugely exaggerated by the Big Brother society. Meanwhile, an endless war in Eastasia keeps the wheels of arms and industry turning and the minds of the people distracted from making trouble. Many conspiracy theorists believe this is precisely the situation we have today, with al-Qaeda as Goldstein, and the War on Terror and the Middle Eastern campaigns substituting for the Eastasia conflict.

This is not to say that al-Qaeda does not exist; indeed, as we have seen, it may have been specifically brought into being to provide an outside threat. But its real influence has been much-questioned outside the media.[7] Many suspect that what is probably a loose network of tin-pot militias has been blown out of all proportion to replace conveniently the number one enemy lost when the Soviet Union fell. Fired into prominence by the NWO cornerstone of 9/11, if what is now generically referred to as al-Qaeda *has* become a genuine threat, this may have come about through a self-fulfilling process of inflationary propaganda.

Rule by Fear

In the Orwellian view, then, following the initial masterstroke of 9/11, a general heightened fear of terrorism and attack from foreign forces has constituted a kind of further slow-motion false-flag tool to manufacture our consent for the steps of the NWO's ever-gathering pace towards a regime of implacable control (*see* below) and the centralization of power.

What other techniques might also be used? We have already seen in chapter 7 how some believe that if exaggerated threats from the likes of al-Qaeda are not enough, we might even find ourselves being herded together in the face of a false alien invasion. Fear of outside forces, whether they be foreign invaders, ethnic minorities, climate changes, terrorists or extra-terrestrials, has always been used to control the human race. The policy of divide and rule still holds sway, and the New World Order is seen as its ultimate expression.

But if fear is the key to all this, might the occult be the ultimate lock?

II) OCCULT INFLUENCES

Dystopia or Utopia?

Critics argue that a one world government would be unmanage-able and even undesirable to those whose ambitions are to dominate. They contend that concerns about genuine liberty issues have been warped into ludicrous paranoia, manifested as a fantasy view of the New World Order which takes theorists down cul-de-sacs and draws energy away from serious political activism that could make a real difference. Truthseekers may even be deliberately entangled into such thinking, serious investigations neutered by the time spent imagining occult ceremonies and chasing birth certificates – things easy to marginalize as fanaticism.

But this accusation is simply a conspiracy theory of another kind. Defenders point to Orwell's model of global government as being more than workable in the non-fiction world. If any tyrants were simply thinking of using the NWO for their own ends and didn't really want unification, they might eventually be rooted out by the genuinely Utopian forces at the top, who may themselves simply be using today's warmongers as fall guys to be dispensed with when the real vision nears completion. It is also countered that freedom in society *is* increasingly being taken away by different means, rendering scrutiny of whatever one conceives the NWO to be as vital in any case. It can also be observed that occult symbolism *does* seem to be important to the ones who govern.

Occult Tendencies

Those who have accused the NWO of attempting to instate a 'Fourth Reich' see this term as being rather more than metaphorical. While some view the huge influence of Germany on the European Union as being a new kind of domination, albeit financial, others believe the fascination of its former Nazi rulers with ancient symbolism (e.g. the swastika) and their alleged dabbling with the occult has been passed on to other enclaves.

Secret societies have undoubtedly been a major influence on the development of modern civilization, and their fondness for Egyptian symbolism has given rise to the erection of pyramids and needles in numerous cities, full of numerological and mystical significance. Some conspiracy theorists see them as being there to make a statement, or for actual use as occult talismans to focus psychic power. It cannot be denied that pyramids, in particular, remain in vogue, with glass versions having been constructed at the Parisian Louvre gallery in recent decades, and another built atop Canary Wharf Tower in the middle of Britain's major financial centre, alongside many other examples. These are seen as subliminal proclamations of who is really in charge, whatever their esoteric effects, and they are widely considered to be aligned with other 'temples' and monuments, with streets laid out in symbolic configurations to create vast grids of power.

The Eye of Providence

The symbol of the all-seeing eye above a pyramid on the reverse of the Great Seal of the United States, famously emblazoned onto the dollar bill, has become the most prominent occult target of conspiracy theorists. Officially named the 'Eye of Providence', it is derived from the Egyptian 'Eye of Horus' and is claimed to represent a benevolent God watching over his people. Buddhists, Hindus and Christians have adapted the symbol in centuries past, but its most overt use has come from Masonic orders. As such, it is often seen as a sinister eye; the higher degrees of Freemasonry watching lesser humans beneath, represented by the lower levels of the pyramid. The capstone separated from the main body of the structure is seen to indicate their superiority, and the accompanying words *Novus Ordo Seclorum*, which translate as 'New Order of the Ages', is close enough to 'New World Order' to create discomfort.

Historians challenge the ominous interpretations, pointing out that the symbol was specifically designed for the Great Seal in 1776 (the 13 steps of the pyramids representing the then 13 states of America) and that Freemasonry only adopted it in 1797. Nevertheless, this symbol and the many others undeniably treated as sacred by secret societies do seem to creep into government stationery, banknotes and buildings across the world. They must therefore carry some meaningful weight, or why use them? Are they just in-jokes from canny architects and designers? Some suggested this when the 2012 London Olympics logo appeared to spell the word 'Zion' when slightly rearranged, the Olympic stadium was surrounded by perfectly proportioned Eye of Providence-style lighting gantries and the masses were jollied up by bizarre mascots with single eyes over pyramidal bodies. Or do such examples make a grimmer statement about who is really in charge and what their intentions are for humanity?

The difficulty here is that for all the establishment's protestations of innocence, time and again word leaks out of strange behaviour in high places that authorities don't generally like to advertise. And sometimes the word is true.

The Bohemian Grove Ceremony

When information began to circulate about the existence of a cult where world leaders worshipped giant stone owls and sacrificed children, it was at first laughed away or believed only by those on the furthest fringes. But when secret intruders, and then journalists, started claiming they actually had witnessed the owl ceremony, the mood changed. So began the controversy over the Bohemian Club, one of the most discussed secret societies believed to be at the centre of the New World Order.

Founded in 1872, this California-based group was initially, as its name suggests, centred around artistic types (it still includes major celebrities, actors and musicians). But soon it began to attract a different kind of membership, drawing in politicians, heads of corporations and other glitterati to become one of the prime orders of its kind. Rapidly wealthy, the Bohemian Club bought up local woodland and christened it 'Bohemian Grove', and, as the years went by, its annual gathering there began to attract attendances of thousands from around the world. Anyone with a high political profile has reportedly shown up there at one point or another, with members said to include figures such as Kissinger, Nixon, Bushes Junior and Senior, Cheney, Blair and many other presidents and prime ministers. Women, naturally, are excluded, raising questions about what the likes of Margaret Thatcher, Hillary Clinton and Angela Merkel might do instead to 'bond', which is one of the primary functions, it would seem, of the Bohemian Club.

But then women might not feel too comfortable in such an environment, with infiltrators having spoken of the bawdy, childish atmosphere of crassness and sexual innuendo that pervades the campfires at the annual conventions. All of which might sound like a harmless playground for male buffoonery (as indeed actor Harry Shearer has claimed it is), were it not for some of the murkier occult tinges to the accompanying ceremonies.

Long rumoured, but only fully exposed when journalist Jon Ronson (*see* p. 220) broke into Bohemian Grove, accompanied by conspiracy theorist Alex Jones in 2000, the grand opening of each yearly gathering embodies a ceremony called the 'Cremation of Care'. The secret videoing reveals a melodramatic pageant comprising a narrated performance in which players dress in robes and parade with flaming torches on an altar placed in front of what may indeed be a giant stone owl. Some have claimed it represents the pagan god Moloch, a bull-headed creature, but other exposed Bohemian Club imagery unambiguously incorporates images of owls, signifying 'knowledge'. The rumours of live sacrifices appear to be derived from the fact that during the ceremony an *effigy* of a child is brought across a lake by boat – an effigy which is then burned on the altar as triumphant (and apparently prerecorded) music plays. With this, the participants cremate the 'dull cares' of the world's affairs and are thus free to cavort without conscience and get on with the rude jokes and fireside banter.

To some observers of the smuggled footage, now freely available on the internet, it appears to be somewhat overblown but essentially innocuous entertainment (as Ronson more or less concluded in the resultant episode of his Channel 4 series and subsequent book). Others, such as Jones, believe the whole thing is uncomfortably wrong and constitutes further evidence of occult, if not Satanic, agendas behind the NWO.[8] Certainly, the ceremony employs occult elements that have traditionally been seen as rather more than innocuous, and the use of child imagery for the 'sacrifice' seems at best in dubious taste.

Perhaps what matters here is the fact that the Bohemian Grove ceremony, whether light entertainment or dangerous ritual, is kept hidden from the masses who fund the lifestyles of those attending. Members of the order ask for our trust in weighty matters that affect lives around the world, yet don't seem to think we have a right to know they dress in robes and watch fake children being sacrificed to owls in their spare time. Conspiracy or no conspiracy, this is not fair. Although the Bohemian Club's existence isn't denied (indeed, Bill Clinton once famously joked about it at a press conference), it isn't discussed either, a policy emphasized by the statue in Bohemian Grove of the club's patron saint, St John of Nepomuk, standing with a finger held to his lips.

Mainstream sources tend coyly, and perhaps foolishly, to dismiss the order as a 'gentlemen's club'. But if that is all it is, why should membership be considered so important to so many influential names involved in very serious matters? It is, for example, said that the first meeting to discuss the development of the atomic bomb took place at Bohemian Grove, perhaps sensibly beyond the eyes of the world but also far outside any semblance of a democratic process.

The Cremation of Curiosity

Once again, with such disdainful attitudes to those whose 'dull cares' they are supposed to shoulder, it must be asked if it is any wonder that minds with even a tiny inkling into the underground activities of the ruling classes no longer respect what they are told by them? If truthseekers begin to believe in almost anything after a while, from blood-drinking monarchs to fake alien invasions, can they really be blamed for doing so in the face of such deception? Or, as intimated above, is the very plan to lead the few who dare to ask questions down avenues the NWO authorities know will never be treated seriously by the mainstream media, even though, or perhaps *because*, the media's own envoys also regularly stand beneath the owl? For all the openly available footage and published accounts of the Cremation of Care ceremony, thousands of protestors surrounding Bohemian Grove each year, demanding their right to know what's going on, generally fail to materialize. All the New World Order gets is the likes of Alex Jones with a bullhorn. Curiosity has been well bred out of the population.

As we saw in the previous chapter, if the worst conspiracy nightmares are true it may be that the real human sacrifices go on behind doors closed even to some of those attending Bohemian Grove. A further worry, however, is that persons who might sacrifice a child, or even just the effigy of a child, might also be quite capable of sacrificing *everyone* but the chosen, in due course.

III) SOCIAL CONTROL AND DEPOPULATION

A World of Control

How might the New World Order go about ensuring that no one stands in the way of a path to totalitarianism? Orwell's fictional vision envisaged control of information, blanket surveillance and the deconstruction of language as the tools of oppression, while another dystopian tale, Aldous Huxley's 1932 novel *Brave New World*, imagined chemical containment, sexual distraction and depopulation policies. Hardline conspiracy theorists believe that *all* such approaches are being used today, in plain sight, and argue that if most people have been conditioned to have no interest in something even as bizarre as the Bohemian Grove rituals, they would be unlikely to notice these going on either.

Since 9/11, fundamental freedoms once taken for granted have unquestionably been eroded. Some of this has occurred through overt legislation (as with the Patriot Act – *see* p. 193), but most have slipped under the radar as changes to small print. Relaxed rules for those at the top of the pyramid now effectively enable unlimited 'emergency powers' to be introduced at any moment of the leaders' choosing, as with Executive Directive 51, quietly brought in under George W Bush in 2007. The 'Operation Garden Plot' and 'Rex 84' procedures had already established grounds to implement full military control in a designated crisis, but, meshed with the new regulations, the path to US martial law and detention of any designated disruptive influences has become even easier, presenting rather too many opportunities for another 'Reichstag fire' (*see* pp. 72–5).

Truthseekers say that calculated amounts of civil unrest (but not all-out revolt) are sometimes purposely stirred or allowed, to enable the gradual removal of human rights, as was suspected in Britain when days of mass rioting broke out in 2011, aided enormously by the police inexplicably failing to act decisively on the first night.[9] Previous chapters have highlighted the core belief that even terrorist atrocities may be staged when the fear dial needs turning up, 9/11 being the ultimate piece of theatre. In this view, mass shootings in colleges and shopping malls may also be set-ups, with hypnosis and brainwashing techniques used to control the perpetrators. Some saw the Norwegian massacres of 2011, in which racist fanatic Anders Behring Breivik killed 77 people in bomb and shooting attacks, as a possible example. Such tragic events add to the calls for more social controls and bring the terror just a little closer to home. They also generate calls for gun controls, to the dismay of certain right-wing militias, who see this as disarming their ability to combat the coming NWO coup.

Those anticipating mass detentions claim that FEMA (the US Federal Emergency and Management Agency) has built a network of vast internment camps across the USA. Although some of these 'camps' have turned out to have mundane explanations, a number of enigmatic compounds *have* been built and currently stand empty. When pressed for an explanation, authorities have implied they are simply standby holding pens for 'immigrants'.

The suspicious prefer to see them as NWO concentration camps, being prepared for a final solution of a new kind.

Because society does seem to be kept under constant fear of outside threats, the alleged cleverness of the control agenda is that measures brought in to 'protect' us are often welcomed. They are even begged for by the less inquisitive members of society, compliantly alarmed by the continual media squall over terrorism, crime, rioters, immigrants, global warming, swine flu, bird flu and foreign nations with deadly weapons. Duly rewarded by responsive authorities, we have given our collective consent to a forest of surveillance cameras (more in Britain than in any other country in the world), full body scanners and other intrusive procedures at airports, extended police and military powers, heavy environmental taxes, Kafkaesque bureaucracy and 'health and safety' restrictions that go far beyond the call of duty. In the same breath we also give the green light for questionable wars and invasions.

Truthseekers complain that freedom of speech is additionally contained by induced social prejudices which see people policing each other's thoughts and actions through simple fear of ridicule or judgement, thus maintaining the status quo. Where social engineering fails to quieten louder individuals, we have seen how they appear to be removed through strange accidents, bizarre suicides or other means (*see* chapter 5). Yet the subjugation of expression is not the same as the erasure of feelings, and privately people will often share opinions somewhat different to those they might convey in public; what the mainstream presents is not necessarily the world that most of us inhabit.

The Future of Surveillance

In addition to hovering spy satellites, drones and CCTV surveillance – which we are told prevents crime, despite statistical studies that show otherwise[10] – the last few years have seen a cascade of increasing legislation which enables governments to pry into electronic communications. Every email we write and every website we visit is now, in theory, logged and monitored. This raises crucial liberty issues. Not only does it treat everyone as a potential criminal, but a future regime with a bent towards fascism, NWO or otherwise, could easily misuse this information. The coming programme to install microchips into the human race is likely to strengthen this unfolding pattern of open season on private communication and free movement. Already, platoons, police forces and pets are being microchipped with ID tags, and the process is likely to widen and take over if there is no serious resistance.

In time, an electronic ID will regulate our every movement and financial transaction, raising the question of what will occur if those considered as subversives are targeted by authorities, however unfairly. Their implants could be switched off at a stroke, creating outcasts unable to interact socially – a persuasive bargaining tool. Those who welcome such developments seem to forget that angels do not run the world and that they themselves could easily fall foul of such a system. Some conspiracy theorists go further, anticipating the potential for microchips, with who knows what embedded within them, to be employed as mind-control devices. Evangelical Christians believe they would also fulfil the biblical prophecy of the restrictive 'Mark of the Beast' (Revelation 13:16–17), without which no one is able to 'buy or sell', raising further fears that the NWO heralds the arrival of the Antichrist.

With the surge in technology that will before long enable brains to interact directly with computers (early experiments are already proving successful), the benefits of being permanently hooked to social networking and the internet, screened directly into the mind's eye, may frighten older generations, but will be highly desirable to those brought up on technological convenience. Concerns that a whole civilization would be very controllable by such means do hold some currency.

The problem presented by a 'global brain', of which the internet is the genesis, is that it will be very vulnerable to authoritarian influence. Already, much of society has unwittingly ensured that the word of Wikipedia, for instance, has become the modern orthodoxy on almost everything, yet there are many concerns about its contributors' recurring biases, particularly against alternative thinking. When everyone drinks exclusively from the same pool, the risk of contamination becomes a major issue. Internet censorship, held back for years before the authorities realized a genie had been let out of its bottle, is already creeping in via the back door. The continued freedom of this vital tool that has transformed the effectiveness of many kinds of activism should not be taken for granted.

A number of remarkably draconian internet restrictions are slowly being introduced under the veil of 'copyright protection' issues. At the same time, planned introductions of improved systems promise faster and more versatile interaction, but may also come with new licensing laws and package deals which could see independent voices that have thrived since the internet's inception quietly marginalized into silence. No provocative banning will be required; it could simply happen by a process of gradualism and social conditioning that once again polices itself, saving the NWO the trouble of direct intervention.

Social Programming

The ubiquity of propaganda has already been explored in these pages; it has been used since time began, to rally political support or instil certain mindsets into the populace. Some truthseekers consider that such programming goes much further, however, and believe we are intentionally kept in usefully lethargic indifference by social, chemical and psychological means. The claimed techniques used to weaken the glue that once held society together include the breakdown of the family unit, the erosion of community bonds, the loss of spiritual values, the denigration of language, the flooding of young minds with music that stimulates the basic instincts but doesn't inspire, and increased exposure to fast and highly sexualized or violent images. The 'dumbing down' of radio and television, and the magazine shelves groaning with little but celebrity gossip and salacious conjecture, are all thought to be part of the psychological warfare being deployed against us. Beyond the content, even the medium has come under question, with some pointing to the proliferation of microwave masts and wireless broadband as being another line of attack. Their potentially negative health effects have been raised even in mainstream circles.

By all these methods, while burdened with debt and increasing pressures, it is said we are blasted into a state of apathetic distraction which fosters not revolution, but a sinking into a kind of underlying depression whereby we are prevented from accessing our higher and more proactive natures. Thus the New World Order keeps the masses away from the gates of Bohemian Grove or Bilderberg meetings, while the few troublesome characters aspiring to awareness can be easily dealt with by ridicule or, when really necessary, simple removal.

New Age interpretations see this as a lowering of the collective energy vibration, holding humankind back from making the evolutionary leaps that psychics and ancient prophecies (*see* p. 27) have been promising for centuries. Indeed, it has been proposed that one of the reasons for the acceleration of the control agenda in recent decades is that there is a real awareness of the potential of a cosmic disaster to strike some time soon. This could manifest as a huge solar flare, asteroid strike, galactic superwave, geophysical upheaval or the return of the Anunnaki and the planet Nibiru. It is likely that those with an interest in the occult and ancient symbolism would be very aware of prophecies from previous times and modern astrological predictions. The wide belief that the period following 21 December 2012 would be one of global transformation will surely not have been lost on the New World Order's more mystically inclined overseers. With their plans coming along nicely, there would be great wariness about the possibility of such a disruptive development, and the idea of the human race energetically transforming beyond the NWO's oppressive grip would be of concern. Perhaps this is why they might be taking no chances and are therefore assailing our mental and physical well-being.

Chemical Compromising

Where social programming fails, chemical suppressants might do the job. There is great anxiety, in and outside conspiracy circles, about the amount of unpalatable additives and preservatives that go into most mass-marketed foods. Many are known to produce dangerous side effects, particularly hyperactivity in children – who are then diagnosed as having ADHD (attention deficit hyperactivity disorder) and prescribed drugs such as Ritalin as a suppressant, creating a vicious chemical circle. An incredible one in ten American children are said to be taking Ritalin, while a similar percentage of adults are on anti-depressants, often needlessly. To the cynical, all this is evidence of an active NWO incentive to dope us into submission – on top of the 'recreational' street drugs that ruin whole communities. There is a broad conspiracy consensus that the so-called 'war on drugs' is a sham and that the real mandate is to keep their flow going, as the total failure to destroy opium crops in Afghanistan after a decade of Western occupation might suggest. Why? Because people busy tripping, fighting, robbing or pimping each other are unlikely to be storming parliaments any time soon or trying to change the world.

As a civilization we do seem extremely keen to guzzle down pharmaceuticals of one kind or another, as was demonstrated when swine flu was promoted as the next great plague in 2009.

Sales of the anti-flu drug Tamiflu duly soared, despite its inability to combat that particular strain of the virus. This led some to wonder if the whole thing was a cash-in from its manufacturers, Roche Laboratories, or an attempt to flood the world's bloodstreams with pathogens that might be triggered by a killer virus at some later stage (*see below*). The news that former US Secretary of Defense Donald Rumsfeld (who presided over the 9/11 crisis) was involved with the companies that patented Tamiflu was not taken lightly by the conspiracy community. That Rumsfeld was also one of those behind the ubiquitous artificial sweetener aspartame, much-criticized on alleged safety issues, hardly helped. The grip of the big pharmaceutical companies is seen as another important component of the ultimate plan.

Fluoridation of water and vaccination programmes are also staple areas of confrontation from truthseekers, who see them as further evidence of chemical suppression offered as health miracles, questioning both their safety and effectiveness. Medical experts who attack such heresy as irresponsible scaremongering are often quick in turn to scorn other paths – including alternative medicine, homeopathy and high-dose vitamins – as being the real killers, claiming they lead to people avoiding the allopathic treatments they really need in favour of 'quack' science. Bodies such as the Codex Alimentarius, the food safety body of the World Health Organization (WHO), are tightening regulation of the alternative health industry year by year, to the point where conspiracy theorists believe it will eventually disappear completely under these ill-founded and restrictive policies.

A few small voices who fight the Codex rules, such as the National Health Federation and Alliance for Natural Health, highlight the irony that the WHO seems perfectly content for everyone to down aspartame and Tamiflu, and supports pharmaceuticals which are known to cause hundreds of thousands of deaths every year, yet it attacks natural products that can statistically be shown to have barely hurt anyone.

To the gloomiest theorists, it is almost as if the powers-that-be would be happier if we all dropped down dead . . .

Depopulation Policies?

One of the curious traits of the New World Order is its apparent propensity for subtly letting people know what its intentions are, as if it can't help its own boasts or somehow feeds off the speculation around it. There are two very overt examples of this which, if taken at face value, appear to declare an audacious and worrying plan to wipe out over 90 per cent of the global population. Over-population is a genuine anxiety of the times, but is the NWO planning a drastic remedy?

In 1980, a perplexing monument was erected at Elbert County, Georgia, USA, describing itself as the 'Georgia Guidestones'. Based on plans submitted under the alias 'R C Christian', its sponsors have never revealed themselves. The four Stonehenge-like slabs, arranged around a central pillar and capstone to form astronomical alignments, are engraved with platitudes in several languages, laying down the rules for an idealized Utopian world. The monument appears designed to survive the ages so that its advice might one day become the new ancient wisdom for some post-apocalyptic world. Amidst some more sensible suggestions sit ones which have caused the stones to become targets of anti-NWO vandalism over the years: they shockingly advocate the need for eugenics, a 'world court' and, most disturbingly, directly recommend that the global population be kept under 500,000,000. Given that this is just a tenth of the current numbers, there is understandable concern about what is planned for the billions of people seen as surplus to requirements.

Although the Guidestones could be dismissed as the mere folly of a wealthy eccentric, supplementary information provided anonymously in the official booklet accurately duplicates the aspirations of some of the world's best-known academics (such as the aforementioned Wells and Russell), who openly expressed similar thoughts in their works.

Other US artworks also appear to petition for eugenics and depopulation, such as the striking but overtly miserable murals at Denver International Airport, Colorado, which opened in 1995. These unaccountably depict epic scenes of death and destruction, one of which includes an image of a boy in Bavarian costume – the originating country of the Illuminati – beating swords into ploughshares. This has been seen as a blatant representation of the Illuminati implementing the Fourth Reich under cover of civilian activities. The dead babies and youths in coffins depicted in the murals remind conspiracy theorists of the NWO's fondness for effigies of sacrificed children. While art critics may disagree, there are really few excuses that can be made for exposing holiday travellers to these horrors unless an important subliminal point is being made. The pale horse with evil glowing eyes outside the airport appears to cement the message.[11] The Cheyenne Mountain Directorate, a NORAD facility (*see* p. 178), is situated in the Denver region and designated an emergency government shelter. It has been presumed to be a future NWO stronghold in the event of trouble kicking off – hence, perhaps, the message of the local murals.

The more one looks for evidence of authorities and figureheads praising the merits of a vastly depopulated world, the more one finds it, with references made by everyone from Bill Gates and Prince Philip (no surprise to reptilian agenda aficionados) to doctors and professors. Agenda 21, a UN initiative begun in 1992 to help achieve environmental 'sustainability', has also been accused of harbouring Malthusian population-control policies and supporting the enforced annexation of private land. The problem is, when qualified people start to think about something, they can be prone to planning it.

If there is even a spark of truth to all this, how might such a reduction of the population be achieved? Some believe a killer virus could be released at an appointed time (seeing AIDS as a deliberate and discriminatory trial run), while others, as we have seen, claim that the first stage of weakening has already begun, through slow chemical infiltration. A large number of people, however, think that the very air we breathe is also being poisoned.

The Chemtrails Mystery

Imagine waking up each morning, afraid for one's life *because there are strange clouds criss-crossing the sky.* This is the reality for an increasing number of truthseekers as they fearfully peer up from their windows, believing that aeroplanes are now deliberately strafing the human race with dangerous chemicals. If not mass hysteria, is the claimed surge of unusual vapour trails in recent years evidence of an ongoing depopulation programme, or is a huge climate engineering experiment in process?

The 'chemtrails' phenomenon is one of the fastest-growing seams of conspiracy alarm, as evidenced by a daily procession of morose web posts displaying the latest 'violated' skies across the globe. It hits hard because the idea that covert forces are contaminating the air itself means there can be no escape.

Aeroplane contrails have long been a feature in our skies, forming as water vapour and gases condense into icy cloud in sub-zero temperatures. War-time photos from the 1940s display them, and people living under international flight paths have for years become used to the wispy bands of thin cloud. The conspiracy world, however, contends that something has been added to these multiplying trails in recent times, in a plot so all-encompassing that the majority of the population simply hasn't noticed, blinded by its very enormity. These new embellishments reputedly last longer and spread wider than standard contrails, laying gauzy veils across the sky, allegedly creating illness and lethargy among those below. Commercial air liners have supposedly been adapted or duped into dropping the deadly toxins, but military activity is also claimed to have been observed.

Despite intense fascination with what truthseekers have christened chemtrails, this particular debate is muddied by some awkward areas of uncertainty. Bloggers' assertions that 'spraying' is taking place on any given day tend to make the assumption that most of the vapour trails we see are abnormal, but this indiscriminating approach alienates scientific minds who might otherwise show curiosity towards an area surely worth a little further study. The notion that a deliberate contamination or adjustment of the atmosphere is taking place has, naturally, been met with blanket dismissal by authorities and scientific bodies, which state that so-called chemtrails are quite normal, if sometimes unusual, meteorological interactions, deemed to be anomalous through a simple lack of professional knowledge. Likewise, aviation experts claim that the complex grids of crossing lines can be explained by all manner of flight path and altitude decisions made to accommodate varying weather conditions, which is why trails appear on some days and not others.

Problematically, unlike, say, 9/11 – where a significant number of mainstream professionals have broken ranks to challenge what they see as clear breaches of the laws of physics in the official story – the supporting evidence of the chemtrail theorists has so far relied mostly on unqualified research (with the exception of ex-neurosurgeon Dr Russell Blaylock, who believes harmful 'nano-aluminum' may be present in the trails) or the testimony of unnamed or biased witnesses. Further fragmentation is caused by uncertainty over what the motivation of a 'spraying' programme might be. The assumptions tend to fall into one of the three following categories:

- Chemtrails as a depopulation strategy – in this view, the sprays, although plainly not intended as instant killers, are introducing harmful toxins into our bodily systems and the general environment, weakening our resistance to viruses that might be released later. (The chosen NWO survivors would presumably be immunized against all stages of the programme or hidden in their shelters.)

- Chemtrails as climate engineering – alternatively, chemtrails may be an extension of HAARP-type projects (*see* below), introducing elements into the atmosphere necessary for the easier manipulation of weather and climate.

- Chemtrails as solar protection – the now mainstream concern about the potential of the Sun to throw out a dangerous solar flare some time soon (*see* p. 28) has led to speculation that the chemtrails might in some way be designed to fortify our atmosphere against it. The secrecy surrounding the spraying might therefore be justified in the name of not wanting to create widespread panic.

Quite *how* such a massive scheme could be implemented without generating more concerned whistleblowers is unknown. Substantial chemical vats would have to be stored somewhere, with or without cabin crews' knowledge, together with the equipment necessary to release the contents. Would not several technicians have come forward by now to call attention to such strange extra cargoes? The internet does play host to occasional anonymous testimonies from frightened staff claiming the chemicals are loaded from what outwardly appear to be sewage tankers, but they have never been authenticated. It has been argued that military vehicles would be more likely to be used for this, yet most of the witnessed 'sprayers' appear to be commercial flights. If such accounts are *not* conjured by the imaginations of theorists keen to validate their beliefs, then clearly they give genuine cause for disquiet.

The internet is full of accounts of detrimental health effects in areas below what are perceived as chemtrail flight paths, many complainants describing respiratory ailments, flu-like symptoms, headaches, nausea and a general depletion of energy, particularly on days when trails appear to linger, spreading out to weaken the sunlight. Authorities across the globe have received numerous calls for investigations from alleged chemtrail sufferers, but requests have fallen on deaf ears. Media investigations have sporadically taken up the call, but with few results. Tests carried out by the Louisiana-based television station KSLA News 12, for instance, at first suggested unusually high quantities of radioactive barium in local water supplies below claimed chemtrail areas, but later analysis showed the figures were, in fact, perfectly normal.

A key difficulty here is that of proving a correlation between events 30,000 feet or more above with those on the ground, neither open sky nor miles of land below providing very useful calibration points. This becomes an issue with the stories of web-like 'angel hair' sometimes seen floating in the air on days of chemtrail activity. Given the several possible natural sources of such fine threads (webs, etc.), and with no conclusive physical analysis available, convincing connections have yet to be demonstrated.

Other objections to the notion of a 'spraying' programme have revolved around the sheer scale and cost that such a monumental task would entail. To cover the entire planet with a network of chemical layers, though not impossible, would surely be one of the most ambitious projects ever mounted by humankind, absolutely requiring (unlike 9/11 or the Moon landings) the participation of thousands of operatives. Is it feasible that such a vast enterprise could be undertaken without a convincing exposure occurring? Yet some believe so, and consider it one of the biggest cover-ups of our times.

The major superpowers, especially China and the USA, *have* openly experimented with weather control and cloud seeding with silver iodide to encourage rainfall. Between 1962 and 1983, for example, Project Stormfury was an ongoing US attempt to alter the behaviour of tropical cyclones with the iodide technique, using planes flying into the hearts of storms. There have been many other publicized schemes, so the concept of spraying something into the air to create atmospheric change is not without precedent. It has been argued that there must be easier ways to kill a population, hence the atmospheric augmentation theories, but high-altitude tampering clearly *does* occur from time to time, and the idea that some long-term effect, planned or unplanned, might result from this cannot be entirely discounted. It is likely that many of the perceived chemtrails are merely normal phenomena – but perhaps not all.

HAARP: The Ultimate Weapon?

The suggestion that chemtrails are being used to fortify the atmosphere in some way has led to another theory – that the chemical changes enable a more versatile use of the HAARP facility: the High Frequency Active Auroral Research Program. This military research project was set up in Alaska in 1993, with its Ionospheric Research Instrument (IRI) – 180 antennas covering 33 acres – coming online in 2007. Although primarily a US initiative, other HAARP facilities have been built around the world since with the cooperation of a number of different countries.

The scientific bodies that run HAARP claim it is a simple military communications exercise, 'exciting' the ionosphere with directed electromagnetic pulses to help extend signals to submarines and aid underground scanning, among other capabilities. But the conspiracy world has almost unanimously declared it the deadliest weapon of the NWO.[12] The high-minded intentions given in official information on HAARP seem not to reflect those buried in the patent applications, which make clear a more lurid military vision, auguring future opportunities for both weather and mind control. Such a tool would plainly prove invaluable, as one USAF document on the potential for electromagnetic weapons makes very clear, promoting the advantages of producing 'mild to severe physiological disruption or perceptual distortion or disorientation . . . The ability of individuals to function could be degraded to such a point that they would be combat ineffective.'

The intentions of the authorities thus revealed, and with the complex science of HAARP barely understood by the public, the project has almost inevitably been held responsible for triggering everything from general malaise to earthquakes, volcanoes, tsunamis and hurricanes, and indeed any unexplained event. 'Weather wars' have long been postulated. The scientists at HAARP claim to despair at such misrepresentation, protesting that their work is openly accountable and that the facilities are regularly opened to the public. But truthseekers are having none of it. To them, HAARP is the weapon of choice, the ultimate bargaining chip of the New World Order, directed at foreign enemies and internal enemies of the state alike. We must submit or be pulsed into ineffectiveness anyhow; surrender or be vanquished by sudden 'natural disasters'.

All this might be laughed away as the final paranoia to end all paranoia – were it not for a telling quote from that father of today's political landscape, Zbigniew Brzezinski, in *The Grand Chessboard*:

Political strategists are tempted to exploit research on the brain and human behavior. Geophysicist Gordon J. F. MacDonald, a specialist in problems of warfare, says accurately-timed, artificially-excited electronic strokes could lead to a pattern of oscillations that produce relatively high power levels over certain regions of the earth . . . in this way one could develop a system that would seriously impair the brain performance of very large populations in selected regions over an extended period.

If geophysical weapons do still remain on the drawing board, then, mind control *is* clearly seen as within reach. That suggests that even if HAARP is not the tool this time around, something very like it probably is, or will be soon, for it is human nature to find a way to create what it imagines, even if what it imagines are nightmares.

An Invincible Force?

And so the New World Order theories have developed into a vision of an invincible global regime with the power of life and death over us all. But is it accorded too much power, by the very people who feel they are its victims? Perhaps so, as our epilogue will explore.

IN SUMMARY...

New World Order Conspiracies: Arguments Against

The Illuminati is a long-disbanded order with no influence in the world today – Countries working in close alliances do not indicate a desire for global unification – Claimed occult tendencies are nothing more than the novel affectations of 'gentlemen's clubs' – The so-called 'control agenda' is simply necessary social guidance blown out of proportion – The idea that populations are being assailed by mind control and chemical poisoning is crazed paranoia – How would it benefit authorities to kill the very people they need to make any kind of society work?

New World Order Conspiracies: Arguments For

Secret societies are clearly a powerful part of Western civilization, Illuminati or no Illuminati – Intentions to create a world of political unification under centralized control have been openly stated by people in positions to realize them – Occult references are too overt in ceremonies and symbolism for them to mean nothing – Increasing global controls on freedom extend far beyond necessity – The technology to affect human minds is being developed, and therefore the will to use it probably lies not far behind – A NWO with a desire to depopulate has surely worked out precisely what it needs to create a tailor-made replacement society.

CONCLUSION: A CRUCIAL CHOICE

It has come to this, then. The centuries of deception, evasiveness and the many abuses of command have taken their toll on the collective psyche. If any lesson can be drawn from the resulting growth of belief that a New World Order run by a remote, self-interested and amoral elite wants not only control but also to see most of us dead, it is that the establishment's own behaviour has brought it about, whichever way it is looked at.

One of two things must be the case: either some or all of the truthseekers' views are true, in which case the population needs to stand up as one *now* and urgently challenge the powers-that-be before they go too far with a programme that has consequences even they may not have banked on. Or the now-ingrained mistrust held towards authorities who have hardly shown themselves to be caring or reliable in a number of areas has become so extreme that a giant collective fantasy has been created which threatens the psychological well-being of society – in which case the targets of the fantasists urgently need to go out of their way to show a more compassionate, truthful understanding of how this has happened.

Ridicule and marginalization has not removed the growing doubts, and without a new and radiant integrity in the halls of power, free from arrogance and the need to suppress, conspiracy theories will continue to thrive and fester.

There is a choice to be made here as to which way we go. The question is, will anyone take it while there is still time to make a difference?

EPILOGUE

A world of control, of oppression, of habitual deception. Is this really how things are, or simply human nature massively distorted through a dark lens? The truth probably lies somewhere in the middle.

Most conspiracy theories are centred around the concept of someone *out there* doing something to *us*. Life can undeniably work this way but, at the same time, those 'out there' are merely reflections of what is buried deep in the collective psyche, projected onto egos that enact our shadow sides for us. The uncomfortable reality is that any kind of deceptive elite playing chess with civilization can only do so because we allow it.

If all those with the slightest awareness of the games being played were to put aside their nominal differences, stand together and galvanize the rest of the population to create a society free from the perceived faults of the present authorities, those who front those authorities would doubtless adjust accordingly. They are what they currently are because of people's tendencies to give away responsibility. We too often neglect our own capacity to co-create the environment around us. The solution surely begins by accepting responsibility in our own lives. Behaviour we hate to see in the halls of power must also be changed in our living rooms and offices; despised cultures of untruthfulness must be remedied with personal authenticity. This is where transformation begins.

It may be that truthseekers accord 'the elite' too much influence. Its ambassadors share the same planet and breathe the same air as us (probably), and appear equally prone to mistakes and factional in-fighting. They might only succeed as often as they do because we wrongly presume omnipotence on their part and fail to act in balance. If a solution to the undoubted transgressions of leadership is to be found, we must take back the power that is rightfully ours. Apathy, fostered or innate, is not yet wholly triumphant, and we must never allow it to be so.

Becoming informed has traditionally been seen as a path to empowerment, and never has so much free information been available as it is today through the internet. We should take advantage of this gift before those feeling threatened succeed in retracting it. Knowing where to start with conspiracies can admittedly be daunting. One useful technique is to begin by seeking the view of an overtly mainstream website such as Wikipedia. This is notoriously unreliable on alternative subjects, but is what the everyday world tends to read – something always vital to know. If this fails to debunk a viewpoint entirely, it is usually a sign of a theory with substance. The next step is to find a site giving the hardline conspiracy view, before tracking down a sceptical or middle-ground source (if one can be found). From this procedure, a flavour of the overall truth can sometimes emerge. If not, explorers will at least be better aware of the different areas of confusion.

An immersion in conspiracy consciousness can be overwhelming, but discernment and balance is the key. Falling into paranoia and depression will not help humankind, nor will aggressively demanding that others listen to 'the truth' make them do so. Polarization is one of the very problems. Only reasoned presentation of evidence, moderate tones and compassionate understanding of the public's conditioned outward reluctance to risk ridicule will really make a difference. The polls, after all, show that, deep down, some of the concerns felt by conspiracy theorists are shared by more people than we are told.

So we can dismiss all conspiracies as entertaining fantasies if we wish, and take the risk of running 'free' and easy while walls of control are built up quietly around us, or we can sit in terror, fretting that the New World Order is bugging our homes and zapping our minds. Neither approach would seem wholly sensible. Yet if the worst-case scenario is true, is not giving into fear the very aim of those who would control us? Better, perhaps, to throw off the anxieties, enjoy the good things we have, and simply do what we can to make a difference.

There are many grounds for optimism. By their nature, conspiracy theories are not the happiest of contemplations, but if forewarned is forearmed, spreading awareness of worst-case scenarios might stand a chance of preventing them from ever happening. Speculation can also call attention to areas that benefit from being illuminated in any case. Together with the application of positive, constructive thinking, a difference can surely be made. Indeed, the growing science of consciousness research strongly suggests that when many minds focus together, particularly with positive intent, the energetic environment around us subtly but detectably changes. It may be that exploiting that mechanism, combining it with assured social action and the encouragement of a new, more honest political system will take our civilization on to brighter horizons. There is much work to be done, but a conscious admission of what has been wrong so far is a beginning at least.

The claimed intentions of the ruling elite, misguided though their means may be, are probably right in a few respects. Cooperation is more likely to bring peace and prosperity than division, and some sensible, ordered approach to the future would seem to be wise, founded in reason rather than reflex prejudice. But forcing such a world into being through the moribund processes of militaristic might and policing of expression, denying the legitimacy of those with other beliefs, is unlikely to create lasting success. Only by embracing the realities of diversity and hearing the voices of everyone can there ever be a real new world order.

NOTES AND REFERENCES

Numerous websites, tomes and journals, in addition to my own research, were used to formulate the overview in this book. In an age where information on almost any subject can be accessed by a simple internet search, most quotes and references can easily be traced, so I have only included notes here of things which were of specific help, which give information unavailable from mainstream channels, or which indicate further resources of particular interest.

Introduction

1 **British Humanist Association conspiracy conference:** This took place in London on 25 September 2011. An interesting review of the event, by Ben Emlyn-Jones of Hospital Porters Against the New World Order, can be found at: http://hpanwo.blogspot.com/2011/09/british-humanist-association-conspiracy.html

1. What Is Conspiracy Theory?

1 **US government on conspiracy theories:** This quote is taken from 'Conspiracy Theories and Misinformation', US Department of

State's Bureau of International Information Programs, June 2010, and can be found at: http://www.america.gov/conspiracy_theories. html

2 **The Manchurian Candidate:** The phrase 'Manchurian candidate', oft-used in conspiracy circles, generally refers to the 1962 film directed by John Frankenheimer and starring Frank Sinatra, based on the 1959 novel by Richard Condon, in which a Korean War veteran is brainwashed by the Soviets to assassinate a US presidential candidate. Many believe just such mind-control techniques are used today. The film (remade to lesser effect in 2004) is discussed well at: http://www.filmsite.org/manc.html

3 **Paul McCartney's facial structure:** Andrew Spooner Jr carries out a compelling forensic comparison between the 'real' pre-1966 McCartney and the later allegedly 'replaced' one at: http://james-paul-mccartney.150m.com/fc6.html

4 **McCartney theories:** Andru J Reeve's book *Turn Me On, Dead Man: The Beatles and the 'Paul-Is-Dead' Hoax* (AuthorHouse, 2004) is a good compilation of the McCartney controversies.

5 **The Skeptics' Dictionary:** This debunking website can be found at: www.skepdic.com

6 **NASA warnings on solar activity:** NASA's June 2010 meeting with the world's top-level scientists and politicians to alert them to the dangers of high solar activity is reported at: http://www.telegraph. co.uk/science/space/7819201/Nasa-warns-solar-flares-from-huge-space-storm-will-cause-devastation.html

   The administrator of NASA, Charles F Bolden, posted up a surprisingly frank video to his employees on 10 June 2011, concerning 'emergency preparedness' in which he urged them to be more ready for an unspecified 'emergency'. Some think this might refer to coming solar flares. The clip can be seen at: http:// www.youtube.com/watch?v=ESWp7SHD05s

7 **Noam Chomsky defends free speech:** A statement on the imprisonment of Holocaust questioner Vincent Reynouard, described by Chomsky as 'inconsistent with the basic principles of a free society as these have been understood since the Enlightenment', and a subsequent interesting discussion thread can be found at: http://amkon.net/showthread.php/29354-Noam-Effin-Chomsky-defends-imprisoned-Holocaust-denier

8 **George W Bush on implicit support for terrorism:** The notorious quote 'Either you are with us, or you are with the terrorists' was made at the President's address to a joint session of Congress on 20 September 2001. The full text of this speech can be found at: http://yc2.net/speech.htm

'Let us never tolerate outrageous conspiracy theories' was spoken in Bush's speech to the United Nations on 10 November 2001, and can be watched at: http://www.youtube.com/watch?v=6K5M0xtxQVQ

2. Historical Conspiracies

1 **Gunpowder Plot explosion:** ITV's programme *The Gunpowder Plot: Exploding the Legend*, presented by Richard Hammond, was first broadcast on 1 November 2005. The relevant clip of the 'Houses of Parliament' being blown up can be seen at: http://www.youtube.com/watch?v=eFytcsA9mU8&feature=related

3. False-Flag Conspiracies

1 **Churchill and *Lusitania*:** Quotes from Winston Churchill's letter in which he appears to wish for a ship to 'get into trouble' are included in a useful middle-ground discussion which contentiously claims that there may have been as much 'foul-up' as conspiracy, available at: http://www.rmslusitania.info/controversies/conspiracy-or-foul-up

2 **Vice Admiral Beatty on Pearl Harbor:** This quote is included and discussed with other interesting evidence at: http://www.lewrockwell.com/kreca/kreca6.1.1.html

3 **New independent inquiry into USS *Liberty*:** The quotes about President Johnson's seeming desire to see *Liberty* sunk were reported in the 'Findings of the Independent Commission of Inquiry into the Israeli Attack on USS Liberty, the Recall of Military Rescue Support Aircraft while the Ship was Under Attack, and the Subsequent Cover-Up by the United States Government' (Capitol Hill, Washington DC, 22 October 2003).

4. Political Conspiracies

1 **Nixon's call to Apollo 11:** The full text of this historic phone message can be found at: http://en.wikisource.org/wiki/ Richard_Nixon%27s_Phone_Call_to_the_Moon

2 **John F Kennedy's Moon mission speech:** The full text of this influential speech can be found at: http://history1900s.about.com/ od/1960s/a/jfkmoon.htm

3 **Lunar hoax opinion polls:** US Gallup figures from 1999 are quoted in a *Time* article at: http://www.time.com/time/specials/ packages/article/0,28804,1860871_1860876_1860992,00.html. The UK's *Engineering and Technology* 2009 poll is discussed at: http:// abcnews.go.com/Technology/Apollo11MoonLanding/story? id=8104410#.TzuGeq7ubyC

4 **Apollo 16 astronaut 'dangles':** This fascinating footage can be seen at: http://www.youtube.com/watch?v=7ciStUEZK-Y&feature=related

5 **Lunar rover footage:** A good sequence demonstrating the debated effects of 'Moon soil' being spun from the rover wheels can be seen at: http://www.youtube.com/watch?v=sRSpntQ-VtY

6 **BBC response to 'Libya' footage error:** Attempts have been made to pin down the BBC further on how video of the Indian demonstration could possibly have been broadcast as being from Libya, to no avail. A telling exchange of correspondence between truthseeker Mike Raddie and BBC spokesmen is required reading and can be found at: http://www.mathaba.net/news/?x=628673?rss

7 **Tony Blair's closeness to Rupert Murdoch:** A good report on the news that Blair had quietly become godfather to Murdoch's daughter can be found at: http://www.telegraph.co.uk/news/ politics/tony-blair/8740530/Tony-Blair-is-godfather-to-Rupert-Murdochs-daughter.html

8 **David Cameron's closeness to Murdoch and News International:** The revelation that Cameron or his cabinet met with News International staff over 100 times in a year is discussed at: http://www. dailymail.co.uk/news/article-2019009/Rupert-Murdochs-chiefs-met-ministers-100-times-Osborne-Gove-list.html. Cameron's own personal meetings with Murdoch are highlighted at: http:// www.independent.co.uk/news/uk/politics/revealed-camerons-26-meetings-in-15-months-with-murdoch-chiefs-2314550.html

5. Assassination Conspiracies

1 **Lee Harvey Oswald:** A good source of information on Oswald, and also his killer, Jack Ruby, with several embedded film sequences, is available at: http://www.spartacus.schoolnet.co.uk/JFKoswald.htm

2 **Mysterious deaths of JFK witnesses:** A worrying list detailing the strange demises of 21 people with potentially important information on the shooting of John F Kennedy can be found at: http://www.cassiopaea.org/cass/jfkdeaths.htm

3 **Polls on Diana:** UK opinion polls claiming that 90 per cent of British people believe Diana was murdered are referred to in discussions about the white Fiat driver at: http://www.express.co.uk/posts/view/17797/Diana-Killed-by-Fiat-driver-says-police-chief, and at many other sources, although links to the original poll seem to be elusive. The more concrete one-in-three result, conducted by Sky News, is broken down and discussed at: http://news.sky.com/story/543024/one-in-three-backs-diana-conspiracy
    Less dramatic but still significant US opinion polls on Diana are reported at: http://www.cbsnews.com/2100-500160_162-613064.html

4 **MI6 plot to kill Colonel Gaddafi:** Ex-MI5 staff member David Shayler was sent to prison in 2002 for exposing an official MI6 plot to kill Libya's former leader, along with revelations of secret Western deals made with Osama bin Laden. Details of these and other claims by Shayler and his then partner Annie Machon are widely available, including in Machon's book *Spies, Lies and Whistleblowers: MI5, MI6 and the Shayler Affair* (Book Guild Ltd, 2005), but a useful summation is available at: http://www.propagandamatrix.com/shayler_gate.html

5 **Camilla Parker-Bowles's car crash:** A resource on this little-reported but potentially important incident can be found at: http://www.cremationofcare.com/the_nwo_di_camillacrash_june1997.htm

6 **David Kelly timeline:** A useful compact timeline on the David Kelly affair is featured at: http://www.telegraph.co.uk/news/politics/8566789/David-Kelly-timeline.html

7 **Polls on David Kelly:** UK opinion polls showing that only one in five citizens believe Kelly committed suicide are discussed at: http://www.dailymail.co.uk/news/article-1303356/Dr-David-Kelly-Just-believes-suicide.html

8 **Mystery helicopter at Kelly death site:** This curious episode is exposed at: http://www.dailymail.co.uk/news/article-1386967/ Mystery-helicopter-landed-scene-Dr-Kellys-death-body-found. html

9 **Kelly's sister's testimony:** Sarah Pape's denial that Kelly was suicidal is covered at: http://www.guardian.co.uk/politics/2003/ sep/03/huttonkeyplayers.huttonreport2

10 **Norman Baker, MP, on Kelly:** Before the publication of his book *The Strange Death of David Kelly* (Methuen, 2007), Baker's findings were usefully précised in the *Mail on Sunday* in his article 'I Believe David Kelly Did Not Commit Suicide – And I Will Prove It', 23 July 2006, pp. 51–4.

11 **Mysterious deaths of Clinton contacts:** A list detailing the shocking number of people with connections to Bill and Hillary Clinton who have died in strange circumstances, a phenomenon described as 'Arkansas Sudden Death Syndrome', can be found at http://www.prorev.com/WWDEATH.HTM

6. 9/11 and Related Conspiracies

1 **Tenth anniversary 9/11 polls:** The high levels of doubt expressed ten years on about the veracity of the official version of 9/11 were significant. The British ICM poll, conducted on behalf of Reinvestigate 9/11, found that 'of those who expressed an opinion 37 per cent agreed that rogue elements in the American intelligence services may have made a decision prior to 9/11 to allow a terrorist attack to take place'. In France, the doubt was more specific, a HEC poll showing 'that 58% have doubts compared to 31% who accept the official story. Half suspect that US authorities deliberately allowed the attacks to take place while a third suspect they were implicated in the execution of 9/11.' The polls are discussed at: http://www.911truth.org/article.php?story=20110909085546680

2 **Resources on 9/11 truth:** The internet is crammed with 9/11 truth websites, but a good starting point is provided at: http://www. ae911truth.org/links.php. In terms of books, readers are probably best advised to start by searching out some of the ten or so meticulously researched titles by David Ray Griffin (which began with *The New Pearl Harbor* (Olive Branch Press, 2004)). Griffin's level-headed analyses quickly leave most people convinced that

the true facts of 9/11 have been obfuscated, whatever the ultimate reality.

3 **Flight 77's cockpit doors:** A report on the claim that the cockpit doors were never opened during Flight 77's final flight is available at: http://www.sodahead.com/united-states/flight-77-cockpit-door-never-opened-during-911-hijack/question-821961

4 **Nano-thermate in WTC dust?:** Gregg Roberts summarizes the scientific analyses of thermitic particles in the dust around the fallen towers at: http://www.ae911truth.org/info/57

5 **David Ray Griffin on WTC 7:** Griffin's book, *The Mysterious Collapse of World Trade Center 7: Why the Final Official Report About 9/11 is Unscientific and False* (Interlink Publishing Group, 2009), is a devastating and essential critique of the official line on WTC 7.

6 **Mysterious deaths of 9/11 witnesses:** A video examining the unusual pattern of deaths among key people present at the 9/11 events can be watched at: http://911blogger.com/news/2010-03-03/mysterious-deaths-911-witnesses

7 **Benazir Bhutto on bin Laden:** Bhutto's comments that bin Laden had died some years before his claimed shooting by the US are reported at: http://english.pravda.ru/world/asia/15-01-2008/103426-benazir_bhutto_osama-0

8 **Jan Blomgren on Moscow bombings:** Blomgren's prediction of Kremlin-sponsored false-flag attacks was published in *Svenska Dagbladet*, 6 June 1999.

9 **Polish air crash cover-ups?:** The shocking claim that Russian troops shot surviving passengers from the Smolensk air disaster is discussed at: http://www.dailymail.co.uk/news/article-1278175/Footage-Polish-air-crash-emerges-claiming-Russian-speaking-men-shooting-survivors.html. Claims of discrepancies in the post-crash autopsies are reported at: http://news.yahoo.com/poland-exhumes-2010-plane-crash-victims-075014615.html

10 **Helicopter crashes:** The investigation into the Chinook accident that took the lives of 25 Northern Ireland counter-terrorist staff is covered at: http://www.guardian.co.uk/uk/2010/jan/04/software-link-1994-chinook-crash

The news that several of the US Navy SEALs who allegedly shot bin Laden were killed themselves in a later helicopter crash is

documented at: http://www.dailymail.co.uk/news/article-2023123/
Special-forces-helicopter-shot-Afghanistan-mission-rescue-
fellow-Navy-SEALs.html

11 **7/7 train explosions:** The quoted survivor testimony describing a
blast looking as if it had come from *beneath* the train is from the
Cambridge Evening News, as discussed at: http://julyseventh.co.uk/
july-7-mind-the-gaps-part-1.html

7. Extra-Terrestrial Conspiracies

1 **Cydonia/Avebury alignments:** The claimed geometrical simi-
larities of the Martian 'monuments' with the Avebury complex
in Wiltshire, UK, are demonstrated in the Appendix to David P
Myers and David S Percy's book, *Two-Thirds* (Aulis Publishers,
1993, revised 1999).

2 **Artificial structures on Mars and the Moon:** Analyses of orbital
pictures allegedly showing unnatural features on Mars can be
found at: http://metaresearch.org/solar%20system/cydonia/asom/
artifact_html/default.htm

    Claimed artefacts on the Moon are examined at: http://
paranormal.about.com/od/lunaranomalies/ig/Strange-Things
-on-the-Moon

3 **Phobos probe incident:** The loss of *Phobos 2* and its last transmitted
images are discussed at: http://www.bibliotecapleyades.net/marte/
marte_phobos05.htm

4 **Nephilim quote from Genesis:** This translation is from *The New
American Standard Bible*.

5 **Airship 'abduction':** The story of the first attempted alien
abduction is featured under the 'Mystery Airships' entry at: http://
en.wikipedia.org/wiki/Mystery_airship

6 **The Fatima apparitions:** The events at Fatima are examined in
more detail in this author's own book *The Truth Agenda: Making
Sense of Unexplained Mysteries, Global Cover-ups and Prophecies
for our Times* (Vital Signs Publishing, 2009, revised 2011), chapter
4, 'Miracles and Prophecies'. Information on *The Truth Agenda* can
be found at: www.truthagenda.org

7 **The Disclosure Project:** The official website for Steven Greer's
ongoing attempt to expose government knowledge on UFOs is
available at: www.disclosureproject.org

8 **Reagan's statement at *ET* screening:** Ronald Reagan's curious exclamation about the truth of ET contact, made in front of Steven Spielberg, is discussed at: http://www.openminds.tv/ spielberg-confirms-reagan-705

9 **JFK instructs CIA to share UFO information:** Kennedy's (reportedly resented) order to let the Soviets have access to US records on both UFOs and space technology is examined at: http://www.examiner.com/article/kennedy-linked-us-ussr-space -missions-with-classified-ufo-files

10 **Reagan's statement on 'alien threats':** President Reagan's speech to the UN was made on 21 September 1987. This and several similar references made by Reagan are compiled, with embedded videos, at: http://www.bibliotecapleyades.net/exopolitica/exopolitics_reagan 03.htm

11 **Colonel Robert Salas's nuclear base/UFO claim:** Salas records this experience in his book *Faded Giant* (BookSurge Publishing, 2005), while a full account of this remarkable, but not unique, incident is also available at: http://www.nicap.org/malmstrom67-3.htm

12 **David Icke on the reptilian agenda:** Icke's first book to detail this issue was *Children of the Matrix: How an Interdimensional Race Has Controlled the Planet for Thousands of Years – and Still Does* (First Impression, 2001, later republished by Bridge of Love). Many of his subsequent books expand on the theme. General information on Icke can be found at: www.davidicke.com

13 **Reptilian agenda summation:** A useful summary of the reptilian issues is unwittingly provided by a piece presumably intended as satire, but which accurately encompasses the overall beliefs, available at: http://uncyclopedia.wikia.com/wiki/ Reptilian_Agenda

14 **Jon Ronson on David Icke:** Ronson's experiences with David Icke are described in his bestselling book *Them: Adventures with Extremists* (Simon & Schuster, 2002), while the relevant episode ('David Icke, the Lizards and the Jews') of his Channel 4 series *The Secret Rulers of the World* was broadcast in May 2001 and can be watched at: http://video.google.co.uk/ videoplay?docid=-2912878405399014351

15 **The Hollie Greig case:** The ongoing campaign to bring Hollie Greig's alleged abuses to proper attention can be kept up with at: www.holliedemandsjustice.org

8. New World Order Conspiracies

1 **Origins of the New World Order:** Terry Boardman's book *Mapping the Millennium: Behind the Plans of the New World Order* (Steiner Books, 1999) is an intelligent look at the geopolitical seeds of the NWO. A potted take on his views is available in Boardman's 2008 article 'The Roots of the New World Order', which can be found at: http://www.monju32.webspace.virginmedia.com/NWO14.htm

2 **George W Bush and God:** In 2005, Palestinian Foreign Minister Nabil Shaath reported that when asked why he invaded Iraq, George W Bush claimed that divine inspiration was behind the action, as reported at: http://www.guardian.co.uk/world/2005/oct/07/iraq.usa

   Shaath and Palestinian Prime Minister Abu Mazen describe their meeting with President Bush in the BBC series *Elusive Peace: Israel and the Arabs*, broadcast on BBC2 in October 2005, details of which can be found at: http://news.bbc.co.uk/1/hi/programmes/elusive_peace/4268184.stm

3 **The *Guardian* on the Bilderbergers:** Charlie Skelton's telling article 'Bilderberg 2011: The Tipping Point' can be read at: http://www.guardian.co.uk/world/2011/jun/16/bilderberg-2011-tipping-point

4 **'Goldman Sachs rules the world':** This shockingly honest interview with trader Alessio Rastani was broadcast on the BBC News channel on 26 September 2011 and can be seen at: http://www.youtube.com/watch?v=kpg76VjTa58

5 **Presidents and secret societies:** An at-a-glance list of former US presidents and the secret societies they belonged to is available at: http://www.directoryupdate.net/presidents.html

6 **The Grand Chessboard:** Zbigniew Brzezinski's influential book was published in 1998 by Basic Books. Many useful and revealing quotes from it are compiled at: http://www.wanttoknow.info/brzezinskigrandchessboard

7 **Al-Qaeda myths:** Adam Curtis's acclaimed 2004 BBC2 series *The Power of Nightmares* was one of the only media sources to tackle the myths around al-Qaeda, but it quickly vanished from repeat schedules, was never shown in the USA, and never released on DVD, which may indicate something of its importance. Unofficial uploads can be found on the internet, and information on the series can be found at: http://en.wikipedia.org/wiki/The_Power_of_Nightmares

8 **Bohemian Grove:** Jon Ronson's aforementioned bestseller *Them: Adventures with Extremists* (Simon & Schuster, 2002) discusses his experience of the Cremation of Care ceremony, while the footage was included in an episode ('The Satanic Shadowy Elite?') of his Channel 4 series *The Secret Rulers of the World*, broadcast April–May 2001.

Alex Jones's much darker take on what he sees as a Satanic ritual can be seen in his documentary *Dark Secrets: Inside Bohemian Grove* (available from Jones's site www.infowars.com), an extract from which can be viewed at: http://www.youtube.com/watch?v=r5dHhvpHIjM

9 **2011 British riots:** Many truthseekers ventured the observation that the nihilistic mass rioting across the UK (sparked initially by a police shooting) between 6 and 10 August 2011 seemed to have been deliberately allowed. This view was bravely voiced, to audience derision, by a woman on BBC1's *Question Time* the week after, which can be watched at: http://www.youtube.com/watch?v=Sbe95TEFOSQ

10 **Surveillance statistics:** Several studies have shown that while it may help to identify offenders, crime is not actually prevented by CCTV, with numbers of incidents sometimes having *increased* in areas where cameras have been brought in, as a 2009 *ABC News* article by Marcus Baram discusses at: http://www.abcnews.go.com/US/Story?id=3360287&page=1

11 **The Georgia Guidestones and Denver murals:** The Vigilant Citizen website examines these with some interesting observations at http://vigilantcitizen.com/sinistersites/sinister-sites-the-georgia-guidestones and http://vigilantcitizen.com/sinistersites/sinister-sites-the-denver-international-airport

12 **HAARP:** One of the best-known conspiracy takes on HAARP is the book *Angels Don't Play this HAARP: Advances in Tesla Technology* by Dr Nick Begich and Jeane Manning (Earthpulse Press, 1997). The authors also sum up their work at: www.haarp.net

CONSPIRACY
RESOURCES

There are, of course, countless websites and books available on conspiracies. This list is just a very quick starter guide, highlighting some of the best-known, immediately useful or related sources of information, in alphabetical order. Please note that their inclusion here is not necessarily an endorsement of the views or beliefs expressed in them.

Websites

www.ae911truth.org (Architects & Engineers for 9/11 Truth)
www.anhcampaign.org (Alliance for Natural Health – alternative health)
www.astrologicalinsights.co.uk (Helen Sewell – astrology)
www.aulis.com (lunar hoax theories)
www.coasttocoastam.com (George Noory – web radio station, general conspiracy)
www.cropcircleconnector.com (crop circles)
www.davidicke.com (David Icke – general conspiracy)
www.diagnosis2012.co.uk (2012 prophecies)
www.earthfiles.com (UFOs, general alternative/conspiracy)
www.emtvonline.co.uk (Edge Media TV channel – general alternative/conspiracy)
www.fluoridation.com (fluoridation issues)
www.glastonburysymposium.co.uk (conference – general alternative/conspiracy)
www.ianrcrane.com (Ian R Crane – general conspiracy)

www.infowars.com (Alex Jones – general conspiracy)
http://julyseventh.co.uk (7/7 London bombings)
www.nexusmagazine.com (*Nexus Magazine* – general alternative/
   conspiracy)
http://noosphere.princeton.edu (Global Consciousness Project)
www.prisonplanet.com (more Alex Jones – general conspiracy)
www.redicecreations.com (Red Ice web radio station – general
   alternative/conspiracy)
www.rense.com (Jeff Rense – general conspiracy)
www.stj911.com (Scholars for 9/11 Truth & Justice)
www.thenhf.com (National Health Federation – alternative health)
www.truthagenda.org (Andy Thomas news and *The Truth Agenda* book)
www.ufocasebook.com (UFO reports)
http://uncensored.co.nz (*Uncensored* – magazine, general conspiracy)
www.vitalsignspublishing.co.uk (Andy Thomas publications)
www.xzoneradiotv.com ('X' Zone web radio station – general
   alternative/conspiracy)

Books

Baker, Norman, *The Strange Death of David Kelly*, Methuen, 2007
Begich, Dr Nick, and Jeanne Manning, *Angels Don't Play This HAARP: Advances in Tesla Technology*, Earthpulse Press, 1997
Bennett, Mary, and David Percy, *Dark Moon: Apollo and the Whistleblowers*, Aulis Publishers, 1999
Boardman, Terry, *Mapping the Millennium: Behind the Plans of the New World Order*, Steiner Books, 1999
Cooper, William, *Behold a Pale Horse*, Light Technology Publications, 1991
Friedman, Stanton T, and Don Berliner, *Crash at Corona: The U.S. Military Retrieval and Cover-up of a UFO*, Marlowe & Co., 1997
Good, Timothy, *Above Top Secret: The Worldwide UFO Cover-up*, Sidgwick & Jackson, 1987
Good, Timothy, *Beyond Top Secret*, Pan Books, 1997
Griffin, David Ray, *Debunking 9/11 Debunking: An Answer to Popular Mechanics and Other Defenders of the Official Conspiracy Theory*, Olive Branch Press, 2007
Griffin, David Ray, *The New Pearl Harbor Revisited: 9/11, the Cover-up and the Exposé*, Olive Branch Press, 2008

Griffin, David Ray, *The Mysterious Collapse of World Trade Center 7: Why the Final Official Report About 9/11 is Unscientific and False*, Interlink Publishing Group, 2009

Griffin, David Ray, *9/11 Ten Years Later: When State Crimes Against Democracy Succeed*, Haus Publishing, 2011

Henshall, Ian, and Rowland Morgan, *9/11 Revealed: Challenging the Facts Behind the War on Terror*, Robinson Publishing, 2005

Icke, David, *The David Icke Guide to the Global Conspiracy (And How to End It)*, Bridge of Love, 2007

Mack, John E, *Passport to the Cosmos: Human Transformation and Alien Encounters*, Crown, 1999

Marrs, Jim, *Alien Agenda: Investigating the Extraterrestrial Presence Among Us*, HarperTorch, 1998

Marrs, Jim, *Rule by Secrecy: The Hidden History that Connects the Trilateral Commission, the Freemasons, and the Great Pyramids*, HarperCollins, 2002

Marrs, Jim, *The Terror Conspiracy: Deception, 9/11 and the Loss of Liberty*, Disinformation Co., 2006

Radin, Dean, *Entangled Minds: Extrasensory Experiences in a Quantum Reality*, Paraview Pocket Books, 2006

Ronson, Jon, *Them: Adventures with Extremists*, Simon & Schuster, 2002

Ruppert, Michael, *Crossing the Rubicon: The Decline of the American Empire at the End of the Age of Oil*, New Society Publishers, 2004

Sitchin, Zecharia, *The Twelfth Planet*, originally published 1976, new edition Harper, 2007

Stray, Geoff, *Beyond 2012: Catastrophe or Ecstasy*, Vital Signs Publishing, 2005, US edition Bear & Co., 2009

Thomas, Andy, *Vital Signs: A Complete Guide to the Crop Circle Mystery*, SB Publications, 1998, revised 2002, US edition Frog Ltd, 2003

Thomas, Andy, *The Truth Agenda: Making Sense of Unexplained Mysteries, Global Cover-ups and Prophecies for our Times*, Vital Signs Publishing, 2009, revised 2011

Tips, Scott, *Codex Alimentarius: Global Food Imperialism*, National Health Federation, 2007

Wisnewski, Gerhard, *One Small Step? The Great Moon Hoax and the Race to Dominate Earth from Space*, Clairview Books, 2007

INDEX

Bold numbers indicate significant sections/chapters.

INDEX